Preface

This is the final report of a study carried out by the Policy Studies Institute for the Home Office Research Unit between November 1979 and May 1981. The project was entitled 'Policy Implementation in the Field of Racial Disadvantage' and the summary of the approved research proposal stated that:

> the study is to investigate local implementation of central government policies relating to racial disadvantage. The focus will be upon policy making and service delivery in education and social services. After exploratory interviewing at national, regional and local levels, six authorities (each containing substantial proportions or significant local concentrations of West Indian and/or Asian settlement) will be chosen for intensive fieldwork. The study will attempt to identify factors bearing on the assimilation and interpretation by these local authorities of advice, guidance and statutory requirements, in order to illuminate the context of policy implementation and to establish the opportunities for and constraints upon effective central influence. The final report will seek to indicate the relative efficacy of the several ways of exercising such influence and to make recommendations of practical significance for the relationship between central departments and local authorities.

The following chapters present our findings. Chapters I and II introduce the study, and set it in context. Chapters III, IV and V deal with aspects of the corporate practices of local authorities. Chapter VI discusses policy and practice in the field of personal social services while Chapter VII explores a number of issues relating to education in schools. Chapter VIII summarises some of the more significant national influences on local policy development. Chapter IX presents our overall conclusions and addresses the issue of how central government might best assist local authorities to respond to the particular needs of a multi-racial community.

The project was directed by Ken Young; Naomi Connelly and Gerald Rhodes carried out the greater part of the work in social services and education respectively. David Smith and Freddie Ruffett served as consultants to the project. Chapters I to V, and Chapter IX, are by Ken Young. Chapter VI is by Naomi Connelly. Chapter VII is by Ken Young and Gerald Rhodes, and

Chapter VIII by all three. Cindy Manderson assisted in cataloguing part of the collection of research material and Sue Johnson provided invaluable library support throughout. The PSI typists under the supervision of Elsie Moore coped magnificently with the draft final report.

We should like to acknowledge the helpful co-operation of a considerable number of local authorities and in particular the six which feature prominently in this report. Draft chapters were discussed with officers or members in each of the six authorities and we are indebted to them for their comments. We are also grateful for the helpful comments offered by members of the interdepartmental committee set up by the Home Office Research Unit to advise on the project.

As will be seen, this is not just a study of the local implementation of national policy; it is equally an account of the varied ways in which local authorities have responded to the exigencies of their own circumstances. For this reason we have chosen to publish the report under a title which more nearly does justice to policy makers and practitioners throughout local government.

K.Y.
N.C.

Contents

page

I Introduction

The Race Relations Act of 1976 embodied a number of new departures in policy for a multi-racial society. There was, for example, the extension of the concept of racial discrimination to cover indirect as well as direct practices. The Race Relations Board and the Community Relations Commission were replaced by a single body, the Commission for Racial Equality (CRE), with the responsibility for both law enforcement and the promotion of change. Section 71 of the Act[1] established the new requirement that local authorities should 'make the appropriate arrangements' to ensure that their operations paid due regard to the need to eliminate racial discrimination and 'to promote equality of opportunity and good relations between people of different racial groups'. This new duty — general, ambiguous, and supported neither by sanctions nor incentives — reflected the growing awareness that local authorities are in a key position to affect the wellbeing of ethnic minority groups.

The research project reported here has its origins in concern as to how that responsibility has been discharged both before and since 1976. Our remit for this study, completed some five years after the passage of the legislation, was to appraise how far and in what ways central government has influenced and is able to influence local authorities towards the more positive acceptance of their role in multi-racial areas. More generally, it is a study of the ways in which the local authorities themselves have responded to the presence within their areas of large numbers of people of Asian or West Indian origins.

Immigration has brought successive flows of individuals and families to various destinations in London, the Midlands, and the North. Most were attracted by opportunity; some were refugees. They vary in the length of their settlement, in their family structures, in their skills and economic activity, in their culture and in their faith. Above all, their diversity of origin — national, regional, island — is often maintained through distinctions that most policy makers are accustomed to obliterate (as we have just done) with such generalities as 'Asian' or 'West Indian' or with such shorthand or blanket terms as 'immigrant', 'New Commonwealth' or 'ethnic minority'. Yet if a diversity of origins and culture defies such general categories, there are still

---

[1]Throughout this report, where reference is made to S.71, this refers to Section 71 of the Race Relations Act 1976.

common factors, above all, the common threat of racism and discrimination and widespread (but by no means universal) material disadvantage. To this extent diverse minority groups share some common circumstances and this convergence underlies the increasing prevalence of such general terms as 'black' or 'black British', which emphasise the distinctiveness of colour in a white society.

Our own discussion in this report cannot possibly pay due regard to the diverse characteristics of the populations who settled in the cities and towns which we visited. At our level of generality we are obliged to use the broad terms 'Asian', 'West Indian', 'ethnic minority', 'multi-ethnic' and 'multi-racial'. We use these terms throughout this report, but with an awareness of their descriptive inadequacies.

We must also make clear at the outset that the coverage of this report is circumscribed by our principal focus upon the actions of local authorities in multi-racial areas. We have not set out to ascertain the circumstances of the minority communities in the areas which we studied, nor the impact upon them of the various local authority policies and practices. Still less are we able to consider the broader relationship between public policy and the minority communities: immigration controls and nationality laws, policing, or the vulnerability of black workers at the margins of a depressed economy. We recognise both the limits of local authority action and the corresponding limits of our own study.

We are, however, concerned with the ways in which local authorities attempt to meet (or ignore) the needs, rights and aspirations of the ethnic minority communities. The extent to which local authority policy and practice impinges upon the welfare of ethnic minorities as, for example, in the fields of education, social services and employment, is only gradually coming to be recognised. During the summer of 1981 two reports — those of the Home Affairs Committee of the House of Commons and of the Rampton Committee — have illuminated the crucial importance of local decisions in tackling racial disadvantage. In some authorities this aspect of policy is recognised and responded to; the following chapters show how far and in what ways this occurs. Yet, even there, because of the gulf between intention and outcome we cannot be sure that those attempts are ever carried fully into effect. Nor can we hazard a judgement as to whether well-intentioned actions produce the expected benefits to the minority communities. Such questions require a different study and cannot be answered by the one which we were commissioned to carry out.

We have tried in this study to describe the contexts in which an ethnic dimension has been taken into account in the policies and practices of local authorities. As we show, all manner of marginal adaptations can be made by practitioners (even without the authority of 'policy') to provide services more appropriate to a multi-racial society. Moreover, there are areas in the provision of an essentially personal service where the most important adjustments have to be made at the level of the individual practitioner. Yet there are other areas of broad corporate and departmental policy where change cannot be made without the explicit recognition and discussion of race and its implications for public policy. In the broadest sense, explicitness is a necessary (though never a sufficient) condition for appropriate action. It seemed nonetheless to be rarely achieved.

We were ultimately concerned to explore the feasibility of national policy initiatives to encourage such local development. The multi-racial character of many British cities is, historically speaking, a recent phenomenon which has gradually come to be recognised as containing important implications for national policy makers. The response from central government has, to date, taken the form of increasingly stringent immigration control, of anti-discrimination legislation, and of programmes of compensatory funding channelled through the local authorities. In the 1980s, the situation is different. Immigration has been severely restricted. Public expenditure limits and economic priorities have in recent years constrained the growth of the traditional urban programme. Yet the events in Bristol in 1980 and in Brixton and elsewhere in 1981 urgently argue for a new initiative.

In this situation, the performance of local authorities assumes a central importance. Within the prevailing political and economic realities the redirection of limited resources, the re-orientation of existing local programmes and the re-consideration of local practices represent one of the few remaining options in the field of race relations. In a sense, the policy framework for such initiatives already exists. The 1975 White Paper, the Race Relations Act of the following year, and the subsequent departmental circulars established the contours of a national policy for local implementation. It rests on three linked objectives: the eradication of racial discrimination, the reduction of racial disadvantage, and the positive acceptance of cultural diversity.

If anything, the potential role of local authorities is seen today as even more important than in 1976. It is now widely understood that they could play a central role in any strategy for achieving 'equality of opportunity and good relations between persons of different racial groups'. It is accepted, for example, that local authorities, often the largest employers in their localities, can have important effects on the 'opportunity structure' of their local labour markets. They may revise their own employment practices; they may foster training programmes for the disadvantaged; they may influence the private sector by exemplary action and by the positive use of their own considerable purchasing power. It is accepted that in their role as allocators of benefits in housing, education or recreation and as regulators of land use and the public health, local authorities can go a long way towards achieving the objectives of the Race Relations Act 1976. A handful of local authorities have had some years' experience of innovation and experiment and it is no longer disputed that local government could play a key role. The problem is now one of identifying the most effective means towards these ends. Given that the actual performance of local authorities is highly variable, a major question for public policy is *how* local authorities can be encouraged to re-orient their policies and practices.

We have therefore attempted to identify means by which local authorities may be encouraged to tackle racial discrimination and disadvantage as they arise in the particular circumstances of their own local communities, within the prevailing realities of the current economic situation. Our findings, as will be seen, indicate that there are no simple answers. The policy processes within the local authorities are complex and diverse. Any effective initiative from the centre must adopt a mix of direct and indirect methods aimed ultimately at encouraging self-sustained local change. No single or simple approach is appropriate to the variety of circumstances and the different postures of more than thirty local authorities who, taken together, bear a major responsibility for the wellbeing of our minority populations. That conclusion is elaborated and its implications considered in our final chapter.

During the course of our research, we held discussions with officials of the relevant central departments, the CRE and a large number of promotional groups, professional associations and other organisations. We collected material relating to local authority policies by means of a postal inquiry to all the relevant local authorities. Our main activity, however, was a closer study of six local authorities, all with substantial minority populations. We examined the ways in which they organised the discussion of ethnic issues within their own policy processes and how they consulted and liaised with community groups. We studied their practices in their roles as employers. We explored a range of issues in the fields of education and social services. We tested out our interpretations with the authorities themselves and we explored the issues further by visits to other authorities outside our main sample.

We do not pretend that this is anything more than an exploratory survey. Nevertheless, by relating our more focused inquiries to the wider experience of authorities in other multi-racial areas we are more confident that we have unearthed a range of common issues. There are many areas where we need to know more. But the very generality of the experiences which we noted in our work with the local authorities underscores the inferences which we draw. The following chapters describe what we found and, we hope, illuminate the constraints and the opportunities which would be encountered in any new central initiative which sought to work with local authorities toward policies and practices more appropriate to multi-racial Britain.

References

Committee of Inquiry into the Education of Children from Ethnic Minority Groups, *West Indian Children in Our Schools*, Interim Report (Rampton Report), Cmnd 8273, (HMSO, London, 1981).

Field, S., Mair, G., Rees, T. and Stevens, P., *Ethnic Minorities in Britain: A study of trends in their position since 1961*. Home Office Research Study No. 68, (HMSO, London, 1981).

Home Office, *Racial Discrimination*, Cmnd 6234, (HMSO, London, 1975).

House of Commons Home Affairs Committee, *Racial Disadvantage*, Fifth Report, Session 1980-81, HC 424 (4 vols.), (HMSO, London, 1981).

Nixon, J., The importance of communication in the implementation of government policy at local level, *Policy and Politics 8,* 1980, 127-44.

Race Relations Act 1976, (HMSO, London)

Smith, D. *The Facts of Racial Disadvantage,* Report No. 560, (Political and Economic Planning now Policy Studies Institute, 1976).

II   The Local Authorities

Any investigation of the policies and practices of local authorities faces a basic and inescapable dilemma: within the constraints of limited resources, should the research design emphasise range or depth? A survey of the entire population of relevant authorities would maximise coverage and probably provide some reasonably complete data on 'the facts of provision'. The alternative, of conducting a study in depth of a smaller number of authorities, forfeits the claim to comprehensiveness but raises the possibility of discovering *why* 'the facts of provision' are as they are. We were asked to pursue the latter course, and the core of our study was an exploration of the context of provision in six authorities. However, in order to judge the representativeness of our 'case study' authorities we also carried out a postal survey of the remaining authorities.

Choosing the case studies

Our brief for this project enjoined us to enquire particularly into the ways in which local authority social services and education departments have responded to the needs of ethnic minority communities. It was agreed that we should also explore some of the more general practices of authorities: the ways in which they organised corporate consideration of ethnic issues, their practices of consulting community opinion, and their roles as employers of staff. These considerations defined the focus of our interest as those authorities who had both social services and education responsibilities: the shire counties, the metropolitan districts, and the outer London boroughs.

We were primarily concerned with those authorities which had within their areas substantial settlements of Asian and West Indian populations. Just what is 'substantial' is a matter for arbitrary decision, especially as up-to-date and comprehensive data are unavailable. We therefore studied a number of data sources (from the Office of Population Censuses and Surveys — OPCS — and the National Dwelling and Housing Survey — NDHS) before deciding to take a minimum threshold of 14,000 New Commonwealth-born population in 1971. In no case is this figure a guide to present population levels (which in some cases may have doubled) yet the 1971 figures isolate a group of eight outer London boroughs and eight metropolitan districts. The counties, with their lesser degree of urbanisation, had to be sampled rather differently. Here a threshold of 5,000 New Commonwealth-born population in the 1971 Census in any one district provided a similarly satisfactory threshold and provides us with seven counties.

We had a wide choice of cases from within this population of 23 relevant authorities and a number of factors in mind. It was important to try to include authorities with substantial Asian population as well as those with substantial West Indian or mixed populations, and we wanted a rough balance of political control. We were also conscious that the willingness of authorities to participate in an in-depth study (with access to files and meetings as well as interviews) would be crucial.

We drew up a shortlist of authorities which met these criteria and which also represented a range of demographic experience from rapid recent growth to relative stability. From this short list, we approached six authorities at different points during the eighteen-month period of our study and all six agreed to co-operate. In some cases we had to wait for committee and council meetings to approve our request for access. In other cases, co-operation was volunteered at senior management levels and we proceeded informally. While the authorities varied in their openness to our inquiries, all were helpful.

In our approach to the authorities we were conscious of the need to assure them of complete confidentiality. We have therefore chosen not to identify particular authorities except by the rather neutral labels Ayeborough, Beeborough, Seeborough, Deeborough, Exeshire and Wyeshire. We have also tried to avoid identifying them *indirectly* by the provision of data that would enable the curious to ascertain with little difficulty their precise identities. In some cases we have deliberately obscured crucial organisational aspects or features of provision that might identify these authorities to the more knowledgeable. In places we have simply referred to 'one authority', either to suppress some important feature or, sometimes, to avoid identifying statements made by particular individuals to colleagues who might read this report.

There are limits on the extent to which researchers can effect concealment. We hope we have struck the right balance between the protection of our sources on the one hand and the presentation of a coherent picture of local policies, politics, and practices on the other. The concealment of sources, of course, impedes any kind of validity check upon the account which we have given. For this reason, as well as to meet our responsibilities to our informants, we have fed back the relevant chapters to key actors in the authorities themselves. In this way we have achieved some factual checking. We also gained the opportunity to test out and argue our judgements with the people concerned. In some cases, we have revised those judgements and in others reinforced them. They remain our own judgements and we were gratified that some of those who helped us in this way were prepared to recognise their plausibility.

We now turn to the authorities themselves. Ayeborough to Deeborough are drawn from the London boroughs and metropolitan districts. One was under Conservative control at the outset of the study, as were the two counties, Exeshire and Wyeshire. The size and type of their minority populations varied.

7

Table II.1   Pool of local authorities

Authority	New Commonwealth-born population 1971			Live births to mothers born New Commonwealth or Pakistan — per cent of total live births	
	Number	Per cent of total population	Predominant ethnic group	1974	1977
Outer London boroughs:					
Barnet	16,325	5.3	Asian	14	17
Brent	39,180	14.0	Mixed	36	43
Croydon	16,980	5.1	Mixed	12	15
Ealing	33,440	11.1	Asian	34	40
Haringey	34,595	14.4	West Indian	34	37
Hounslow	14,305	6.9	Asian	20	26
Newham	20,135	8.5	Mixed	30	37
Waltham Forest	14,505	6.2	Mixed	22	31
Metropolitan districts:					
Birmingham	69,140	6.3	Mixed	22	27
Bradford	22,815	4.9	Asian	19	26
Coventry	15,190	4.5	Asian	15	17
Kirklees	14,390	3.9	Asian	15	20
Leeds	14,725	2.0	Mixed	6	7
Manchester	17,295	3.2	Mixed	10	12
Sandwell	15,630	4.7	Asian	18	23
Wolverhampton	20,065	7.5	Asian	24	28

Non-metropolitan counties:

Avon:					
Bristol	8,775	2.1	West Indian	n.a.	6
Bedfordshire:					
North Beds (Bedford)	5,505	4.4	Mixed	13	18
Luton	8,335	5.2	Mixed	15	18
Berkshire:					
Reading	5,655	4.2	West Indian	9	10
Slough	8,710	8.8	Asian	27	32
Derbyshire:					
Derby	7,765	3.5	Asian	13	16
Lancashire:					
Blackburn	5,415	3.8	Asian	19	30
Leicestershire:					
Leicester	23,280	8.2	Asian	26	32
Nottinghamshire:					
Nottingham	10,860	3.6	Mixed	11	12

Sources: OPCS, *Census 1971: England and Wales*. County Reports, and County Reports as constituted 1 April 1974 and *OPCS Monitor*, FMI: 76/1 and 79/1.

Note: The DoE's National Dwelling and Housing Survey (1978) gave for 1977-78 the proportion of those describing themselves as West Indian, or as Indian/Bangladeshi/Pakistani, for London boroughs, six of the eight metropolitan districts listed above, and for Bristol. The information was too incomplete to be used as an alternative to the Census data, but what was available reinforced our view of the relevance of the authorities listed above. (The second volume of the NDHS was published in 1980, after the pool had been established and the case study authorities agreed.)

Beeborough, for example, has very large Asian and West Indian populations. Others, while mixed, tended to be predominantly Asian rather than West Indian in origin, although some had sizeable minorities from other communities. None was predominantly West Indian.

We chose, then, a rather mixed group of authorities in terms both of their characteristics and, as we were to discover, the provision they made for their minority communities. Ayeborough, Beeborough and Seeborough gave us unrestricted access and, where necessary, we worked through departmental files and regularly attended meetings in these authorities. Deeborough was less easy to penetrate although documentation was made available whenever we sought it. In the two counties, our work was confined to the operational level and to senior managements. Wyeshire was the last authority approached and we have less detailed knowledge of practices there, having had less time to build up relationships and no opportunity to visit schools.

In every case we sought to establish the basic facts as to policy and provision at the corporate and departmental levels. Wherever possible, we relied on documentary sources for this purpose. Our main concern, however, was not so much with *what* was being done, but rather with *how* and *why*. Put more formally, we were concerned with *the organisational and appreciative context of provision*. In the case of the first context, we sought to understand the organisational structures and processes within which questions of ethnicity were handled. In the case of the second, we were concerned with how policy makers and practitioners 'define the situation'.

These two contexts will overlap, for special organisational arrangements for considering the ethnic dimension are made only when ethnicity is seen as in some way relevant to the responsibilities of the local authority. And, at the other extreme, an organisational context that grants considerable autonomy (or 'action space') to the practitioner enables service delivery to be infused more (sometimes for better, sometimes for worse) with the practitioners' own 'appreciations'.

These linked concerns run right through this report, whether we are dealing with the work of a race relations sub-committee in Beeborough or of an individual social worker in Exeshire. Thus, when we characterise an authority as more 'departmentalised' or more 'responsive' we are saying something, in shorthand, about the organisational and appreciative contexts of service provision. An example may clarify this concern. In one authority a thoughtful chief executive pondered: 'how do we get ethnicity in care on to the policy agenda?' Here he was highlighting one of the vital interstices of the organisational and appreciative contexts; his eventual answer involved proposing adjustments in committee and departmental responsibilities that would go some way towards making the discussion of ethnic issues more explicit.

We assume that every organisational and appreciative context — the internal *milieu* of policy-making — is unique to an authority at a particular point in time. There are in this sense no 'typical' authorities. Nevertheless, there are broad parallels between the experiences of authorities in multi-racial areas that establish our six as representative of the 'mainstream' of experience.

Our concern for the common organisational context of education and social services excluded the inner London boroughs, some of whom are regarded as the pacesetters in this field; our concern for the maximum feasible access to the policy processes ruled out other authorities who, while they possess substantial minority populations, are apparently unconcerned about their implications for policy. If our six authorities are representative of anything, it is of the middle ground of those who are trying as best they can to consider and adapt their forms of provision.

The wider data-collection exercise

It was a concern for the representativeness of our findings that led us to approach the remaining seventeen authorities in our original 'pool' for documentary information, and also to approach the relevant inner London boroughs for non-education related material. The response to our postal inquiry (and visits to a number of these authorities) confirmed our judgement that our six authorities were, while dissimilar in many ways, in the broad mainstream of policy development.

A second feature of this wider exercise is that it brought us into closer touch with a larger number of authorities. Apart from our six, we wrote to a further 29 authorities. We have had contact with 26 of them. In some cases, we received bare statements as to why no special policies or arrangements had been adopted. At the other extreme we visited authorities, had extended discussions with officials and received a considerable volume of documentation.

We also received requests for information in response to our own enquiry. In some cases, this led to our building relationships with authorities, advising on practice elsewhere, submitting papers, or facilitating the exchange of experience between one authority and others. That we sought at the outset neither to play such a 'development role' nor to engage in dissemination leads us to suggest in our final chapter that there is both need and scope for such work to be properly provided for by central and local government.

The sheer volume of material collected and the obvious need to consolidate the collection persuaded us not to attempt to draw upon it in writing this report. It has informed our judgements but it is not yet feasible to consider writing the more general appraisal of local authority provision for ethnic minorities. Moreover, our documentary collection is no more than that. It provides us with a mine of facts and examples, even with some yardsticks; it cannot address the more subtle issues of the organisational and appreciative contexts of provision which we pursue in the following study of six local authorities.

References

Department of the Environment, *National Dwelling and Housing Survey*, Phase I, 1978; Phases II and III, 1980, (HMSO, London).

Office of Population Censuses and Surveys *Census 1971: England and Wales,* County Reports and County Reports as constituted 1 April 1974. (HMSO, London).

Office of Population Censuses and Surveys, *Birth Statistics,* Series FMI. (HMSO, London).

Young, K. and Mills, L. *Public Policy Research: A review of qualitative methods*, (Social Science Research Council, London, 1980).

III   Corporate Arrangements

Our principal focus within this project was upon the development of policies and practices in the fields of social services and education. Such developments had to be viewed in the context of authorities' overall approaches to the multi-racial community. Certain issues cut across the departmentalism of local service provision: an authority's own employment practices, for example, or its arrangements for consultation and liaison with the minority communities. These issues are specifically covered in Chapters IV and V. In this chapter, we are concerned with how far and in what ways our sample of authorities adopted specific organisational arrangements to ensure that ethnic issues were considered on a corporate basis.

Local authority services seem unlikely to take explicit account of race where the ethnic dimension has failed to secure a place on the policy agenda of the authority. The creation of corporate 'race relations' machinery may indicate that the significance of the ethnic dimension has been recognised. But in practice we found that the existence of such arrangements in itself signified very little. Race relations machinery may be a necessary condition for the re-orientation of corporate policy but it is clearly not a sufficient one. To use the terminology introduced in the previous chapter, corporate arrangements are an important aspect of the 'organisational context' of provision for ethnic minority populations. Whether or not they will be effective in re-orienting provision depends to a considerable degree on the 'appreciative context', that constellation of attitudes and values in which the particular needs of minorities may or may not be explicitly and favourably regarded. These needs may, of course, be taken into account within individual committees and departments when their own policies are framed. Yet it is readily apparent that considerable variation in these matters occurs between departments in the same authority. Moreover, it may be argued that the wellbeing of minorities is an issue which touches many local authority departments. If it is not considered corporately, it runs the risk of slipping through the lattice of long established policy concerns.

That the corporate aspects are crucial to overall service development has been the view of the CRE's Public and Community Services Section. Recent statements by CRE officials which view the local authority as 'possibly the most important agent for social change' give a central place to 'the authority's overall approach to serving a multi-racial area and the co-ordinating and monitoring machinery which it adopts.' For this reason, 'the Commission would like to see every local authority adopt clearly defined machinery for dealing with ethnic matters. (But) every local authority varies in its internal structure and it would be inappropriate for the Commission to suggest any standard model.' General advice has nonetheless been given as to the need to identify a 'lead committee' and to appoint a specialist sub-committee to deal with ethnic issues, while it is stressed that 'officer level corporate arrangements are equally, and sometimes more important'.

The possible arrangements advocated by the CRE may then be summarised as: (i) a committee comprising senior elected members, possibly with co-opted members from community groups; (ii) an inter-departmental officer group to make recommendations to such a committee or, in its absence, directly to a co-ordinating committee of the council; and (iii) a single focus of administrative responsibility for ethnic issues either in the form of a designated officer or some variety of 'race relations unit'. A number of possible paths of administrative development exist and the adoption of such arrangements is very uneven. Two features of this general picture are noteworthy. The first is that London boroughs tend to have the more fully developed arrangements. The second is that the shire counties tend not to create such arrangements and generally seem less likely to introduce the ethnic dimension into their policy considerations.

As the previous chapter indicated, the shire counties with some exceptions, contain only the smaller minority settlements and these until recently have been generally concentrated within their most urbanised districts. It is, however, also important to recognise that counties have tended not to develop corporate structures for policy making. Similarly, in the metropolitan areas the presence or absence of race relations machinery must be seen in the context of an authority's broader approach to corporate issues. In some authorities, corporate groups on ethnic minority issues proved unable to make headway against a very strong tradition of departmental autonomy. Conversely, an authority which is given to establishing corporate groups more readily may be easily persuaded to set up yet another to deal with ethnic issues; but such a body may lack any policy commitment. Indeed, in an authority whose broad dispositions are hostile to racial explicitness, the creation of formal corporate mechanisms for reviewing ethnic issues may serve to retard the development of departmental policy.

Special mention must also be made of the partnership and programme arrangements established under the Inner Urban Areas Act. It is customary for a network of working groups to be created to review issues for the partnership or programme committee and to assess and develop projects for funding. To set up such a body to deal with ethnic minorities (or with, for example, disadvantaged groups in the labour market) is common. Designation under the Inner Urban Areas Act provides (in marked contrast to the traditional urban programme) an unparalleled opportunity to open up the policy agenda to a number of new actors and (inter alia) to new issues: issues ranging from the local economy on the one hand to racial disadvantage on the other, gearing their consideration to an annual policy cycle. Once again, however, a caveat must be entered. In reality, a 'corporate minded' authority with strong leadership will respond very differently to partnership or programme designation than would a highly 'departmental' authority. It is always the case in local government that processes shape the outcome of policy at least as much as structures do and these crucial processes cannot always be inferred from the existence of administrative arrangements.

We begin by examining the impact of the recently made partnership arrangements on the corporate consideration of ethnic minority issues in Deeborough. We then turn to examine the operation of a similar officer working party of some years' standing as it operates in Seeborough. Ayeborough provides a less common example of a high-level member committee. Each one of these three sets of corporate arrangements was explicitly established in order to provide a corporate forum for policy discussion; none was entirely successful. Are corporate arrangements then unimportant? Some light is shed on this question by the example of Beeborough and we chart the course of incremental development in the operation of the race relations sub-committee there. Finally, we draw some conclusions as to the relative significance of corporate arrangements for handling ethnic minority issues.

The limits of imposition

Deeborough is a large metropolitan district which was granted partnership status under the Inner Urban Areas Act. Within the web of working parties geared to the partnership committee is an officer group concerned with ethnic minorities. It is, then, both a relatively low-powered and a very recent development. Moreover, it has to be seen in the context of Deeborough as a large and highly differentiated authority in which the departments have long enjoyed a high degree of autonomy. The chief executive title is still formally linked with that of town clerk and the chief officers' group meets monthly. In several departments, we met officers who strongly emphasised the absence of a corporate process; some saw this as an obstacle to the pusuit of such issues as race, deprivation or the economy, others as their protection from 'interference' from the town clerk's department. The pressures for corporate, or at least interdepartmental, action tend, therefore, to be entirely *ad hoc,* as corporate minded officials strive to promote the recognition of issues that extend into the 'action space' of other departments. Race is one such issue; the local economy another.

In both areas the planning department has been active in producing a flow of information to committees, striving to encourage moves toward a necessarily corporate strategy. These moves are not conspicuously successful, not least because of the absence of any open forum for policy discussion and owing to the very strong defence that departments and sections within them have been able to mount. Where interdepartmental working groups exist they have made relatively little impact upon departments. As a senior officer commented, 'it's not part of the style of the authority to have review from the centre'.

Moves to promote the establishment of new groups have typically relied upon external events for their justification. The 1978 Home Office document setting out the government's proposals for the replacement of Section 11 of the Local Government Act 1966,[1] prompted discussions within the council machinery. The policy committee accepted the argument that, in order to operate within the new provisions of the expected Ethnic Groups Act, the city would need to consider 'an intergrated Strategy to combat racial disadvantage'. The management team were asked to report upon the essentials of such a strategy but this initiative apparently expired with the Ethnic Groups Bill itself.

The establishment of the partnership committee was the next major attempt to bring the issue of race on to the policy agenda. Within this emerging structure the Home Office were also pressing the view that race should receive particular attention. Accordingly, the Inner Area Programme statment gave some attention to the need to promote equality and good race relations. Race was also emphasised by the partnership research group who produced papers indicating the marked concentrations of Deeborough's ethnic minority population within the inner city area. Once fully developed, the partnership machinery included provision for an officers' working group on ethnic minorities and, as inner city responsibility had been given to one of the assistant town clerks, this group was to be serviced by the inner city unit of the clerk's department.

These moves were apparently reinforced by a visit which the CRE paid to Deeborough. The need to service the partnership committee and the need to be seen to be making a serious response to the CRE's urgings converged in the establishment of the Ethnic Minorities Working Group (EMWG). The EMWG was to consider the basis of Deeborough's 'strategy' for race relations, and its terms of reference permitted it to consider ethnic record keeping, employment issues, service delivery and training, special cultural needs and the machinery for consultation.

The terms of reference for the group were unusually broad, reflecting the fact that they originated from the report on the CRE visit. They included a requirement that the EMWG have 'direct contact' with appropriate outside bodies and members of ethnic minority groups, a requirement which was met by establishing a two tier structure with an 'inner' group of council officers meeting more frequently than the larger group which included representatives of the CRE, the local community relations council (CRC), the Home Office, the Department of Employment's Race Relations Employment Advisory Service, the Department of the Environment's inner cities officers, the police, and the probation and after-care service.

After fairly sustained pressure from the CRE and the local CRC, some adjustment was made to this structure to admit a CRC representative to the

---

[1]Subsequently in this report we make reference to S.11; this refers throughout to Section 11 of the Local Government Act 1966.

'inner' group. The reservations which some officers expressed in relation to this proposal indicated the very considerable sensitivity of the issue; we ourselves were very strongly advised not to press for admittance to the group on the grounds that certain officers were barely willing to discuss the issues even in a semi-private forum. The sensitivities were evidently rooted in the delicate interdepartmental politics of Deeborough and the very distant relations with the CRC. The social services department representative on the EMWG openly held the view that the group were seeking to 'interfere' in the affairs of that department. While the representatives of education, environmental health, planning and cultural services departments were to varying degrees enthusiastic about this new initiative, social services and housing were clearly resistant.

Consequently, there is little to be said about progress in Deeborough. In April 1980 a report was drafted for policy committee on the terms of reference of the group. This covered a number of the issues which the group had discussed: data sources, research needs, communications, the need for service reviews, employment policy, training, translation services and the use of S.11 grants. In several of these areas the EMWG had had no discernible impact whatsoever on departments. A fairly substantial paper on S.11 opportunities was produced by the inner city unit but it clearly failed to move the two departments at which its suggestions were directed. Employment policy was the subject of a separate report to the policy committee; this report was not favourable to racial explicitness or record keeping.

Apart from the council's role as an employer, the EMWG's main concern was with reviewing individual services. The group strongly recommended for each service a 'review (of) policies and procedures as they affect ethnic minority residents' with the aim of identifying areas of improvement. Such reviews should cover: reasons for possible low service uptake; possible special needs; staff comprehension of the circumstances and culture of ethnic minorities; possible inadvertent discrimination; extension of S.11 use; and ethnic record keeping. It was recommended that responsibility for such reviews should nevertheless rest with the service committees. This deference to the service committees, taken together with the policy committee's unwillingness to provide a strong lead, has effectively nullified the proposed service reviews.

Even the officers most closely involved concede that the EMWG is not a forum for policy change; 'we've produced all the information that's available; it needs someone to say that we want now to have the policy'. It seems unlikely that the management team will place such a suggestion before policy committee. Most directors, with the exception of education, are seen as antipathetic to the arguments advanced by the EMWG. Partnership meetings and a CRE visit had influenced the council's leaders 'into recognising that other people think there's a need for action'. But the apparent disillusion with the partnership arrangements and the absence of *continuous* CRE pressure works to ensure that this will not be a powerful influence.

In this sense, Deeborough's corporate machinery has been *imposed* upon a diffuse and largely unsympathetic organisation. For a while, partnership created an illusion of corporate working but the machinery which it developed was not powerful enough to draw together divergent service departments. Even so, had the EMWG worked solely to a partnership remit the sense of disappointment, openly confessed by some of the key officers, might have been less sharp. The very much broader remit of the EMWG embodied unrealisable expectations of this particular local administrative context. The group set up initially as a response to CRE pressure, not surprisingly failed to develop under that merely episodic encouragement. Unless there is a major initiative to which the council will have to respond, there is unlikely to be much scope for this new group to contribute to policy development.

Corporatism without commitment

This example of Seeborough provides both parallels and sharp contrasts with that of Deeborough. The two authorities are similar in that both have an interdepartmental officer group charged with considering ethnic minority issues; Seeborough's political leaders have similarly shown little interest in the explicit consideration of the ethnic dimension in policy making. Yet two other factors seem *prima facie* to give more weight to ethnic issues in Seeborough. The first is the generally more elaborate structure of corporate policy making there and the openly corporate inclinations of the chief executive. The second is far longer experience of corporate consideration of ethnic issues by the Working Group (Minority Ethnic Groups). This group is no recent innovation but came into being when the council's management structure was established on local government reorganisation in 1974. It has, then, a more substantial history than any other comparable body in our study.

The structure established for the new council brought together all chief officers in a management team which itself contained an 'inner cabinet' of a permanent management team consisting of the chief executive and a few of the service directors. Corporate policy preparation is facilitated by a network of 'multidisciplinary' groups of interdepartmental membership reporting to the management team on at least a quarterly basis. The groups are encouraged to 'consider the need for input of viewpoint of policy direction from either management team or members of council'. In this latter case, however, 'no approach should be made for a member input other than via the management team'. Within this somewhat hermetic environment the groups are given, notionally at least, a free rein: 'staff are encouraged to discuss and explore issues which may not necessarily be consistent with the views of their directorate . . . obvious constraints of strict adherence to previous policy decisions or to limitations of finance should be avoided.'

In July 1974, the chief executive's office asked departments to appoint representatives to a Working Group (Immigrants) which would meet under the chairmanship of the deputy director of administration. The departments of planning, social services, education, environmental health, finance, housing and leisure services were to form the core of the group. The original memorandum defined 'immigrant' as 'groups of new arrivals who have not yet integrated themselves', specifically excluding Poles and Irish. The focus of the new group was to be 'people mostly from Asia, Africa and the West Indies'.

Before the first meetings of the group took place there was a prolonged dispute over the proposed terms of reference. The starting point for the first meeting was a statement that education, 'colour and culture', housing, health, and work were identified as 'possible spheres in which the presence of immigrants might either cause or aggravate existing problems within the general society'. By November 1974, the group had refined their aims, adopting the term 'minority ethnic groups' in preference to 'immigrants' on the grounds that this would broaden their remit to include 'non-coloured immigrants'. The 'specific aims' of the Working Group (Minority Ethnic Groups) were agreed to be:

(i)   the investigation of special needs arising from the pressure of different Minority Ethnic Groups and the recommendation of such action as seems desirable;

(ii)   the investigation and the recommendation for implementation of possible solutions or palliatives where particular problems have been identified;

(iii)   the monitoriing of the action taken by local government services to ensure the fulfilment of the aims expressed above;

(iv)   the consultation, invitation to attend, and where considered appropriate, the co-option onto the Working Group of the representatives of any relevant group.

This last provision proved to be important and considerable use was made of it during the following six years. In particular, the senior community relations officers (SCROs) of the two CRCs within Seeborough's area were co-opted at an early stage. Invitations to attend on an *ad hoc* basis were fairly freely extended: representatives of the Minority Rights Group, the probation service, the Quakers, the Polish community, the Pakistan Association, the local minority group committee and the Caribbean Association attended on occasion. By this means, the group has been able to hold a series of discussions informed by the direct and immediate articulation of minority viewpoints.

Similarly, a range of substantive issues has been discussed, beginning with a paper on multi-racial education presented at the first business meeting of the group. Other topics have included census data, gypsies, multi-occupation, improvement grants, Saturday schools, police liaison, urban aid, community centres, monitoring, West Indian social workers, the Select Committee report on the West Indian Community, Asian surnames, health education, interpreting services, housing improvement areas, staff training and youth unemployment.

The group has also generated a number of modest initiatives. Improvement grants literature has been translated into Gujerati, Urdu and Punjabi. A project to encourage a more standardised use of Asian surnames within the community has been initiated. A further project to encourage electoral registration and to improve public education in the field of registration and voting has been considered. In addition, the group has considered and advised on a number of issues of more specifically 'departmental' concern.

Our general impression, however, and one confirmed in conversation with a number of participants and observers, is of a considerable gulf between the potential of the group as a pacesetting policy forum and its actual achievements. Three problems in particular seem to underline this relative failure and there are reasons to believe that these problems are not specific to this particular situation. First, there is the predominant disposition of the authority which is summarised in Seeborough's often-quoted 'policy to not have a policy on race'. Second, there is the ambiguity of the group's position as mediator between the separate directorates and the minority communities. Third, there is the fact of the powerlessness of the group, bypassed as it is by the departmental streams of policy development and resource allocation. Each of these may be considered in turn.

The group's terms of reference and co-optive powers appear to reflect a presumption that the ethnic dimension in local services should be explicitly identified and discussed. This was probably the intention of the chief executive in establishing the group; his personal commitment to good race relations is widely recognised within and beyond the authority itself. Nevertheless, the chief executive can only pose the question of 'how to get ethnicity in care on to the policy agenda'. The dispositions of the council are recognised as militating against 'racial explicitness'. When put to the test these dispositions are probably shared by some members of the working group itself. A proposal for a 'policy seminar' on the Race Relations Act 1976, mooted by the director of social services, elicited the opinion that 'a specific policy on the provision of services to minority ethnic groups . . . might be construed as discriminating in favour of such groups'. The seminar proposal made no further progress though it was recommended to the management team. One of the group's notable failures concerned a proposal from the Caribbean Association for a community centre to be included in the Urban Programme submission for 1977. The centre was supported by the police and the social services department. Representatives of the Association attended a meeting of the working group, and a number of suggestions for enhancing the prospects of the proposal were made and followed. Although the working group formally endorsed the proposal it was rejected by the social services committee after only brief consideration as an inappropriate use of resources.

This incident was complicated by the working group's lack of formal standing in the Urban Aid process, to which we shall return. A second failure, however, concerns a matter central to the group's own remit: the monitoring of the authority's employment policy. In March 1977, the group discussed the 1976 Race Relations Act, and several CRC and CRE publications on education, housing and social services were tabled. The general issue of monitoring was discussed and the chairman supported a monitoring exercise. But the sole outcome of this discussion was a proposal from the group for an exercise to determine the ethnic composition of the Council's staff. The social services department's representative pointed to 'the difficulties in categorising persons under their ethnic origins' and the group determined upon a 'visual check' of each department, to be undertaken by senior management to a common set of criteria.

When the management team was asked to endorse the group's proposal it was vetoed on the advice of the chief executive. There was some feeling that the (literal) 'head count' exercise was a clumsy device but a deeper aversion to racial specificity is revealed in the management team's conclusion that the proposal 'serves no useful purpose' would 'involve members of the group in a great deal of useless work' and, significantly, that 'it could be regarded as divisive'. The group's chairman was rather sharply informed of this veto and of the hope that 'no action has been taken'.

The community centre and staff 'head count' proposals not only illuminated the extent to which the group would ultimately be constrained by the shared view of the council and its senior administrators on racial issues, but also pointed up the ambiguities of the group's position. The impetus in the group's discussions comes in part from its 'outsider' element, in particular from one of the SCROs. Moreover, its co-option of the two SCROs and its openness to the attendance of representatives of the minority communities bestows upon the group a multiple constituency. A responsibility to the minority groups themselves is added to the lateral and vertical responsibilities to directorates (which are felt to be real despite the 'working rules') and to the management team. These possibly conflicting responsibilities have been brought into the open through a number of incidents.

The failure of the Caribbean Community Centre proposal embarrassed the working group. Apart from supporting the bid they had held a further meeting at which a West Indian social worker had addressed them on the problems of the West Indian community. The chairman of the Caribbean Association, having himself attended the previous meeting of the group, now denounced the authority for 'adopting a negative attitude to the West Indian population'. His attack received front page coverage in the local press. One member of the borough engineer's staff reacted very strongly to these events, submitting a paper to the group, claiming that its meetings 'have in my opinion helped the group (and myself in particular) to find a sense of direction'. He noted the broader 'diffusion of responsibility' which led him to ask 'is there a policy?' and to conjecture whether Seeborough 'is not prepared to do anything specifically for the West Indian community'. The group was left 'in a vacuum': 'they need to know what the authority's objectives are, limited though they might be at this time, and what is expected of the community itself, in terms of self-help.' The group, he argued, was 'unable to become effective' and should 'consider its (continued) existence'.

The uncertainty which pervaded the group's discussion at this point owed much to its having become the focal point for minority group representations. The chief executive, clearly anxious to avoid a further episode of this type, acted promptly to separate the group's consultative functions from those of internal policy consideration. He immediately instigated the establishment of a 'joint consultative council' (JCC) in the area of Seeborough where the West

Indian population was concentrated in order to create a separate forum to 'discuss the special problems of these groups'. Shortly afterwards, he attended the working group to clarify the persistent ambiguities of its role. He spoke at length on the proper relations between the group, the new JCC and the CRC and proposed further discussion (outside the group) on 'consultative procedures'. Henceforth, the working group should concentrate on 'the development of policy' toward minority ethnic groups; some months later he attended another meeting to urge that the working group 'should be self-generating' and 'an informal platform from which advice to the council might flow'.

The increased intervention of the chief executive in this group's affairs indicated the need to resolve the sense of near-bewilderment as to the group's role. Although a minor crisis had been averted by a decision to continue meeting (not that the group could have properly done otherwise), the development of a separate consultative machinery had merely re-defined the role of the group. The task of testing and communicating the feelings of the minority communities was hived off (although the two SCROs remained active and vocal members) but 'policy development' was arguably fraught with even greater hazards.

One of the two SCROs consistently pressed the view that the group 'had to be seen to be achieving success'. However, in its isolation from mainstream policy development its achievements were limited. Its recently prescribed role of advising the council was hardly feasible in a system where member contact was precluded and where the management team necessarily represented departmental interests. The group is obviously regarded with some suspicion in both the education and the social services departments: there is growing disinclination of either department to send senior staff to meetings. Its lack of a *de facto* corporate role is symbolised by the chairman's apparent lack of previous acquaintance with education department officers attending there and at other meetings.

Since mid-1979, the group has appeared to be pursuing its new 'development' role by attempting to secure a place in the mainstream of policy. The processing of applications for Urban Programme assistance is one obvious area in which the group could seek to have a presence. At the time of the Caribbean Centre failure it had proved necessary to reassure those concerned (discernibly the social services department) that 'it was not the group's intention to interfere with the existing procedure of the authority for processing applications under the Urban Aid programme, but to make a positive contribution by way of report to the management team for possible assistance to the appropriate committee'. Even so, some members of the group have recently urged the need for further discussion on the Urban Programme bids and indeed on the use of S.11 funds.

The present method of handling Urban Programme submissions in Seeborough is that bids are considered by the social services committee after their collation by the social services officers. During 1980, it was agreed to ask all directorates to submit details of Urban Programme proposals to the working group for comment. The management team had agreed this new procedure and late in 1980 the group considered submissions to social services committee for responses to Circular 21. Our general impression of the meeting was of continued departmental dominance of the process. Departmental prerogatives were rarely far from the surface of discussion and while the working group were able to record their particular support for some projects they were unable to comment adversely or make any real attempt to establish priorities. The most important outcome of the process was the opportunity given to the SCROs to reiterate with greater force than before their complaint of exclusion from the consultative process advocated in the circular. We return to this issue in Chapter IV.

The future position of the working group in relation to Urban Programme bids is necessarily uncertain. The chairman has repeatedly advocated a 'rolling programme' of bids assembled in advance of the circular. Such a process would probably give the group or more central involvement in assessing priorities but the social services department are unlikely to relinquish their own grip on the process. This conclusion is reinforced by the inability of the group to secure for itself a significant role in other areas of corporate policy affecting ethnic minorities, in particular the use of S.11 funds and policies towards black youth. Thus, while formally the group represents a further channel of policy development, from itself through the management team and chief executive to the policy committee, this channel is notional rather than real. Power continues to lie with the committees and their directorates.

The ineffectiveness of Seeborough's working group is unlikely to be overcome by administrative means. If the council's policy committee were prepared to take a lead on the ethnic dimension in local services, influence and advice could indeed flow *from* the working group, *through* the management structure to the policy committee and with their authority *to* the service committees who, at the end of the day, will formally or actually take the crucial policy decisions. Political commitment on the part of leadership is, however, the *sine qua non* of such a development.

Strategy without substance

Ostensibly at least, Ayeborough's arrangements provide for the engagement of political leaders in the consideration of ethnic minority issues in a manner that contrasts notably with Deeborough and Seeborough. Ethnic issues are discussed within the private forum of the member-level Ethnic Minority Strategy Group (EMSG), yet there are thus far, few indications of any significant adjustments in provision being considered as a result. Ayeborough is an authority with a distinctively corporate style: there is a one-party policy group, a fortnightly meeting of the chief officers' board, and a system of policy review. Nevertheless, officers in many departments remain sceptical of corporate initiatives and openly stress the gulf between image and reality in the authority's working.

Ayeborough's Ethnic Minority Strategy Group met for the first time in October 1979. There have been nine meetings of the group, all but two of which we have attended. The group's starting point was an internal report on responses from various departments to the Race Relations Act 1976; the review exercise was carried out at the behest of the chief executive. The group was to consider this report, to investigate each department in depth, and to report to the policy group. An approach from the local SCRO with a view to his joining the group was rejected. The strategy group is chaired by the chairman of the education committee and members include the leader of the council, the chairmen of the plannng, establishments and housing committees, and two backbench councillors.

The chief executive invariably attends and other chief officers are frequently present, even on occasions when their own departmental business is not on the agenda. No 'outsider' is allowed to be present (apart from a member of the PSI team). Relations between senior councillors and chief officers are notably informal (first names being frequently used); discussion seems to be entirely open and is not noticeably steered from the chair. As a result, departures from the agenda are frequent and new issues are often raise by members.

The EMSG has considered a wide range of issues including the council's general responsibilities under S.71, ethnic record keeping, language teaching, voluntary schools, careers service, leisure services, community education, ethnic record keeping in education, housing applications and transfer arrangements, improvement grants, employment of ethnic minorities, further education, NDHS tabulation, equal opportunity statement, the experience of schools, racial harassment, environmental health, and social services. Housing issues have, however, occupied the greater part of the EMSG's deliberations. Councillors displayed a close interest in aspects of lettings policy and frequently returned to the question of whether or not their various formal and informal practices were discriminatory. Next to housing, employment and the general issues of record keeping stimulated a great deal of discussion. The proposed series of final meetings to consider the draft report and to settle the record keeping issue has been repeatedly postponed because of the pressure of other council business. While it is possible to anticipate neither the report nor its reception by the policy group, some general observations may be made.

First, what changes to policy or practice may be expected? The answer to this question is that very few changes are likely to be mooted. The overwhelming weight of the submissions from the several directorates sought to justify existing policies. Although formal CRC submissions were rarely considered (for reasons detailed in Chapter IV), several directors and councillors argued against what was seen as 'the CRC/CRE view' when rejecting the case for changes in policy. Some marginal adaptations have been made — for example, on the eligibility for housing of members of a family currently living overseas — but these have been exceptional. Meanwhile, the directorates and service committees have responded to separate representations from community groups, for example, in the provision of mother-tongue teaching on a pilot basis. The strategy group, with its service-by-service reviews, has perhaps been less susceptible to the arguments for change than the mainstream committee and management structure.

To understand why this might be so it is necessary to consider the strategy

24

group's mode of operation. The leader of the council and the senior chairmen have been openly sceptical about the relevance and propriety of the issues raised by the CRE and by local bodies since the 1976 Race Relations Act. The general disposition of this group of leaders is of stern resistance to 'discrimination'. This resistance is carried over into discussion of disadvantage and multiculturalism, where moral arguments for a 'colour blind' approach are punctuated by apprehensive references to possible white backlash against any alternative. These leading members may be said to accept very little of the case made by what they see as 'race relations pressure groups'; their reception of papers from their directors has been strongly conditioned by this view. Discussions have tended to vindicate and endorse existing practices, although there has been an obvious concern on the part of councillors both to understand service procedures and to treat individual cases fairly and to this end hypothetical cases have sometimes been raised in order to test out the operation of the departments' standard operating routines. 'Decisions' as such are nevertheless rare and no votes have been taken. The function of the series of meetings has been to estabish gradually a sense of what the council's posture toward the minority groups and their needs should be.

That this mode of operation predominates is due in part to the membership of the group. There are no opposition members present. A single backbench councillor has repeatedly attempted to raise more searching questions and to challenge both officers and senior colleagues. Our detailed notes of such exchanges indicate that these challenges are usually suppressed or over-ridden, usually in a comradely spirit but sometimes with thinly veiled impatience. In a minority of one among the politicians, this councillor has been unable to affect the course of the discussions. Some council officers, called before the EMSG as the agenda requires, have questioned the council's position from their own field manager and practitioner viewpoints. Such appearances are, however, episodic and their views are, at best 'noted'.

In the absence of CRC representation, the leading role in policy scrutiny has fallen to the chief executive. This role seems to be accepted by members and the chief executive is recognised as strongly committed to the more radical interpretations of S.71 and of 'equal opportunity'. It is undoubtedly true that both the initial review of council practices and the subsequent establishment of the EMSG were chief executive initiatives. However, it would be surprising if from his largely neutral and inter-professional position he were able to mount effective challenges to policy. In each meeting of the EMSG, we have witnessed the chief executive consistently broadening the issues, questioning established assumptions and returning to the questions of equal opportunity and responsiveness to community needs. But with the single exception of the development of an equal opportunity policy statement (which is considered further in Chapter V) the feeling of the group has consistently appeared to be against the chief executive's proposals.

Ayeborough's 'corporate' initiative in race relations would appear then to be hamstrung by the broad disposition which dominates the council's affairs: first, the rejection of racial explicitness; second, the departmentalism of the administration; third, the 'broker' style of leadership with its emphasis on resolving conflicts between separate committee chairmen. The corporate-minded and innovative chief executive is virtually isolated in this diffuse structure. He is uniquely well placed to raise questions of policies towards ethnic minorities, yet nonetheless ill-placed to determine the outcome of discussions. In itself, then, a corporate forum for considering the ethnic dimensions of policy at the highest political level within a local authority is in itself no guarantee of policy change. Without the critical input from the CRC or minority groups it may simply serve to confirm existing practices.

Incremental change

The experience of Ayeborough, Seeborough and Deeborough exemplified the problems of establishing race relations machinery in the absence of political commitment and in highly departmentalised authorities. Of course, both factors are to be found in varying degrees in each of the authorities considered. It remains to ask: what factors are crucial to the introduction of an ethnic dimension into local policy making? The case of Beeborough throws light upon this question. In particular, Beeborough had until very recently few pretensions to operate as a corporate authority. The council's administration was headed by a long-serving town clerk and the management structure strongly reflected past conventions. Moreover the committee business and, in particular, relations between members and officials appeared to be conducted with unremitting formality.

It is perhaps indicative of the different climate of race relations politics in Beeborough that our own approach to the authority was made (on authoritative advice) to elected members rather than to officials. The election manifesto on which the Labour Party fought the 1978 borough elections had included a commitment to implement the 1976 Race Relations Act. A number of black councillors had been elected and were crucial in creating a climate in which ethnic issues were discussed openly and explicitly.

In July 1978 the council's policy and resources committee established a Race Relations Working Party (RRWP) with the following terms of reference:

(i)   to consider what are the obstacles in Beeborough to the attainment of greater racial harmony and the removal of racial disadvantage;

(ii)   to examine in what ways the Council's policies might be extended or altered so as to contribute further towards overcoming these obstacles;

(iii)   to establish priorities in any such policy developments; and

(iv)   to report from time to time with recommendations to the Finance and General Purposes committee, to other committees of the Council, to the Beeborough Community Relations Council and other interested bodies

It had been envisaged that the RRWP would co-opt additional members from the ethnic minority communities.

The membership of the RRWP was also bi-partisan and the subject of consultations between majority and minority leaders. Its members included four majority party members, three from the minority party and (after some disagreements among the councillors) representatives from the local CRC, the Indian Association, the Islamic Centre (later replaced by Indian Women's Association), the Pakistani Workers Association, the West Indian Women's Association and the West Indian Community Centre.

The RRWP continued in this form for about two years and held thirteen meetings. During 1980, a decision was taken to formalise the RRWP's operations by reconstituting it as a sub-committee of the Policy and Resources Committee. This change was apparently associated with a revision of the management structure of the council and the establishment for the first time of the post of chief executive. One consequence has been, though, that the Race Relations Sub-Committee (RRSC) has met rather less frequently than its predecessor. The membership is unchanged.

During the sixteen or so meetings of the RRWP and RRSC a wide range of issues has been discussed, over and above the general approach to race relations adopted by the council, to which we return. Topics have included staff training, housing, record keeping, police liaison, recruitment, conditions of contracts, advertising policy, use of S.11 funds, immigration controls, social survey, publicity, evidence to the Royal Commission on Criminal Procedure, West Indian children in schools, multicultural education, proposed visit by CRE, ethnic record keeping in recruitment, training and promotion, the Nationality Bill, and evidence to the House of Commons Home Affairs Sub-Committee on Race Relations and Immigration. It is important to note that some of these topics have recurred at several meetings. Unlike the analogous bodies in our other authorities, Beeborough's race relations bodies have engaged in continous discussion of what are clearly seen as the key issues for improving the situation of the local minority communities.

The tone of these discussions — searching and often heated — was set at the first business meeting of the RRWP. One particularly active West Indian councillor presented a paper on racial discrimination and disadvantage. The RRWP's minuted conclusions are significant for their grasp of the issue of explicitness in race relations policy:

> The Working Party accept the general approach portrayed in the paper and in particular the conclusion that these racial inequalities will not be overcome simply as a result of general programmes designed to combat urban deprivation for the population as a whole. The specific racial dimensions of urban deprivation need to be considered as a separate issue in all local authority policy making.

In accordance with this view, the RRWP (and RRSC) have frequently referred issues to the service committees. They recommended, for example, that the housing committee move toward the appointment of S.11 funded advisory officers for ethnic minorities. They have also insisted on discussing a document on multicultural education despite education department views that this was properly within the province of the education committee. Their most significant exercises have been those concerned with employment and training practices, the creation of a race relations post under the chief executive, and the consultations with community groups contingent upon these developments.

The particular developments in employment and training initiated in Beeborough are discussed further in Chapter V. The council's consultative practices are also discussed more fully in Chapter IV. The creation of a race relations advisory post is an ambiguous issue, inextricably bound up with training matters yet, as will be seen, inseparable from the progressive expansion of commitment observable at the meetings of the RRWP and its successor.

The origins of the race relations adviser post lay in the study of the training needs of the council carried out by the Industrial Unit of the Runnymede Trust. Runnymede's report, which took a critical view of some departmental managements, had a rather unfavourable reception among chief officers. The various comments from departmental heads indicated deep disagreement over the validity of Runnymede's conclusions. There was, however, considerable pressure to respond positively to the report, and subsequent discussion was deliberately steered toward the implications of race relations for staff training. Accordingly, a Runnymede proposal for an important training post for race relations work both attracted substantial support (for it was difficult to argue against it) and deflected attention from the more contentious allegations.

This development, although originally independent, quickly converged with the RRWP's espousal of an equal opportunity policy statement, backed up by a system of record keeping and monitoring. The subsidiary aspects of this proposal led to considerable discussion, and some opposition from minority party members of the RRWP. It was nevertheless endorsed by the RRSC, the Policy and Resources Committee and the council itself. When the new chief executive came into post in 1980 the chairman of the RRSC asked him to review the proposal for a senior training post. He reported that 'it may be felt that the post could be more productively used if it had a wider brief' and suggested a redesignation of the post as principal race relations adviser on the grounds that the council needed advice to be given to certain departments on race relations and a central point of contact for ethnic groups. The adviser would follow up the implementation of any monitoring arrangements, co-ordinate the council's race relations activities, review departmental services, encourage increased take-up by ethnic groups of available provision, and monitor advice to committees. The chief executive stressed that the adviser should report direct to him in order 'to ensure direct access to the head of the council and the ability to influence major policy decisions'.

Training needs, the desirability of monitoring the equal opportunity policy and the obvious requirement that a new chief executive establish structures which give him a grasp on the council's administration equally contributed to the movement towards creating an advisory post. Pressure from the minority groups represented on the RRSC may have contributed to this drift; at one meeting a co-opted member pressed strongly for the creation of a race relations unit. The West Indian councillor who had played a distinctive role in each meeting of the RRWP and RRSC had earlier tabled a paper outlining a possible job description for an advisory post; his own views (invariably expressed with some force) were probably instrumental in persuading the RRSC chairman and other leading figures to extend the training post to this new and more significant form.

The adviser proposal did not have a smooth passage. The minority party recognised the transition from what had been previously agreed (because widely agreeable) rather late in the day and moved unsuccessfully to defer the post. The RRSC chairman and the chief executive meanwhile moved rapidly to elaborate the job description, settle a grading and advertise for candidates. They moved too rapidly, perhaps; the need to resolve the issue without conflict (and outside the full RRSC) led to an agreed grading which some felt inadequately reflected the importance of the post. Minority group representatives and some councillors joined forces to refer back the proposal against the very strongest advice of the RRSC chairman. Eventually the policy and resources committee reversed their previous decision and, on the recommendation of the RRSC, revised the grading upwards.

As will be apparent, a series of mutually reinforcing events had proved crucial in maintaining the momentum of incremental change in Beeborough. Each new departure could be justified by reference to some past decision. There were no marked discontinuities in the development of these corporate arrangements, but rather a gradualist expansion of both commitment and provision. The structure of the RRWP probably contributed to this process. The presence of minority group representatives clearly affected race relations discussions. The awareness that these representatives could not conceivably speak for all minority groups in the borough encouraged a process of consulting opinion more widely. Those consultations themselves served to confirm, as some leading councillors had alleged, that Beeborough needed to make a sustained and highly visible attempt to reorient its services in the interests of a multi-racial community. The basic dynamics of their situation largely shaped the direction in which the RRWP and RRSC moved. Two other particular factors doubtless contributed to this incremental progress. These were respectively embodied in a forceful West Indian councillor who tended not only to initiate the major departures in discussion but was invariably well prepared with material to counter the consequent objections; and a respected, accommodating and skillful RRSC chairman.

Concluding comments

In this chapter we have attempted to convey something of the different corporate structures and styles of operations in four of our six authorities. Each of the four appears on paper to have gone some way to making provision for race relations discussions at the corporate level, although none would conventionally be regarded as 'brand leaders' in this respect. Probably they are typical of that broad group of authorities who are neither pushing back the frontiers nor refusing to recognise that there are issues to be discussed. Each may develop in different directions or at a different pace. Our work during the period June 1981 — May 1982 will be concerned with monitoring these developments in corporate arrangements, and the implementation of the decisions taken within them.

Some tentative conclusions may be drawn on the basis of our work so far, and these can be presented as comparisons among the four situations. Ayeborough's 'strategy group' is handicapped by the absence of any external voice and its deliberations may well serve only to confirm the elected members' implicit policy of discounting the racial dimension. Seeborough's officer group could make some contribution to policy development but this is unlikely to occur unless the group is reinforced by acceptance at the political level and perhaps by the creation of an advisory post within the authority. Deeborough's officer working group may well decline with the partnership arrangements themselves; again a political initiative would be necessary to overcome the reverses which this modest corporate initiative in race relations has already suffered. Beeborough are likely to continue to develop their corporate arrangements, but a striking feature of their RRSC meetings has been the lack of any departmental officer presence. The new chief executive has taken a more participatory and interventionist role than his predecessor; even so, Beeborough's problems are likely to occur in the field of securing effective implementation for proposals which, however modest they may seem to those who make them, may outrun the slowly-developing commitment of many of those who have to put them into effect.

This last consideration reinforces the most basic point about these four contrasting sets of corporate arrangements. Whatever the success of a member, officer or mixed group *as a group* it must ultimately be judged by its overall impact on the council's affairs. In most cases, that impact appears to be vitiated by one or both of two factors: the absence of a genuinely corporate management structure or the absence of a group of committed senior councillors. The example of Beeborough indicates that political will, if ambivalent at times, can ultimately achieve a distinctive authority-level policy position. The example of Seeborough suggests that a management structure, however well elaborated, can achieve little in so sensitive a policy area if political commitment is not forthcoming.

This is not to say that corporate arrangements are unimportant. We argued at the beginning of this chapter that the impact of local authority action on the wellbeing of ethnic minorities is likely to remain unconsidered in the absence of some forum in which an across-the-board appraisal can be made. Ultimately, a vital element in that appraisal must be the voice of the minority communities themselves, and it is to the question of consultation that we now turn.

References
Commission for Racial Equality, *Local Government and Racial Equality* (London, 1981)
Department of the Environment, Memorandum (July 1980) to House of Commons Home Affairs
    Sub-Committee on Race Relations and Immigration. Published in House of Commons Home

Affairs Committee *Racial Disadvantage*. Fifth Report, Session 1980-81. HC 424. Vol. II, pp.274-83, (HMSO, London, 1981).

Home Office, *Proposals for Replacing Section 11 of the Local Government Act 1966: A consultative document*, (HMSO, London, 1978).

Robinson, C. The origins of corporate structures for race relations policy in inner London borough councils. M.Sc. dissertation, London School of Economics, Department of Government, 1980.

Stewart, J., *The Responsive Local Authority*, (Charles Knight, London, 1974).

IV Consultation and Liaison

In this chapter we consider the ways in which authorities have provided for the expression of minority community opinion within their policy-making processes. All authorities in multi-racial areas face the same dilemma of whom to consult, to what end, and by what means. Not surprisingly, such practices vary widely. On one hand, there are authorities who have no special arrangements for consultation with the minority communities over and above an often distant relationship with a local CRC. On the other hand, there are authorities with extremely elaborate networks of consultative committees where officials or councillors regularly meet representatives of the communities. There are a host of other arrangements in between, which include special one-off exercises in sounding minority opinion in order to gauge reactions to a specific policy initiative.

It is only too easy to fall into the trap of regarding consultative machinery as an end in itself. The content and consequence of consultation may to some extent be independent of its form. The fact remains that consultative arrangements may serve a variety of conflicting purposes (and may thereby meet the apparently contradictory interests of a number of parties). Image-building and symbolic politics are often readily apparent; moreover, an evidently genuine consultative exercise may be used by some officials to strengthen their own position by enlisting 'community opinion'. The importance of consultation lies then not in its form but in its substance and its consequences. The key questions are how far an authority can take account of the range of minority opinions in the community and to what extent it is prepared to create channels for the expression of those opinions.

The structure of this chapter will be as follows. First we look at the longest-standing of all consultative modes: relations with a local community relations council (CRC). Next we examine two *ad hoc* attempts to extend the range of consultation yet further, to the entire range of identifiable minority organisations in the locality. Third, we discuss the experiences of those authorities which have created a special forum in which a dialogue can occur between the local authority and a selection of community representatives. Finally, we discuss the general merits of these modes of consultation and consider how far they illuminate the 'response style' of authorities.

Consulting the Community Relations Councils

In some areas, the CRC is still seen as the 'voice' of the minority communities with consultative arrangements reflecting this perception. In other areas we found that this representative role was denied by local authority policy makers. It is often difficult to make an accurate appraisal of the relations between CRCs and the groups they purport to represent. Owing to the ethnic, social class or age structure of its members, a CRC may fail to reflect the diversity of opinion in the locality. Nevertheless, an authority in an area of great ethnic diversity may be faced with few easy consultative options and a CRC may at least appear to aggregate what are in reality different and conflicting opinions and interests. Moreover, a comfortable relationship with a CRC may channel or subdue pressures for change in local authority services.

We found few instances of CRCs successfully initiating new developments. There were instances of CRCs publicly criticising local policy, calling for change or pressing for greater support from the local authority to the CRC; but these public or semi-public activities were rarely matched by any participatory role in policy making. In the absence of such a role the CRC contribution to local policy is necessarily reduced to one of commenting *post hoc* on proposals which are already being mooted or, indeed, have already been discussed and agreed. This point is exemplified by the committee of senior council members established in Ayeborough. The local SCRO was not invited to attend meetings of the committee; he met leading members of the council shortly after their first meeting and submitted a note establishing areas of concern to the CRC. Thereafter, members repeatedly referred to their intention to open discussions with the CRC at the conclusion of their series of meetings. In another area an SCRO, reflecting on his eleventh hour co-option to an officer committee on the 1976 Act, recalled that he was 'invited to go along to discuss a document already finalised . . . I resent this still . . . (being) used as a rubber stamp'.

Such *post hoc* consultation itself presupposes at least an amicable relationship between the council and the CRC, such as obtains in Ayeborough. In Deeborough, on the other hand, the local CRC barely figured in the minds of policy makers as a source of advice and opinion: the CRC had been divided and lacking in direction, while other 'umbrella' ethnic organisations had greater claims to representativeness than the CRC itself. Time and again the accusation of 'unrepresentativeness' was levelled by respondents in the case study authorities. Where (as is often the case) councillors sit on the executive committee of the CRC, they feel justified in dismissing its claim to representativeness, perhaps pointing to the predominance of one major ethnic group. The reserve with which the CRC in Beeborough was treated reflected a similar recognition that many of the Asian organisations preferred to operate outside the CRC framework and the council's consultative practices made allowances for that situation. In Exeshire county officers dismissed the city CRC as largely representing the professional classes, while the city, concerned about the CRC's largely Asian affiliation, dealt with West Indian groups direct.

Where relations between the authority and the CRC were particularly close

33

(with, in some cases, local authority officers sitting on or even chairing CRC sub-committees), awareness of the CRC's limitations as a source of advice on the community might be sharpest. In one case, where we attended a CRC sub-committee, much of the meeting (largely of Asian professionals) was given over to consideration of the self-confessed inability of the members to represent 'community' opinion. Some suspicion of organised groups was apparent, and discussion here and in a later interview with the SCRO turned readily to the feasibility of survey research as a more reliable measure of 'consultation' for need-determination.

Consultation with CRCs could be undertaken for a range of very different motives. A local authority would probably be mistaken in undertaking such consultation in order to test 'community' opinion but there were evidently circumstances when the CRC's representative role was a convenient fiction for an authority. Some CRCs and their staff will encourage this fiction: 'I speak for the people' was the grandiose claim of one CRC representative in a discussion with the local authority at which we were present. A more candid and realistic view of what CRCs can and cannot do was however fairly widespread, although its corollary, that consultation should be broader based, was less apparent.

One of the most powerful reasons for consulting CRCs (and councils for voluntary service) is a wish to legitimate an Urban Programme bid made by the authority. Urban Programme circulars issued to date have stressed such consultation as a normal part of the processing of bids. For example, circular 20 (issued in 1979) included the question: 'If the project will benefit ethnic minorities, what are the views of the local Community Relations Council?' The Department of the Environment's 1980 review of the traditional urban programme indicated the scope for improvement in this respect and circular 21 contained a stronger exhortation than hitherto.

Arrangements in this respect are still extremely variable. Voluntary sector participation can occur in determining the criteria for project support, in the project selection process itself, and in the actual sponsorship of projects. Some authorities exclude the voluntary sector (including CRCs and CVS) from the first two stages while admitting or encouraging bids from voluntary organisations. The results are similarly variable: a local CVS conducted a survey of six major authorities; the results showed a striking range of practice from predetermined levels of voluntary sector funding (as low as three or ten per cent in two cases) to open bids with from seven to 75 per cent of the total programme funding going to local voluntary groups.

Broad-based evidence on the situation since circular 21 is not available. Beeborough have a special sub-committee (with CRC and CVS representation) to scrutinise Urban Programme bids, and groups wishing to promote particular projects appear before this subcommittee. The voluntary sector has recently become main beneficiary of the Urban Programme in Beeborough and the 'ethnic dimension' appeared to be in the forefront of the sub-committee's concerns. Indeed, it has been proposed that from 1981 Beeborough concentrate aid on projects of direct benefit to black groups. In

Deeborough the voluntary sector is involved in fairly open debate as to selection criteria but has chosen not to participate in the selection process itself. In Exeshire the city CRC has been effectively excluded from participation in the Urban Programme process in favour of the CVS.

The experience of Seeborough perhaps merits attention. We noted considerable discussion on the role of the CRC and CVS in commenting on the Urban Programme bids. Strong feelings were expressed by one SCRO in several meetings and at one he tabled a paper setting out his criticisms of the authority's apparent practice of claiming (in the DoE submission) that the CRC had been consulted and that it supported particular projects when in reality no such consultation had taken place.

This has been a much-discussed issue in Seeborough. In October 1980, a local CVS (which covers only a small part of Seeborough's area) convened a meeting of local bodies 'to clarify any points regarding local handling procedures for Urban Aid applications' in discussion with the relevant officers of Seeborough, who attended the meeting. Considerable dissatisfaction with processing of Urban Programme bids was expressed and the SCRO's previous criticisms were reiterated by CVS officers. A follow-up meeting in February 1981 pressed for extended consultation in future and resolved to take early steps toward securing it. An inspection of the bids considered by Seeborough for submission under circular 21 indicates the generally high priority given to 'departmental' projects (arguably of a 'main programme' nature) and the generally low priority accorded to voluntary sector projects: of the nineteen proposals, voluntary sector projects were rated sixth, seventh, fifteenth, sixteenth, seventeenth, eighteenth and nineteenth.

The issue of consultation on urban programme bids was also discussed in a meeting of Seeborough's corporate working group. The two SCROs commented in turn on each of the nineteen proposals, a typical comment being that 'I was not consulted in any way on (this) . . . but I fully support it'. The conciliatory line adopted by the CROs at this meeting reflected the fact that the need for fuller consultation had been largely conceded by the working group chairman and a social services department officer at the meeting with the CVS. There was no longer a need to do more than underline the lack of consultation in an amiable manner. At the same time, it is important to note that the apparent repentance of the authority (apparent in the sense that the issue had, at the time of writing, still to be discussed by management team or elected members) owes something to the internal tussle over ultimate oversight of the Urban Programe process. The education and social services departments were reluctant to consult, arguing that there was too little time available between the issue of the circular and the submission of an application. It was also felt that priority should be given to time-expired projects seeking renewal. The working group chairman has argued that the conflict of needs could be resolved by the introduction of a 'rolling programme' or 'continuous consideration' of projects, with consultation taking place in advance of the appearance of the circular. This argument is also intended both to open up the process and to give the working group a role in the *corporate* consideration of projects, a proposal strongly supported by the SCROs who form a natural alliance with the 'corporate' forces on this issue against departmental self-interest.

As we have seen, consultation with CRCs may take several forms. In the first place, the CRC may be seen as the preferred 'voice' of the community itself. Such consultation as would follow from this would suit the authority's own purposes in legitimating policy and insulating the authority from the more direct demands of community groups. There are indications that this type of relationship is being eroded as CRCs are bypassed both by groups seeking to press demands and by authorities genuinely seeking to test opinion. While the Urban Programme arrangements are intended to elicit CRC support for projects with an 'ethnic' content, authorities with a commitment to consultation will need to devise their own, necessarily more complex, procedures than recent circulars have required.

Finally, scope apparently exists for closer working relationships between CRCs and local authority staff at the 'operational' level. Specialist social workers from minority backgrounds may, as in Seeborough, become the focus of such relationships, giving alarm to senior managers. Exeshire's practice of having education and social service department staff appointed to CRC committees (itself a commonplace occurrence elsewhere) provides for some exchange of views (as on the appointment of school governors) but little apparent input to the authority's own operational practices.

Particularly noteworthy is the working arrangement established between the CRC and the social services department in Ayeborough. It is called the Social Services Advisory Group; it is serviced by the CRC and convened by one of the department's area officers. Department membership includes other area officers, a principal officer (development), a hospital social worker, two community workers, and the specialist social worker for the Asian community. The CRC is represented by the SCRO (who has had a close and continuous working relationship with the chief executive and one of the area officers) and by a CRO who formerly worked in the chief executive's department. The meetings have been concerned with current and potential use of S.11, and with a pilot survey of the ethnic origins of new clients in one area office. Training, unemployment, and the CRE's *Youth in Multi-Racial Society* have also been discussed. Given the exclusion of the CRC from top level discussions on race relations in Ayeborough, such operational level relationships may in the long run prove to be the most promising channel for advice and consultation there.

Consultative exercises

The previous section indicated that the patterns of CRC-authority liaison varied widely, but seldom bestowed an important consultative role upon the CRC. Recognition of the fact that the CRC can rarely claim a genuinely representative authority (and in places has effectively relinquished such a claim) may prompt an authority to engage in a wider consultative exercise in order to sound opinion. Three such *ad hoc* exercises are worth considering here: that which dealt with multicultural education in Deeborough, and Beeborough's consultations in respect first of race relations generally, and latterly of staff record keeping.

Deeborough's education committee approved an important report on multi-cultural education early in 1980. The report set out the results of a major consultative exercise authorised by the committee in 1978. The basis of consultation was a series of questions framed by the chief education officer (CEO) with a view to reviewing the effectiveness of the education system in a multi-racial context. Initially, a teacher in charge of English as a second language at a local school and community centre was seconded, on S.11 funds, to head-quarters to carry out the exercise. The appointment was for one year but this was later extended for a second year in order to aid the implementation of decisions taken in the light of the survey.

The survey itself was in two parts, seeking both the views of schools and of community groups. The schools received an elaborate structured questionnaire, but our concern at this point is with the community groups. The community consultation document was a statement by the education chairman expressing commitment to a multi-racial society, followed by the CEO's five questions. The seconded teacher, who was active in community affairs and was himself black, carried out the consultation exercise personally, whereas the schools questionnaire was administered by the education department's inspectorial staff.

The seconded teacher initially approached over 200 community groups and individuals with a letter inviting comments. The response was admittedly 'poor': 'the main response was largely oral — we had to go out or bring them here to discuss the issues and record their replies.' There were 45 written replies and 67 interviews with individuals and groups.

A proportion of the poor initial response may be attributed to confusion on the respondents' part; 'we approached both organisations and individuals — the individuals relied on the organisations to reply'.

There were clear lessons to be learned from this operation. Respondents may have found the written invitation and the framing of the questions both ambiguous and daunting. Some of the concepts — inadvertent discrimini-nation, for example — were handled more easily in discussion. Resistance to monitoring was expressed by some groups and West Indian parents and organisations were reportedly wary of the separate discussion of West Indian children. It is difficult to discern a clear picture emerging from the consultation in Deeborough. The mixed reactions in both the communities and the schools enabled education officials to claim at least a partial vindication of the proposed innovations in education policy. It ensured that the department was in fact more aware, and more *officially* aware, of the feelings of community representatives. Finally, it demonstrated to those influential in the ethnic communities that the authority was prepared to tackle the problem issues, some of which had already been identified in recent years in *ad hoc* representations to the CRC and to the education department. Although it was clearly intended as more than a public relations exercise its effect on the authority's 'image' was probably beneficial. This elaborate consultation exercise was made possible by the full-time appointment for that purpose of an officer who was acceptable to Deeborough's minority communities.

Beeborough's exercises were somewhat different. The most recent arose from the discussions on employment policy recounted in the next chapter; an earlier exercise was carried out in pursuit of the Race Relations Working Party's concern to establish the general climate of race relations in the borough. One of the RRWP's terms of reference required that it consider the obstacles to the attainment of greater racial harmony and the removal of racial disadvantage. At the request of the working party, the town clerk wrote to over 600 local organisations in October 1978.

These organisations comprised tenants', residents' and ratepayers' organisations and all known community groups. Each of these was invited to submit written comments to the RRWP. Some 70 replies were initially received; most were of a fairly bland or limited nature, but 22 of them made specific suggestions which touched in some degree upon policy and practice, and abstracts from these were tabled at a meeting of RRWP. Tabled at the same time were the observations in full of two organisations, one of which, a residents' association in a multi-racial area, had established a sub-committee to collate views and submitted a thoughtful and extensive report. Further views were tabled at later meetings as they were received. Two organisations originally expressed a wish to appear before the RRWP with prepared papers, but in the event neither took up the invitation to do so. The only organisation actually to appear was a local group representing West Indian parents, whose chairman submitted written comments and initiated a heated discussion of discrimination against West Indian children.

The RRWP's response to the initial round of replies was to consider a number of issues raised by the respondents. The list of organisations invited to comment was reviewed; invitation lists for civic functions were scrutinised; further discussions of interpreting services were set in motion; a publicity initiative on multi-racial issues through the council's 'Civic Review' was endorsed; the collection of information from other local authorities on responses to S.71 of the Race Relations Act was set in motion.

Earlier, the RRWP had recommended the collection of ethnic records in the field of housing allocation. When a decision to act on this issue was deferred by the council pending consultation, the RRWP agreed to extend the consultative process to cover employment. In June 1979, the leader of the council appealed to community groups to 'ascertain the feelings of their members' on the issues 'so that as wide a view as possible can be represented in the replies' to the eventual survey. The RRWP decided not only to elicit opinion by means of a letter from the chairman but to inform respondents of the recent council policy on non-discrimination 'by way of support to the Working Party's view that records should be kept'.

The letter set out the considerations which had moved the working party and added 'before reaching a conclusion on this proposal, the council are anxious to have the views of your organisation upon the question of the keeping of ethnic records of their staff'.

38

This was sent to 36 organisations of which some (for example, the Indian Association) were umbrella organisations for a number of other groups. Of the 36, three opposed the proposal, two 'abstained' and 22 supported it. One of the opposing bodies recommended the reservation of vacancies for different ethnic groups in proportion to their numerical strength in the community while one felt that race relations would deteriorate as a result of record keeping. On the other hand, the local Indian Association reported that the proposal, having been considered by the executive committee of its 14 member organisations, was supported by 12 of them. The local CRC considered the proposal at length, and eventually voiced fear that such records could be misused.

The full political significance of this exercise is considered in the following chapter; its broad effect was to ensure that organised community opinion was weighed in the balance along with the somewhat less enthusiastic responses of the trade unions and the authority's own chief officers. Like Deeborough's education exercise, it enabled the proponents of policy change to enlist community support in an internal struggle against the long-established practice of racial inexplicitness.

Consultative committees

Although our lack of information about the practices of local authorities in general enables us to comment neither on the use made of CRCs as channels of advice nor upon any *ad hoc* consultative exercises which might have been carried out, the response to our survey indicated that some authorities have set up consultative machinery, either specifically for that purpose or as one among the several functions of their corporate arrangements. The various corporate arrangements established in each of our four 'district' authorities have already been described in Chapter III. Here we consider how far each provided for an element of consultation by the direct participation of minority group representatives. We then consider the special arrangements adopted in Seeborough to institutionalise consultation.

The consultative value of Ayeborough and Deeborough's corporate machinery can be readily determined. Deeborough's working group of officers were extremely reluctant to admit a CRC representative to their discussions, despite the explicit requirement to consult embodied in their terms of reference. In Ayeborough, the initial internal review of practice had been treated as a confidential exercise but the SCRO was aware of the report which arose from it. His request for a place on the Ethnic Minority Strategy Group was rejected, but he was encouraged to submit papers and offered a meeting with the group at the end of the review process. The SCRO turned his attention to preparing a series of papers setting out the CRE/CRC views on education and social services within the context of Ayeborough's particular local circumstances. These he hoped to submit for the EMSG's consideration. However, as he was not on the circulation list for the EMSG papers he was ill-placed to keep abreast of developments. His paper on education, which he submitted to the EMSG and which he understood to have been fully discussed, was in fact merely noted in a rather perfunctory manner, having been tabled too late for serious consideration by the councillors. The social services paper was prepared in the expectation of a future meeting of the group on this topic; the meeting however had already taken place some weeks earlier.

In contrast, Beeborough is distinguished by the substantial ethnic minority representation on the Race Relations Sub-Committee. With the exception of the local Indian Association, contribution to discussion has perhaps been rather less than might have been expected. One council officer expressed his disappointment to us that the minority members of the committee did not initiate more of the discussions. However, their own role must be considered in the light of the presence of the black councillors attending the RRSC. Not only do these councillors openly speak for the minority interests, but they also serve to mediate between the council and community 'sides'. They thus prevent a polarisation that could undermine the sub-committee's effectiveness.

Nevertheless, there is some dispute as to minority representation on the RRSC. The chairman has made repeated attempts to keep a broad membership but difficulties have been encountered in identifying and contacting the relevant organisations. The Muslim interest in particular has lacked sustained representation since the death of the nominee of the Pakistan Workers' Association. Suggestions made by the minority representatives on the RRSC for contacting the Association or for identifying an alternative organisation seemed to underline the difficulties faced by even this body in identifying and appraising the claims of the many possibly 'representative' groups in a heterogeneous authority with a population of more than a quarter of a million.

Opposition party members of the RRSC have raised particular objections to the irregular attendance of members and the attendance of substitutes, questioning their representativeness. The view of the RRSC majority has been to encourage the maximum participation of organisations rather than individuals. But one of the lighter moments in the RRSC's history was the lengthy reprimand delivered by one opposition councillor to a minority representative whom he had mistaken for the chairman of another (rather more vociferous) group. The limits of representativeness are fairly freely acknowledged in Beeborough; the extensive *ad hoc* consultative exercises decribed above are testimony to the uncontested view that consultation cannot be effective when it is confined to a small regular forum of select organisations.

The narrower view, which stresses continuity rather than range of consultation, characterises the arrangements adopted in Seeborough. Seeborough's distinctiveness lies in the establishment of two Joint Consultative Committees (JCCs), one in the north and one in the south of the authority. The northern JCC is perhaps more narrowly confined to joint CRC-local authority liaison but we shall consider them together here. The southern JCC was founded later and brings local authority officers together with the representatives of West Indian and Asian organisations. These bodies merit a close examination as an experiment in institutionalised consultation.

The northern JCC was established in May 1976 following several approaches by the northern SCRO to the chief executive. The chief executive favours discussion and all modes of participation, and at the inaugural meeting (under the CRC chairman) he 'pledged his support for the JCC and hoped that his chief officers would assist in whatever way possible in this new venture'. He was accompanied at this first meeting by the deputy director of education, the assistant director of housing, the director of social services and the divisional social services officer. The chief executive, chief, deputy and assistant chief officers from several departments have frequently attended the meetings.

The proceedings of the northern JCC are rather formal despite the close familiarity and acquaintance of the members. Topics discussed since 1976 include general education, social services and employment issues; local works and projects; the Urban Programme; the Race Relations Act; housing records; housing action areas; representation on boards of governors; translation and interpreting services; National Front activities; library services; allocation of children to schools; liaison with the health service; youth organisations; nursery education; and town planning and development control matters. Many of these topics have recurred from meeting to meeting, and the discussions have usually been both detailed and closely focused upon the authority's own practices.

The southern JCC presents something of a contrast. It was established on the personal intervention of the chief executive, following the near crisis in the relations with the West Indian organisation and the associated ambiguities as to the consultative role of Seeborough's internal officer working group (see Chapter III). The subsequent separation of functions has ostensibly allowed the internal working group to concentrate on policy issues, leaving the opinion-sounding function to the new JCC which came into being in 1977. In contrast with the northern JCC the minority representatives on this second body were nominated by the local Minority Groups' Council, a body to which a number of West Indian and Asian groups are affiliated. The local SCRO also attends.

The chairman is usually provided from the minority side and in this case the secretariat is provided by the authority rather than the CRC. As the chairman of the first meeting remarked 'There was a very great need for officers, councillors and members of minority groups' communities to meet to discuss common problems and to find solutions to those problems. He thought there was a great need for the development of informal structures. Despite this early reference to councillors, local authority representation at both JCCs has been exclusively at officer level, a fact precisely reflected in the subsequent change of title of this JCC to the 'South Seeborough Minority Groups and Seeborough Officers Joint Consultative Committee'. A suggestion at the second meeting that the membership be broadened to include 'representatives of all three political parties' was not supported.

This officer monopoly of the consultative process has precluded any more extended discussion of the general direction of policy. Officers are able to take refuge where necessary behind the prerogatives of council committees and the established practices of their own departments. Thus, the first meeting of the southern JCC recorded that 'on the more complex questions of policy the group may well have to consider policies which relate to specific issues. It may not be possible to make a blanket policy to cover all of the special problems of the minority groups.'

Discussion has concentrated on a range of issues of which the following are examples: specialist careers officer, specialist social worker post, survey of Asian youth, problems of young West Indians, (specific) planning applications, report of the Select Committee on the West Indian community, appointments to public bodies, the Race Relations Act 1976, employment of minority groups, Home Secretary's Advisory Council on Race Relations, advice centre, nursery facilities, learning difficulties in schools, General Improvement Area, electoral material, and youth unemployment.

In so far as any differences between the two JCCs are discernible they centre on the considerable informality of the southern JCC and its eschewal of policy issues. For the most part, the topics discussed were confined either to matters of local authority practice, or to the general circumstances of the local communities or to developments at the national level. In contrast, our own observations of the northern JCC meetings suggest a greater willingness to discuss broad issues of local authority activity and service provision. It is perhaps significant that one (now departed) member of the southern JCC (whose personal style was evidently more abrasive than that of his colleagues), having earlier lost his proposal for a political element on the committee soon challenged the general approach that had been adopted and expressed concern, on behalf of absent colleagues and of himself, about the direction of the Joint Consultative Committee, the credibility achieved and the absence of long-term objectives. In the discussion that followed, it was agreed that the objectives of the JCC were properly confined to those expressed in the constitution which they had approved. Since this individual left the area, JCC discussions have clearly become more consensual.

Something more than a matter of style is at issue here in what may be judged to be an only partly successful exercise in consultation whose main limitation is the acceptance of current policy as 'given'. The first of these meetings which we attended heard the outgoing chairman speak forcibly against confrontation and argue that 'consensus is the answer'. Consensus was clearly to coalesce around the authority's own priorities. Explaining (for our benefit) the great value of the JCC, the chairman pointed to the value of minority groups being able to meet with 'the policy-makers': 'we don't want to press for things that can't be done. They can tell us what can't be done'. The atmosphere in those JCC meetings which we have attended has been extremely friendly, despite the marked defensiveness on the part of the Seeborough officers. Reference among members to friendship links and professions of friendship appeared almost to be a conventional mode of address in the JCC, somewhat diffused perhaps when extended by the end of the first meeting we attended to the PSI observer himself. Sport has been a common topic not only of pre-meeting conversation but also of allusion during the discussions. One Asian member, making a rhetorical attack on the policies of the present government, was rebuked not only by the committee but more forcibly by a West Indian colleague who insisted 'don't bring politics into it'. That the rebuke came from a member who is also a well-known Labour party activist is testament to the pervasiveness of a consensual and non-partisan atmosphere.

Seeborough's JCC experiment is regarded with great pride by the authority's officers and indeed there are important lessons to be learned from it. As a channel of consultation it is limited by the membership of the two bodies (which some officers will privately describe as 'unrepresentative'). As a channel of policy discussion, the northern JCC has had more success, perhaps in part because of the prominent role played there by the notably policy-minded SCRO. The southern JCC is clearly of limited utility, although it undoubtedly provides some satisfaction to its members.

Perhaps the most telling comment on the southern JCC is provided by comparison with the separate Police Liaison Committee established in 1979. Some of the issues raised in the JCCs have *also* appeared at the meetings of this liaison committee, where senior police officers and the Police Community Relations Officer meet the officers of the several local authority departments. The police representatives appear to initiate to a remarkable degree the discussion of local authority provision.

The crucial link, however, is between these police officers and yet another body, the Minority Groups Police Liaison Committee (see Figure IV.1). In this last forum, the *same* minority figures from the southern JCC discuss local issues with the police, claiming that minority groups 'know the police can exert influence (on the local authority) . . . you can do it for us'. This machinery of police liaison has been described, apparently fairly, as 'very important'. There is a close correspondence of issues discussed there, in the JCCs and in the internal officer working group. Such correspondence complicates the assessment of influence, but other evidence corroborates the indications that in south Seeborough, at least, the police are effective mediators of the consultative process; indeed, the suggestion for a southern JCC was apparently first made in the Minority Groups Police Liaison Committee. Perhaps the fact that the same minority leaders press issues in a police forum indicates their awareness that the JCC is not an effective channel of influence for them.

Concluding comments

This chapter has presented a general view of the specific arrangements for consultation of opinion adopted in our several authorities. CRCs appeared to be rather variable vehicles for sounding opinion and several authorities have made the (necessarily costly) attempt to reach community groups directly. Such attempts cannot be casually made; they demand considerable investment of time and effort. We have devoted extensive space to Seeborough's unusual JCC arrangements. Interesting and perhaps in itself suggestive, the significance of the JCC concept in its Seeborough setting is perhaps the sharp separation between consultation and policy development; compare for example the fusion of these two functions in Beeborough's Race Relations Sub-Committee. The second striking feature of consultation in Seeborough is the absence of any line of communication to elected members. If political commitment is indeed necessary to policy development, then Seeborough's minority groups are ultimately excluded from real participation in policy consideration by the very form of the consultative process.

(North Seeborough)   (South Seeborough)

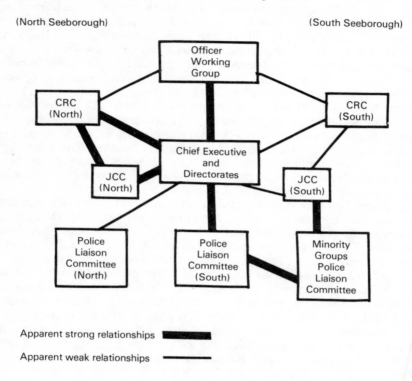

Apparent strong relationships

Apparent weak relationships

This conclusion returns us to the observation made at the beginning of this chapter. Too great an emphasis on consultative forms may obscure the far more important issues of content and consequence. In Ayeborough and Exeshire, CRCs are held at arm's length. In Seeborough the form of consultation largely prescribes the content; it has proved difficult to raise divisive policy issues in such a forum. Beeborough's creation, on the other hand, of an established consultative group at a political level, backed by a willingness to test opinion more directly, provides a continuous stream of ethnic issues onto the policy agenda. The substance of discussion cannot be predetermined and the authority cannot protect itself by ruling issues 'out of order'. Perhaps the greatest danger of 'closed' consultation on the Seeborough model is in fostering an illusion of harmonious race relations, in which genuine conflicts are suppressed by the consultative process.

There is no single touchstone of 'effectiveness' in the evaluation of consultative arrangements; they inevitably embody a plurality of interests. What is satisfactory in one context or to one group of participants may be readily dismissed elsewhere. Our main concern in this project was with the adjustment of policy and practice to the needs of a multi-racial community. From this point of view, effective consultative arrangements are those which provide for the direct expression of minority opinion to those who have the power to make decisions. No single mode of consultation will suffice to meet the requirements of flexible and responsive policy making.

References

Barker, A., *Strategy and Style in Local Community Relations,* (Runnymede Trust, London, 1975).

Commission for Racial Equality, *The Nature and Funding of Local Race Relations Work: Community Relations Councils*, (London, 1980).

V Employment Policies

In this chapter we consider the third general area of local authority activity, that of policies relating to the councils' employees. Some of the issues which arose – for example, the recruitment and training of teachers and social workers from ethnic minority groups, are considered in Chapters VI and VII. Our main concern in this chapter is to present our impressions of the general approach of the authorities to the adoption and interpretation of 'equal opportunity' as a criterion or guideline for their own recruitment and training policies. Inevitably, this question leads into further aspects of employment policy, for example recruitment advertising and record keeping. It also touches upon the significance of national influences on policy development, in particular the Race Relations Act 1976 and the promotional activities of the CRE. These again are topics which we shall examine more closely in a later chapter.

The Race Relations Act of 1976 which replaced the 1968 Act continues the legal prohibition of discrimination in employment. Section 4(1) covers unlawful discrimination in recruitment, section 4(2) covers discrimination in access to opportunities for training, promotion, transfer and other benefits of existing employees. Section 1(1)(a) and Section 3(1) define 'direct' racial discrimination, the intentionally less favourable treatment of an individual on racial grounds. Section 1(1)(b) adds the concept of *indirect* racial discrimination, defined as treatment equal in a formal sense as between different racial groups but unequal in its effects upon a particular group and which cannot be shown to be justifiable on other than racial grounds.

The 1976 Act, however, also embodies the concept of 'positive action' and Section 38(1)(2) sets out the circumstances in which an employer may provide various forms of encouragement to minority groups, including special access to training for a group hitherto underrepresented in some particular activity. 'Positive action', as it is popularly understood however, goes beyond this statutory obligation to remove barriers to the recruitment and advancement of minority workers, and generally denotes a programme to remedy the effects of past discrimination and disadvantage. 'Positive' or 'reverse' discrimination at the point of recruitment remains unlawful, however; like any other employer, a local authority can neither recruit nor promote staff of a particular ethnic group on the grounds that the group have in the past suffered from adverse discrimination. A local authority may on the other hand lawfully take steps to remove certain barriers to 'equal opportunity' with similar effect, and (under Section 5(2)(d), may choose to regard membership of a particular ethnic group as in itself constituting a qualification for certain posts. More generally, Section 71 of the Act contains a general injunction to local authorities to promote 'good race relations' and 'equality of opportunity' and arguably permits almost any practice not specifically prohibited elsewhere.

This brief synopsis of the legal context of employment policy implicitly indicates the enormous scope for diverse interpretation of duties and opportunities under the Act. It is hardly surprising that these provisions seemed to be shrouded in confusion within all of the authorities. The confusion is compounded by the absence of what local authorities would regard as authoritative advice on the interpretation of the Act, particularly in identifying indirect discrimination and in specifying good practice.

The problems arise most notably in the areas of 'positive action' and good practice. The Act leaves it to the CRE to issue guidance on discrimination and the promotion of equal opportunity in employment. A code of practice prepared by the Commission, if approved by the Secretary of State for Employment, may be laid before Parliament and the observance by an employer of such a code would be taken into account at industrial tribunal proceedings. The Commission's draft *Code of Practice* has been subject to consultation and has been informally submitted to the Department of Employment but has yet, at the time of writing, to be approved.

The local authorities do not regard such non-statutory guidance as has been issued by the CRE and its predecessors as authoritative. The Community Relations Commission publication, *The Multi-Racial Community: A guide for local Councillors* is the sole guidance document directed specifically at local government in the employment field. The CRC pamphlet encapsulated the substance of the issue:

> 'Local authorities can be leaders in the field of equal opportunity employment policies, by which it is made known to employees of all levels that stringent precautions must be taken to avoid intentional or unintentional discrimination in all the employment procedures and practices. In order for such a policy to be shown to be working, and in order to assess progress, an equal opportunity policy should be monitored by means of records which show the racial or ethnic origin of employees in all job grades, and their progress in recruitment, promotion, training and access to benefits.'

Our fieldwork suggests that a number of obstacles lie in the way of achieving equality of opportunity in this field and we have accordingly arranged our discussion around them. First, there is the problem of the varied interpretations of what 'equal opportunity' implies. The second obstacle concerns the fundamental confusion as to whether employment policies should be considered in a narrow organisational context or a broader community context. Third, there is the resistance to any steps to provide for effective monitoring on the part of councillors, officers and staff representatives. Finally, we present a brief portrayal of Beeborough's progress towards an equal opportunity policy, as an illustration of how an authority can attempt to overcome these obstacles.

Interpreting 'equal opportunity'

We found the term 'equal opportunity' to be subject to markedly different interpretations throughout local government. The more positive interpretation of the term is broadly that espoused by the CRE. It assumes that opportunity in the employment field (as elsewhere) will be unequal in the absence of intervention to redress the consequences of disadvantage and past discrimination. It accepts that policies to secure equality will need to be monitored and periodically reviewed, and that many detailed practices, in the handling of casual inquiries or in the placement of job advertisements, will need to be changed. Among our six authorities this view predominated only in Beeborough. Elsewhere we found it supported, if at all, by a minority. On the other hand, some individuals were found to subscribe to a more radical view that positive discrimination, currently unlawful, was required. The contrasts between Beeborough and the other four authorities whose practices we were able to examine are very marked and our discussion in this section is therefore confined to what appeared to be common to the remainder.

We found the interpretation of 'equal opportunity' as implying no more than the absence of unlawful discrimination (or possibly only the absence of *direct* discrimination) to be widespread. Usually put forward in the context of assurances that 'we don't discriminate' this was evidently the accepted policy in Exeshire, Ayeborough, Seeborough, and Deeborough. Evidence for the effectiveness of this policy position was sometimes adduced by authorities from the absence of successful cases brought before industrial tribunals, and practices in the fields of recruitment and advertising were normally unquestioned. On the other hand, the need to avoid accusations of unlawful discrimination often gave rise to training programmes designed to familiarise managers and supervisors – indeed, all staff with a recruitment role – with the formal provisions of at least the most explicit sections of the Race Relations Act.

Many authorities have, after careful consideration, adopted some form of equal opportunity statement. This is often seen as a codification of existing (non-discriminatory) practice and as an assurance of fair treatment to potential applicants for employment. In fact, the National Joint Council's Scheme of Conditions of Service for Administrative, Professional, Technical and Clerical staff includes the following provision:

> 'all local authorities' employees should be afforded equal opportunities in the employment context, irrespective of their sex, marital status, race, religion or colour. The National Agreement on terms and conditions of employment does not differentiate in these respects and local authorities, in applying the agreement and in operating their recruitment, training,

48

and promotion policies, are urged to develop and practice positively the concept of equal opportunities for all.'

An 'equal opportunity statement' may then be viewed locally as no more than a ratification of nationally agreed conditions of service. Conversely, the existence of those conditions may persuade an authority that no local declaration is necessary. In Seeborough, for example, a rather legalistic discussion of the implications of the Act concluded that as the employee's 'Statement of particulars of employment' made reference, *inter alia*, to the NJC terms and conditions of employment 'it is therefore evident that the authority already subscribes to the Act in the belief in equality of opportunity for all persons'. Therefore, no special equal opportunity statement was needed.

The increasing number of such locally adopted statements is sometimes seen by observers as indicating a steady incremental progress towards equal opportunity. Our fieldwork suggests that the adoption of such a statement *per se* is evidence of very little and may be intended to do no more than provide a modicum of legal protection to the authority. In Exeshire, for example, the issue was considered by a working party of chief and senior officers under the chairmanship of the county chief executive. The working party inquired into the practices of the largest district in the county, where an equal opportunity statement had been adopted by the council in 1976. The county officials were assured by local officers that

> 'the acceptance of the policy had not resulted in any great change in the City Council's procedures but it had merely codified those already adopted by officers. It also had the effect of making members and officers more conscious of the requirements now included in the Act.'

With the encouragement of this local example, the county council approved (after consultation with the trade unions) a policy statement affirming that recruitment, training and promotion decisions would be taken 'having regard only to the requirements of the job' and affirming the availability of opportunities 'irrespective of race, ethnic origin or sex'.

The clearest example of 'equal opportunity' policy as a reaffirmation of existing practice is seen in Ayeborough where it is noted that 'no form of discrimination has ever been authorised or countenanced on grounds of race, colour, religion, or nationality'. In this case, the 1968 Act had earlier prompted a report to council that 'the Act involved no change of policy, as the Council did not discriminate on grounds of race'. However, in order that 'no reasons shall be given to anyone to doubt the Council's policy or practice' a non-discrimination resolution was formally adopted.

The Ayeborough practices exemplify the more widespread tendency to deny the existence of unlawful racially discriminatory policies: 'we should ensure . . . that no advice is offered to staff making appointments that a coloured person would not be welcome'. Beyond this, 'at interviews, care must be taken not to adopt a different approach to non-white candidates. Similar questions should be asked as for other candidates'. Inquiries from the local CRC during 1975 had elicited the statement that 'the council as an employer is committed to affording *fair opportunity* for members of minority communities to enter its service and to providing a sympathetic working environment for those who join its staff'. (Our emphasis).

The subject was reopened in Ayeborough by the discussions in the Ethnic Minority Strategy Group. The chief executive persistently raised questions of implementing and monitoring an equal opportunity policy; an active 'backbench' councillor repeatedly expressed scepticism about the realities of employment policy in Ayeborough. Faced with these pressures, the personnel director proposed an equal opportunity statement on two grounds. The first was that it would provide the basis for a far-reaching review of training needs, thus maintaining Ayeborough's position as a 'training-minded' authority. The second was that such a statement would serve to head off pressures for a more positive policy, including monitoring, which he felt to be potentially destructive of good industrial relations.

The position in Seeborough and Deeborough is not materially different. Confident claims are made as to the absence of discrimination and the several aspects of the 'positive' approach are discounted. Seeborough have a detailed document setting out the full ramifications of the authority's 'Personnel Policy' which makes no reference whatsoever to equality of opportunity. In September 1978, the SCRO of the North Seeborough CRC made substantial representations to the authority for a comprehensive rewrite of this document to include a number of additional clauses at appropriate junctures, but without effect.

Deeborough on the other hand have made explicit claims of non-discrimination by formally adopting the TUC model clause, which reads:

'The parties to this agreement are committed to the development of positive policies to promote equal opportunities in employment regardless of workers' sex, marital status, creed, colour, race or ethnic origins. This principle will apply in respect of recruitment, training, pay and conditions of employment, allocation of work and promotion. The normal criteria for selecting a person for a particular job will be that person's abilities and the job requirements. The management undertake to draw opportunities for training and promotion to the attention of all eligible employees and to inform all employees of this Agreement on equal opportunity'.

The city's personnel director amplified this commitment for us:

'We don't view the ethnic minority differently from any other sector. We believe that a local authority has to attract the best talent and should not aim its practices at any other group . . . We always look for the people best able to do the job. We feel free as an authority to identify and approach the best candidates — this doesn't work against the ethnic minority *in itself*, but due to other factors . . .'

50

Here the formal non-discrimination policy represented 'an intention' and implied 'an extensive effort in training of our own people and the coloureds' which, however, for resource reasons had yet to be made.

In Deeborough, more than elsewhere, the commitment to non-discrimination was overtly qualified by the commitment to obtaining 'the best person for the job' in order to maintain a high level of service provision: 'in a time of high unemployment you can take your pick and get people with higher qualifications (although) this is something I couldn't defend. In those sorts of times the ethnic minority must lose out very badly.' It is just such an acceptance that marks off these 'negative' interpretations of equal opportunity from the more positive approach recommended by the CRE and adopted by a small minority of authorities.

It seems likely, on the basis of the information from our case study authorities, that the advocacy of equal employment practices has had less impact among local authorities than even casual inspection would suggest. It cannot be inferred that 'positive action' will flow from an equal opportunity statement. In part this would seem to be because local authorities in many cases reviewed their practices in the light of the Act, or often of the Bill, during 1975-76. There was, as an Exeshire officer commented, 'no authoritative guidance' at the time, and the subsequent government circular gave no specific advice on employment policy. Officials were thus left free to make their own interpretations of the Act and these interpretations had been largely codified by the time the CRE began to issue detailed guidance.

That the negative interpretation with its concern merely to avoid direct discrimination predominated is not surprising. Local authority officials, as public servants, are usually scrupulously concerned that their authority should comply with the statutory requirements. The most salient feature of the Act is the requirement that an employer should not discriminate, and in the case of indirect discrmination, the onus is put upon the employer to prove that his practices were not intended to do so. The council, as the authority, is *itself* the employer and would be held liable for the acts of its servants. Thus, the accountability of the officials to the council, and the reciprocal responsibility of the council for the acts of officials, work together as an inducement to ensure that discriminatory recruitment decisions will not be taken. Hence the flood of, for example, 'recruitment point' training schemes in the wake of the Act. The sanctions attaching to this aspect of 'equal oportunity' are such as to make it a central concern. Because the more positive aspects of the term are merely permissive, they have failed to attract the same attention.

Moreover, the common language of debate and discussion in this field obscures a real gulf between the understanding of the CRE and the few 'positive action' authorities on the one hand, and of the greater part of local government on the other. The point of departure concerns the policy base itself: whether the goals of equal opportunity relate to the entire community or to the existing workforce. 'Equal opportunity for whom?' is the implicit but unstated question here. The very organisation and professionalisation of local authorities tends toward the more restrictive interpretation of this question as one of *personnel policy* rather than *employment policy* and it is to this confusion that we now turn.

The policy base: employment or personnel?

The most distinctive feature of the 'positive' approach to equal opportunity is that its aims are very broad. It is often advocated less as an application of the employment provisions of the Act than as an example of the broader responsibility of authorities under S.71. The emphasis in this case is upon the role of the local authority in the *community*, intervening in the field of race relations and racial disadvantage, maximising minority opportunity, setting an example to other large employers, demolishing the barriers of indirect discrimination and eroding 'institutionalised racism'. It is in such a context that the proponents of 'positive action' point to an authority's status often as the largest single employer in the locality. Such a preoccupation has little significance except within *a community frame of reference* in which local government is viewed as operating, wittingly or otherwise, upon the 'opportunity structure' of its area. Given such a view, it is meaningful to speak of an *employment* policy as one in which goals are specified (at least in part) in community terms. Generally, this view receives less support from establishment or personnel officers than from officials engaged in developing strategies within the inner cities arrangements. In this last case, 'disadvantaged groups' may be identified as a priority target for employment-related projects and it is but a short step from there to the espousal of a positive approach to the authority's *own* employment practices.

It is significant that internal advocacy of positive action typically comes from such quarters. Tackling deprivation is a relatively new aspect of local authority activity, and illustrates the kind of new issue often identified through the 'problem search' activities of specialist units: corporate planning, policy analysis, comprehensive community programmes or inner cities units. The *traditional* locus of policy and practice in this respect lies elsewhere, in the network of establishment committees, personnel directors and staff consultative machinery. Within this network personnel directors occupy a central place, bearing as they do the primary responsibility of staff relations and being the main source of advice to committees and council on staffing matters. The logic of their position sharply differentiates them from the 'corporate' problem-identifiers. Their concern is not with the community but with the workforce and with the entrants to it. Whatever the titles of their policy reports, seminars or training courses may imply, the fundamental concern of these strategically placed officials is with *personnel* policy rather than *employment* policy.

Local authorities and private undertakings occupy quite a different position in relation to the community yet the assumptions of personnel directors in both sectors tend to stress the common elements of management in the context of a large organisation. In both the private and the public spheres the frame of reference of personnel directors is bounded by the limits of the organisation itself. Seeborough's personnel policy is the most striking example of this tendency. Employees (referred to as 'manpower') are seen as 'probably the most vital and certainly the most costly of the authority's resources', and the authority stresses 'the need at all times to ensure that the organisation ...is responsive to the concept of value for money'. This ' determined personnel policy' is intended to 'provide a sufficient supply of manpower trained (and retrained when necessary) to the standards necessary to maintain the authority's service programmes' and at the same time to 'fulfil *as far as possible* the ambitions and potentialities of individual employees' (emphasis in original). The manpower policy statement is replete with such terms as 'strategy', 'aptitude and personality testing', 'long term plan', 'management audit' and 'equilibrium'. It is explicitly a resource management plan and may well operate as an effective strategic tool to that end. Naturally the foremost consideration of the personnel director in Seeborough is to operate this policy with its component sections for manpower planning, recruitment, training and development.

We turn now to look more closely at the views of personnel directors (using this term in a generic sense) in some of the authorities in our study. The professional organisation for local authority personnel directors is the Society of Chief Personnel Officers in Local Govenment (SOCPO), a relatively recent creation. Some personnel directors are also members of the Institute of Personnel Management; they are therefore members of a wider professional community than many of their departmental colleagues. In some cases, the views which we encountered in our study may seem contrary to the spirit of the Race Relations Act, and two issues in particular merit attention: first, the exclusive orientation of most directors to the narrower issues of 'personnel'and organisation; second, their more specific assumptions about 'equal opportunity' and ethnic minorities.

One personnel director exemplified the primary concern of his profession while recognising the case for equal opportunity practices: 'I want to achieve more appointments (but) not at the cost of racial disharmony. In my view we can do both things'. Staff relations, however, were in his view firmly against anything which smacked of 'positive discrimination':

> 'I can increase appointments tomorrow but upset staff. It's the chaps out there — and the girls. If your policy was to increase representation they'd be up in arms. The thing that matters profoundly to local government officers is that they are favourably and equitably dealt with . . . They are terribly anxious about promotion . . . People are intensely watchful and will take umbrage at the slightest thing. So someone comes along and says 'lets favour *this* group' . . . the moment you tip the scales you get a furious reaction. And where will that reproach settle? — on the favoured few.'

Another senior personnel officer set out slightly different views but shared the 'fear that you can set this ball rolling without knowing where it can take you' whereas other local authorities 'may be very philanthropic in their approach . . . we do have this difference of standpoint'. The difference concerned the proper purpose of a personnel policy, which clearly was seen as

53

ministering to an organisational need: 'We've been saying for many years that a local authority should look critically at itself as to skill levels and needs (of the authority itself).'

There were no indications in meetings, interviews or files that personnel directors had considered the issue of their authority's broader role in the community. What was evident in some cases was a marked lack of sympathy with ethnic minority staff verging at times on outright hostility. Such views on the part of some personnel directors cast grave doubt on the prospects for equal opportunity policies which they might be required to develop and operate. One director told us a series of hearsay anecdotes about the practices of minority groups and referred repeatedly to 'coloured gentlemen'. His participation in a seminar with CRE staff was less than wholehearted and he was fairly openly antagonistic about this and another event which he attended.

Another personnel director spoke at length about the 'problems' posed by minority staff:

'We *have* coloured people in our employment, including professional people. There are certain problems with coloured people — problems with language and religion . . . These things don't prevent them from becoming a good employee. It's easy in an employment situation to allow that to cloud the situation — in the past we haven't dealt with this.'

He referred repeatedly to ways in which an undifferentiated 'they' could 'cause problems and friction between employees with (their) wanting to pray every two hours from dawn to dusk'. Moreover, so far as employees from ethnic minorities are concerned 'there are disadvantages on the intellectual side arising from genetic functions plus added disadvantage'.

The general impression which arose from our contacts with and observation of personnel directors is of a profession whose ethos and training incline them to a management role which perceives two distinct needs: the manpower and functional needs of the authority as an organisation and the personal development needs of their individual staff. Their professional skill lies in their ability to balance or reconcile these needs within a tradition of consultation with unions and staff associations. Such competing pressures and loyalties doubtless provide personnel directors with a testing and often unpredictable working environment. To expect them to take the lead role in developing the more positive type of equal opportunity practice may be unrealistic; their professional ethos and their managerial role are understandably at odds with the conception of a responsive local authority operating in a multi-racial environment.

Implementation: beyond a profession of faith

The previous section considered the organisational and professional norms which appear to operate against all but the most restrictive view of equal opportunity. Some of these factors — misunderstanding, excessive work force loyalty, prejudice and fear of a backlash — would also operate whenever authorities sought to take a more positive approach. Indeed, while most of our authorities have adopted formal statements of their practice as equal opportunity employers, at least to the extent of disavowing discrimination, their practices rarely progressed beyond the adoption of such statements and the briefing of recruitment staff on the prohibitions of the Race Relations Act.

If 'equal opportunity' amounted in most places to little more than a profession of faith, or at best an aspiration, why should this be so? That personnel directors are oriented to the existing workforce rather than to the employment role of the authority in the community does not, of course, preclude a determined approach to securing equal opportunity in training and promotion, yet it does little to encourage the re-fashioning of recruitment policies, with the necessary reviews of record keeping, advertising, selection procedures, application forms design, and qualification levels. It may be that such measures as these to bring about equal opportunity in the *recruitment* field have to be set in motion before effective steps can be taken to ensure equity within the workforce itself. There is little substance in 'fair' promotion practices if entry to the workforce itself is (unintentionally) restricted.

What then are the obstacles to giving real force to declarations of equal opportunity? They range from simple misunderstanding of the law on discrimination through the conflation of separate issues, to the fear of opposition, the exaggeration of practical difficulties and sheer administrative inflexibility. These, at least, are the overt manifestations of resistance to the substance of equal opportunity. There may well be deeper-seated 'attitudes of mind' which were not overtly expressed in the interviews which we conducted or at the meetings which we attended.

Perhaps the most surprising of our findings is the extent to which elected councillors and responsible officers fail to grasp the nature and limits of the law on discrimination. That such incomprehension is commonly the case and was shared by two of the personnel directors argues strongly for at least an authoritative clarification of the issues and we return to this point in Chapter VIII.

Some of the confusion undoubtedly arises from a conflation of the terms 'positive discrimination' (unlawful discrimination) and 'positive action' (a term which covers the more emphatic attempts to ensure equal opportunity). Thus in Ayeborough, following a wide ranging discussion of employment issues, it was minuted: 'that it would be possible to *positively discriminate* in favour of ethnic minorities by, say, introducing into advertisements a reference to the Borough Council as an 'Equal Opportunity Employer'. In addition, advertisements could be placed in ethnic minority journals.' (our emphasis). During the discussion which this quotation records the chairman of the establishment committee had expressed himself very forcefully: 'we have in fact managed in Ayeborough to preach the need to see people as people . . . If anyone *dares* to suggest — and I mean *dares* — that we should have *pro rata promotion* then I would come out against it publicly if necessary.' Confusion here was widespread.

One officer in Ayeborough had suggested that ethnic minorities should be encouraged to 'come forward' into council employment on the ground that 'there is a massive population of Asian youngsters in this borough'. This suggestion worried the EMSG chairman, who felt that 'It's going too far obviously to start encouraging recruitment.' The establishment committee chairman was hotly opposed to such positive action, arguing that 'It's racialist. It would be blatantly racialist to say we'd welcome black people instead of white . . . . You're automatically admitting that we do discriminate when you do that.'

Other discussion in Ayeborough confirmed this impression of a confusion which persisted despite the concise and precise contribution of the personnel director. Nor was this confusion confined to employment questions. In housing matters particularly, consideration of the ethnic dimension in service provision was equated with the deplored positive or reverse discrimination'. One councillor asked: 'Are we going to try to create a situation artificially through records or are we going to let people get what they want as at present regardless of ethnic origin?' Another argued vehemently against a situation in which 'there might be empty houses due to no Irishman available'. That policy monitoring does not imply either quotas or 'positive discrimination' is not widely recognised; in Ayeborough as elsewhere some councillors seemed to feel that racial explicitness was in itself unlawful.

To some extent the statements made in meetings, reports and interviews reflect the ordinary looseness of everyday language as much as actual misconceptions about policy and law. However, we have observed meetings at which councillors and officers were clearly moving in just such confused discussions toward the authoritative resolution of these issues. Moreover, in one authority the personnel director confirmed that representation from the CRE or other bodies on equal opportunity would be the subject only of *oral* report to his management team or committee. Such oral reports might reflect this officer's own personal interpretation of discrimination:

> 'I have the distinct impression that we would be in breach of the law if we kept records . . . . If we are not discriminating why should we have to keep records? We are only monitoring the skin of those who are alien – we are doing (this) in obeying the law. Surely we are discriminating in doing this?'

It should be remembered that this officer is the major source of advice on personnel issues to a council which employs many thousands of workers.

The technical advice of officers is particularly crucial in decisions over such issues as ethnic record keeping where practicable and locally appropriate schemes have to be devised. It is accepted that classification by place of birth is an inadequate indication of ethnic identity and the CRE proposal to record *origins* features six categories: African, Asian, Caribbean, UK European and Irish, Other European and Other. Recording should be by self assignment in response to such a question as 'I would describe my ethnic origins as . . .'. In the light of the ready availability of this advice in several CRE publications it is all the more surprising to find a personnel director (who was particularly dismissive of 'the Race Commission' as 'wielding the big stick') not only being unaware of the existence of the CRE's draft *Code of Practice* but representing the record-keeping issue in these terms: 'How are you going to establish (ethnic identity)? How many generations do you go back?' Citing the case of an Englishman born in India he asked 'How do we monitor him? Is it colour we are talking about? Do we monitor the Aussies and New Zealanders?'

This type of misapprehension was probably even more common among councillors, who are less likely to be aware of the practical solutions advocated by CRE or adopted in other authorities.

It is, of course, the case that some councillors and officers are opposed to ethnic record keeping in principle. The council leaders in Beeborough and Deeborough, both areas of earlier Jewish settlement, had expressed reservations about the principle of identifying the ethnic origin of individuals. In Beeborough, the CRC opposed record keeping on grounds of the risk of abuse by a possible racialist régime. The fear of political exploitation of ethnic records by right-wing groups was also cited in Exeshire as an important reason for rejecting ethnic record keeping. To other councillors and officers the principle of identifying ethnicity was distasteful rather than politically dangerous. It was variously attacked as 'divisive' and 'unfair'. It was specifically opposed by personnel directors in Exeshire, Ayeborough, Seeborough and Deeborough.

There were however distinctions to be drawn among these critics of record keeping. One thought 'informal' monitoring of equal opportunity both possible and desirable, at least in relation to promotion. Another rejected the possibility of monitoring schemes altogether with the assertion that *'nobody* is monitoring'. These questions of practicability are important. One council leader, asking to be convinced on record keeping, readily conceded that equal opportunity could be no more than a profession of faith without a monitoring system, yet the discussions of monitoring in his council have yet to recognise the practical possibilities of schemes.

Even if (as our judgement inclines us to believe), the misunderstandings as to the *nature* of the law on discrimination are genuine rather than pretended, views on the *practical* difficulties of record keeping (which also touch upon the anticipated costs of such exercises) may often conceal an apprehension that it would be fraught with potentially damaging political difficulties. Record keeping was described in one authority as 'a mechanism which puts horror into everyone . . . You collect it because you want to use it — to intervene in a situation where everything is developing naturally.'
Another committee chairman warned that:

'I think the thing we should have to guard ourselves against is to avoid being seen to give any impetus to any feeling against people in our employment who have lived here all their lives and were born here . . . There are dangers if we are seen to be going too far on this we'll be discriminating against the indigenous population. I'm afraid of repercussions that could occur and harm innocent individuals. We have a thriving relationship with the Trade Unions that come to us. I'm completely satisfied that if there were any discrimination they'd be the first to complain.'

There were also claims by councillors that any aspects of 'positive action' in employment could provoke a backlash among the white majority while an officer claimed that 'even the fairness of an equal opportunity statement will be misunderstood'.

If such obstacles to implementing good intentions as misunderstanding, practical difficulties and anxiety about repercussions were not sufficient to scotch any proposal for a more positive approach, they could be reinforced by an unwillingness to change procedures. The cost and inconvenience of a record keeping *system* was often cited, along with its implications for the redesign of application forms. Another source of resistance to change concerned practices relating to the advertising of vacancies. The claim that few minority candidates were appointed because few applied was sometimes countered with the suggestion that advertisements should be placed in the minority press. In one authority, the revelation that a minority press existed clearly came as a surprise to the officers concerned and the CRO present was invited to supply details.

In another instance, resistance to minority press advertisement was justified (somewhat obliquely) by references to the need to maintain professional standards. Elsewhere, a personnel officer, in response to a general inquiry, claimed that 'We don't advertise in the *Bangladesh Times* . . . We couldn't get an ad. together and the limited circulation makes it economically non-justifiable.' Finally, even the adoption and publication of an equal opportunity statement could be opposed by senior personnel staff: 'We don't say 'Equal Opportunity' in ads — we believe that in just advertising without restriction (as to candidates) we are being 'Equal Opportunity'.' In this case, the officer concerned claimed to have calculated the advertising cost of including such a statement to be £35,000 p.a. for his authority; he opposed it on this ground.

So far this chapter has dealt exclusively with those obstacles to specific policies for equal opportunity which we found to be prevalent among our sample of authorities. Our broader survey indicated that some of these factors are important elsewhere, but our evidence does not point to the impracticability of adopting a positive approach to equal opportunity. Some inner London authorities have pursued such an approach; we decided to look at their experience and have had helpful co-operation from them. But even within our own sample, Beeborough provides an example of an authority facing up to the obstacles and attempting to develop tangible policies for equal opportunity, policies which go beyond what was elsewhere an often unconvincing profession of faith. Beeborough's experience therefore merits separate discussion.

Developing an equal opportunity programme

The obstacles to equal opportunity programmes appear to be present in greater or lesser degree in many authorities. The experience of Beeborough suggests that positive policies for equal opportunity are, though a delicate and precarious matter, nevertheless feasible. Perhaps it is important to stress that Beeborough is not one of the more 'advanced' authorities, but is a council whose members and officers more nearly represent the broad centre ground of English local government. Beeborough *is* unusual both in the large proportion of its ethnic minority population and in the recent involvement of minorities in the Labour party; this has greatly increased their prospects of representation on the council in 1982. Yet Beeborough's 'progressivism' is not attributable solely to black participation; that relationship is probably a reciprocal one.

The attitudes expressed by Beeborough officers until quite recently corresponded closely enough with those which our study brought to light elsewhere. A compilation of chief officers' views on record keeping made during 1973 revealed that:

'The Council's policy is based on equality of status regardless of ethnic background. It does not recognise 'colour' as a qualifying factor either in favour or disqualification of any circumstance. For this reason it has no record of the number of coloured people in the borough nor does it keep records of its own employees . . . . The council believes in, and affords, equal opportunities to all its employees to gain advancement based on merit. Positive encouragement could be an offence.'

It was felt that the authority should 'absolutely not' keep records due to their potential for 'damage to community relations'. Beeborough has moved during the past few years from this 'negative' interpretation of equal opportunity to an acceptance of the need for 'positive action'.

Some aspects of Beeborough's recent developments in the field of equal opportunity are worth singling out here. There is the general climate of councillor-officer relations and the responsiveness shown to the passage of the 1976 Race Relations Act. There is the adoption of a firm and tangible commitment on the part of the council in its Equal Opportunity Statement. There is the deep concern with training matters that forms a common thread in subsequent events. Also important is the extensive process of consultation initiated in the wake of the Equal Opportunity Statement, the steps taken toward assessing and monitoring equal opportunity, and the council's approach to the workforce itself and to the trade unions.

Until recently, Beeborough might have been regarded as a fairly mainstream if rather traditional type of authority. Its highly respected former town clerk was of the 'old school'. The traditional flavour of Beeborough's management style was to be found not only in its formal structures but also in the strong sense of constitutional rectitude that sustained an almost 'textbook' pattern of member-officer relationships. There were many indications in Beeborough of a long-established formality in these interactions. This sense of at least public acceptance of the 'administrative' role of officers, subordinating themselves to 'policy making' members was probably crucial to the development of a positive approach to race relations there and aspects of these taken-for-granted roles permeate several facets of the developments which we recount later. One

59

officer cited this scrupuously 'correct' conception ('if the Council has a wish to do something and I'm an officer of the Council') as underlying the developments towards equal opportunity; moreover, as he observed, probably realistically. 'It's not an area where officers can lead'.

This 'textbook' convention (which from our observation seemed both pervasive and powerful) applied equally to the interpretation of the Race Relations Act. Unlike some authorities elsewhere, where a narrow and legalistic response was adopted, Beeborough seemed to interpret the Act as signifying a government lead that could not be ignored without impropriety. The local SCRO ensured that the council were well aware of the Act's requirements, having sent a package of material (including the Community Relations Commission's guide for local councillors) to all members. The town clerk's immediate response was to convene a chief officers' working party. In November 1977, a fairly full report was submitted to committee summarising the Act and the subsequent circular which explained its provisions, referring to CRC publications and guidance notes and reporting the views of chief officers. Directors had agreed on the need to take action on averting discrimination and on 'the need for clear general instructions to staff, to ensure against direct discrimination, in particular that caused by instructions from one employee to another'. They were evidently prepared to go beyond this familiar 'minimal' response and to consider the wider aspects of employment policy:

'Local government, as one of the largest employers of manpower, has a duty to look carefully at all practices, especially in the area of employment, to ensure that discrimination does not take place nor does it appear to do so. In this connection it was noted that *ad hoc* enquiries in respect of employment may not be dealt with according to the normal practices and it was therefore decided that in future all such enquiries in respect of non-manual non-teaching posts should be forwarded to be dealt with by the Personnel Section. In addition note was taken of the circumstances in which ethnicity could be considered a legitimate qualification for particular posts.'

Thus, early adjustments to both perspectives and practices were made in the light of the Act. Nor was its effect merely transitory. We noted that in the (frequent) arguments about positive action in Beeborough recourse would be made to the statutory requirements of the Act: 'S.71 places a distinct responsibility on this authority'; policy was seen as 'reflecting the Race Relations Act'; and 'we as councillors are responsible — we want to comply with the law'. Significantly, these arguments were not challenged on the basis of any contrary interpretation.

The Race Relations Working Party, as we recount in Chapter III, was established in 1978 to devise proposals for realising the objectives of 'greater racial harmony and the removal of racial disadvantage'. Inevitably, a large part of the RRWP's discussions has been centred on the council's employment practices and the experience of other more advanced authorities has often been adduced in support of positive action. An equal opportunity policy and specific measures for giving it substance were proposed at the second meeting of the RRWP in September 1978. The range of practices endorsed by the working party was referred to the several directorates for comment.

Meanwhile, the council's employment and industrial policy working party was considering the position of disadvantaged groups in the labour market. Prompted by the RRWP's concerns, the working party drafted an equal opportunity statement which was endorsed by the policy and resources committee and publicised by the leader of the council. The statement, which broadly follows the CRE recommended form of words, reads:

'This authority is an equal opportunity employer. The aim of our policy is to ensure that no job applicant or employee receives less favourable treatment on the ground of race, colour, nationality, sex, marital status or ethnic or national origins, or is disadvantaged by conditions or requirements which cannot be shown to be justifiable. Selection criteria and procedures will be frequently reviewed to ensure that individuals are selected, promoted and treated on the basis of the irrelevant merits and abilities. All employees will be given equal opportunity and, where appropriate, special training, to progress within the organisation. The authority is committed to a programme of action to make this policy fully effective.'

The policy and resources committee in approving this statement in September 1979 referred it to the RRWP to take steps towards its implementation.

Before the working party were able to formulate proposals in this respect their attention turned again to the question of training. The original report on the implications of the 1976 Act had highlighted staff training as an area for urgent attention. The first business meeting of the RRWP included an extended session on training needs, which focused on the requirements of the Race Relations Act; briefing on ethnic minority culture and characteristics; special training for 'public contact' staff; staff selection training; promotional training for ethnic minority staff; and recruitment of ethnic minority trainees in, for example, the field of social services.

The directors had considered these suggestions and in January 1979 the town clerk reported to the RRWP that 'the observations of the various directors have identified a particular need for further training' both for recruitment staff (where central training was suggested 'to ensure a common approach') and for staff who deal directly with the public. Several ways of meeting these needs were discussed and the RRWP invited the Industrial Unit of the Runnymede Trust to prepare detailed proposals for these training facilities and for induction training, the activities in each case to be 'relevant to the special needs of the ethnic minorities and to the provisions of the Race Relations Act'. Runnymede's initial proposals were based on the assumption 'that the council will, at some stage, formally and publicly endorse the working party's recommendation for a positive equal opportunity programme and proceed to introduce the necessary arrangements to cover these elements. Ideally, the training provided would include a description and explanation of the council's equal opportunity policy, and the practical implications of that policy.'

On this basis the Industrial unit was authorised to make an 'analysis of training need' and carried out a brief survey exercise among the council's departments.

The Runnymede report led to extensive discussion among the senior managers of the various departments. The contents of the report and the response to it by directors must be treated as confidential to the authority and cannot be discussed here. Certainly, it generated controversy on which some officers were unwilling to elaborate. When the feelings aroused by the report had faded, recognition of the training need remained. As one senior officer commented, 'Runnymede seemed to highlight very effectively that there *was* a training need — people can't expect to get high paid jobs and have thick skins — there's no point in being defensive.' Indeed, even the most staunch criticisms of the report were qualified by such statements by directors as 'I would agree that more training outlined in the report would improve staff contact with the public'.

Once the Pandora's box of ethnic relations within the council's organisation had been opened, the RRWP could not do other than consider a serious and long term programme of training. In September 1980, a report on training by the newly-appointed chief executive was endorsed both by the establishment sub-committee and by the race relations sub-committee. The report ranged wider than the earlier discussion and amounted to a review of the council's entire training needs and provision. At the time of writing, the details of the programme are still being negotiated with specialist training agencies.

One further area of continuous concern has been the placement of the council's vacancy advertisements. This issue has twice come before the RRSC, but the extension of advertising to the ethnic minority press was also being developed by the establishments sub-committee. A report in December 1979 analysed the placement of advertisements on a departmental basis, *West Indian World* and *Garavi Gujerat* featuring prominently. In February 1980, it was decided to cease advertising in a fringe local paper and to apply the savings to further advertisements in *West Indian World* and *New Life*. The basis of the present policy is that a proportion of the advertisements made are to be placed with the minority press.

Beeborough's extended exercise on consultation with minority and community groups was discussed in Chapter IV. Considerable effort was put into eliciting some response from the more elusive organisations and on at least one occasion the RRWP chairman attended a meeting of a local body to explain the council's commitment to equal opportunity. Opinion among Beeborough's councillors and officers at this point was divided although there was apparently no sustained opposition to the momentum of the equal opportunity policy. There was some dissension, however, on ethnic record keeping and by extending the discussion externally, through consultation, the RRWP was able to amass more support on its own side. At least the argument (heard elsewhere) that minority groups themselves opposed record keeping could no longer be advanced by its opponents within the council; the organisations consulted overwhelmingly supported the proposal.

Thus, when the RRWP returned to the question of implementing and monitoring equal opportunity in September 1980 the chairman was able to argue that 'all of us know that we did undergo extensive consultation. I strongly urge that we underscore the policy with monitoring and that it becomes meaningful.' Earlier in the year the directors had been asked to give their views. None overtly opposed monitoring; several were divided as to its merits and their overall response was either reserved, or neutral with some acknowledgement of the potential benefits. The RRSC approved the proposal with no opposition although several members called for guarantees of anonymity, and consultation with the unions representing the council's workforce was urged by all sides.

Much of the discussion on record keeping was channelled into new directions with the proposal to expand the previously approved training post into that of a Race Relations Adviser. The need to agree this new departure in the face of some evident surprise and resistance ensured that the discussion skated over some areas of evident confusion and uncertainty as to the nature and form of ethnic record keeping. As had become common in Beeborough, elaborate references were made to the established practices of other authorities whom Beeborough was represented as trailing behind.

Certainly, being in the second generation of positive action authorities conferred certain benefits. We noticed several instances of Beeborough consulting the leading authorities in this area as to the details of their equal opportunity policies. As one officer put it 'We've generally known all the staff that are engaged in the other local authorities. The one we know most about is (an Inner London borough) — they made the most impression'. The relevant officers also consulted CRE staff, found them 'very helpful' but modified the Commission's recommended scheme of recording. Thus, by early 1981, the RRSC were able to approve the final details of an ethnic origin questionnaire, and, within a few months, a far-reaching re-design of the council's standard application form.

Beeborough now entered the final phase of introducing an equal opportunity policy, that of consultation with the unions. This had been attempted at an early stage, but it was agreed to return to the unions with a set of definite proposals. The teaching unions had long opposed record keeping while the head teachers' association argued that 'the keeping of such records can activate *(sic)* against the wording of the Race Relations Act, it being unlawful to discriminate against an applicant in the arrangements made for the purpose of determining who should be offered employment'. Although some officers had been confident about a change of view there it was not forthcoming. At the time of writing the other unions have yet to respond and have now been given a deadline by which to submit their views. The Labour group has meanwhile re-affirmed its commitment to achieving equal opportunity.

By the spring of 1981 a suspicion had grown that the unions might drag their feet on consultation. However, as the RRSC members — of both the majority and opposition parties — agreed, it was in the final analysis 'a political decision'. The signs are that the council itself has continued to take that view, for equal opportunity is now so firmly established on the policy agenda that it is probably too late to turn back.

Concluding comments

In this chapter we have considered what light the experience of local authorities casts upon the prospects of moving toward equal opportunity employment policies. While our examples have been drawn from our small sample of authorities, the way in which we came to frame the issues owed a great deal both to the comprehensive postal survey which we carried out and to follow-up visits to some of the other authorities which responded to that survey. We have then accumulated a considerable amount of material by post, by interview, by access to files and by observation of some critical discussions of employment questions. We do not pretend to have done more than scratch the surface of a complex and many-layered issue. Nevertheless we are fairly confident that the help and access we have been given have enabled us to appreciate the more common obstacles to equal opportunity.

The first question with which we dealt here concerned the varying interpretations of what the Race Relations Act prohibits and permits. It is cited equally in justification of minimal policies in Exeshire and of positive action in Beeborough, two extremes which are at least based on close readings of the Act. The Act appears to be shrouded in a confusion which the 1977 circular did little to disperse. The fact that it is open to such varied intepretation, in particular through the vagueness of section 71, enables local authorities to claim statutory endorsement for their own varied predispositions. Thus, while the CRE may be able to assist with advice on implementation to the more positively inclined authorities it can hardly hope to achieve shifts in the 'appreciations' of the more negative.

We argued in this chapter that both positive and negative prescriptions may be drawn from the Act and that it is read differently by different professions within local government. The idea that 'equal opportunity' relates to the role of a local authority embedded in and responsible to a community some of whose members suffer discrimination and deprivation on racial grounds can be accepted by corporate planners, policy analysts and, often, the chief executives to whom they report. The personnel management profession of necessity perceives a different legal and administrative reality. The acknowledged ambiguity in the meaning of 'equal opportunity' is the source of some confusion and frustration within local government. It will not be easily cleared away because it touches closely upon professional status, organisational power and the climate of industrial relations. We also considered a range of obstacles to measures required to give force to the implementation of equal opportunity policies. Clearly the most important was the resistance, often based on misapprehension, to monitoring or record keeping. It is understandable that union representatives should be nervous of a council's intentions in this regard, but that local councillors should misunderstand the logic and purpose of monitoring argues a failure of communication. That responsible professional officers — indeed, in some cases personnel directors — should share these misunderstandings was unexpected though it is legitimate that they should express a different view on the merits of record keeping, particularly when grounded in years of professional experience in the personnel field.

Underlying many of these factors ran a barely discernible thread. 'Equal opportunity' and the practical measures to its achievement presume an acceptance of the realities of a multi-racial community. Much of what we heard in interviews and meetings seemed to acknowledge this obliquely rather than directly. At this point, the experience of Beeborough illuminates more than just the practicalities of equal opportunity policy. Few would deny that politics in Beeborough, for all its tensions, reflects a multi-racial reality, a quality so often conspicuously absent elsewhere. In this, as in other areas of public policy, apprehension about racial explicitness is the invisible barrier to the development of equal opportunity policies.

References

Commission for Racial Equality, *Equal Opportuity in Employment: A guide for employers*, (London, 1978).

Commission for Racial Equality, *Monitoring an Equal Opportunity Policy: A guide for employers,* (London, 1978).

Commission for Racial Equality, *Code of Practice*, Consultative draft, (London, 1980).

Commission for Racial Equality, *Why Keep Ethnic Records?*, (London, 1980).

National Union of Public Employees, London Division, *Equal Opportunities: A pack for negotiators*, (London, 1981).

Trades Union Congress, *Black Workers: A TUC charter for equality of opportunity*, (London, 1981).

Wainwright, D., *Learning from Uncle Sam: Equal Employment Opportunities Programme.* Runnymede Trust Industrial Unit Briefing Paper No.3, (Runnymede Trust, London, 1980).

Young, K. and Connelly, N., *Ethnic Record Keeping in Local Authorities,* (Policy Studies Institute Research Paper 81/5, 1981).

VI Social Services

This chapter considers the different ways in which social services departments in the six case study authorities have responded to the presence of substantial Asian and West Indian communities.[1] As with the corporate policies
and practices discussed in previous chapters, wide variation was found in the
extent to which an ethnic dimension to policy and practice was recognised,
both among authorities and among staff within individual departments.

There are many different settings for the provision of social services, and
many ways of organising chains of command, of advice and of guidance.
There tends to be considerable autonomy in methods of organising work,
partly because of the nature of the tasks involved in the different settings, and
partly — as far as social workers are concerned — because of ideas of what is
appropriate to professional roles. At any one time the general picture is one of
considerable variation and diversity within and between departments, even
when the preoccupations are similar. This general picture holds for our six
authorities, where we found a range of ways of dividing responsibilities for
services, great differences in the perceived closeness of relationships between
various levels of headquarters staff and between headquarters and area
offices, and variations in the opportunities for contacts across the department
for discussion of ethnic or other issues.

It is hardly surprising to find a lack of uniformity also in the response to the
presence of substantial ethnic populations. One person interviewed, who had
moved from a post in Ayeborough to one in Beeborough, described the latter
as '150 times more aware' of the ethnic dimension in social services. Response
within individual departments showed a wide spectrum of views, from those
(including an adviser for children's residential care) who assured the inter-
viewer that it was only since the interview had been arranged that they had
given the slightest thought to the possibility of an ethnic dimension to their
work, to those firmly committed to cultural pluralism and concerned with the
implications of this for social services.

---

[1] For a fuller report of the research in the six social services departments, see Naomi Connelly,
Social Services Provision in Multi-Racial Areas (Policy Studies Institute Research Paper 81/4,
1981).

Except for discussions with a number of CROs and SCROs, interviewing in the local authorities was confined to staff of social services departments. In each department a number of headquarters staff were interviewed: director and/or assistant directors, principal officers responsible for particular services, training officers, voluntary sector liaison officers. We visited two area offices in each authority, suggested by headquarters staff as those in localities of greatest Asian and/or West Indian population; we also visited a few other sites, but in general time did not allow for visits to day and residential establishments. We attended meetings of working groups set up to consider ethnic aspects of work, and some meetings concerned with urban aid. In addition, where available, relevant documentary material was examined. We aimed to tease out the various strands in thinking and in practice, and to see whether there was any relationship between the corporate aspects of policy and practice, and what seemed to be going on in social services departments.

In the sections which follow we outline our findings about the apparent salience of an ethnic dimension in social services and perceptions of its nature, knowledge bases, implications for practice (including staffing), training, and influences on change. None of the departments had, at the time of the interviews, issued policy statements concerning their role in providing services to a multi-ethnic, multi-racial community (although one did subsequently); those interviewed disclaimed any knowledge of a departmental policy and variation within departments was obvious. Much of what we report in the sections which follow will therefore be in terms of individual members of staff, rather than departments as a whole. However, as will be seen, there *were* differences among the departments, some of which have implications for those in local authorities and outside who are concerned with increasing departments' responsiveness to ethnic communities.

The ethnic dimension

Great variation was found in the apparent salience of an ethnic dimension. Broadly speaking, those at headquarters were less likely to see such a dimension to their work than those in area offices, but this was by no means invariably the case. For example, in one London and one county authority there was someone just below director level who had a strong interest in the subject and was concerned with developing services for those from ethnic communities and encouraging the training of staff. Those lower down in the hierarchy, whether interested in the subject or not, seemed aware of (and apparently accepted) this stimulus to thought and action.

At one extreme, a director had not been aware, prior to taking up his appointment in 1976, that over 20,000 of the population in the area of his new post were Asian. In another authority, the principal assistant for research and planning stated that within the social services department ethnicity 'almost isn't an issue'. In a third authority, a senior social worker leading a team working in a part of the city whose population he estimated at 50 per cent Asian was at pains to make clear that, as only about 15 per cent of the cases which came to their attention concerned Asians, ethnic minority considerations were 'of little significance' for staff; the 15 per cent were handled on an *ad hoc* basis, as priorities, necessarily lay elsewhere in this deprived inner city area.

On the other hand, in Beeborough many of those interviewed seemed to see the ethnic dimension as a taken-for-granted, inextricable part of the social services task. And in the authority where ethnicity 'almost isn't an issue', a social worker in child guidance spoke of its 'central salience' and the day nurseries manager stressed as strongly as did her counterpart in Beeborough, the way in which awareness of the multi-ethnic composition of the nurseries influenced their thinking and practice.

A major reason given for not seeing ethnicity as salient for the department, or for the work of the individual being interviewed, was that thus far few demands (at least any requiring an obvious ethnic response) had arisen. Respondents recognised the presence of substantial ethnic populations, but saw these as not requiring or not wanting services, or not requiring or wanting *special* services. In Ayeborough, the ethnic population was mainly Asian and was seen by the social services staff as largely middle-class or lower middle-class owner occupiers — not the usual social services clientele. In other areas, it was suggested that Asians were not very well acquainted with services potentially available through the department; or that they preferred to contain or solve problems within the extended family or religious grouping. On the other hand, they might be aware of the services available and in need of them but lacked the necessary confidence to make an approach. West Indians were described in a number of areas as tending to shy away from authority, even when at least theoretically beneficent; a number of those interviewed in one area described their West Indian population as being long-settled, having 'largely integrated' and reluctant to be seen in any way as different, or needing help which had any specific ethnic aspect.

Less frequently a reason given for according low salience was that the ethnic dimension was irrelevant or soon to become so. A principal officer with responsibilities for residential care said 'One never asks whether a child is black or green or purple: one has a child in difficulty and one looks at the individual case and tries to see what will be best. Colour and ethnic origin are irrelevant.' This view was shared by a residential adviser in another department, who argued also that '*all* children in care have identity problems'. An assistant director said with some exasperation that the prevalent view in his authority still seemed to be 'if we work at it long enough and hard enough we'll make them white' and another assistant director in the same authority stressed the 'transitional' nature of the ethnic dimension: integration in schools seemed to him to imply that eventually integration would pervade all aspects of life, and those who advocated special facilities were thus wasting their time on very short-term measures.

Many of those interviewed in area offices also described the situation as a changing one, although not quite in this direction; some headquarters staff mentioned that field or residential staff had, in the previous six or 12 months, begun to alert them to situations which might require more attention to an ethnic dimension, such as the increasing number of blind Asian clients. Housing and welfare rights problems of newly-arrived Asian communities, which might well have been dealt with by CRCs and local advice centres, were seen to be giving way to marital difficulties, juvenile delinquency, and other situations more likely to be within the social services department's province. Questions of provision for the elderly had recently begun to arise, with the occasional referral for meals on wheels or residential care; with a few exceptions, thinking on this subject seemed hardly to have gone beyond vague anxiety.

The growth of more settled communities was seen as having great benefits in terms of the availability of networks of family and other support, but in some cases assumptions about such networks seemed to be used to obviate consideration of possible unmet need. The growth of political consciousness in some of the more settled communities was noted, and there was apparent unease about the form which expression of views on rights to services might take; the issue might suddenly become important.

There were those who rejected an ethnic dimension on the grounds that the societal aim was integration, and a local authority should not be seen to be going counter to this by providing different or extra services. One officer with responsibilities for relations with the voluntary sector went so far as to say he was concerned with 'evening out cultural differences' and in another authority someone with similar responsibilities said 'I dislike the term "ethnic minority". We see (voluntary organisations) as all the same.' More general was the 'like it or lump it' approach, and a meals organiser described the view of those in comparable posts in nearby authorities as 'if people need meals on wheels, let them have the standard one'. Her own view, forcibly expressed, was that whatever the general merits of integration as a policy, as far as old people were concerned 'integration in food is unnecessary and unrealistic'.

The social services department in Deeborough, in a report to the corporate Ethnic Minorities Working Group, stated that:

> 'The customary approach of the Department to its clients is an individual one. Traditionally social work sees people as individuals, not groups, and group work techniques and community work have only become an accepted part of the approach of the Department in more recent years. Part of the individualistic approach is an understanding of the client's culture and circumstances as they affect his behaviour and assist in explaining it. To seek to understand and interpret the cultural differences presented by people from ethnic minority groups is an automatic response and is part of the work with any family, not only with those where such differences are more marked.'

This statement makes plain two important strands in social workers' thinking which seem to inhibit systematic consideration of a specific ethnic dimension to their work. The first is the presumption that, as one senior social worker in Beeborough put it, 'ordinary social work practice should be good enough to encompass all the range of cases'. She was, however, finding that in practice she increasingly passed on cases to her office's specialist social worker for the Asian community. The second strand is the insistence upon an individual, rather than a commuity, frame of reference. A Deeborough area officer, obviously trying hard to understand the views of West Indian organisations with which he was in touch, and the views of those of his staff who saw a clear ethnic dimension to their work, still maintained: 'As far as this office is concerned we're not in the business of community work. We could have community workers here, but I wouldn't expect social workers to take a community consideration.'

Where there was acceptance of the idea of an ethnic dimension, this was viewed in a variety of ways. At a very basic level, one social worker pleaded for frankness about the difficulty white people had, at least initially, in differentiating black faces, with consequent anxieties on one side and hurts on the other. Another very basic difference is that of language, but in a field as complex as social services, concerned with relationships and feelings and bound by statutory obligations, translation and use of interpreters (rarely available on an adequate scale) were seen as helpful only as very minimal responses.

The next level in the ethnic dimension was seen as communication, including manner and body language as well as understanding of concepts and contexts. Several of those interviewed drew attention to difficulties presented by different manners of speaking and behaviour. The 'florid' nature of West Indian mental illness was commented on, and one area officer spoke of the 'hysteria and volubility' of some West Indians when describing problems at intake; his social workers found this difficult to cope with, even when they expected it. A social worker noted that the way some Asians presented requests induced exasperation, even though it was recognised that this was at least in part because of different patterns of language use. She commented that some of her younger colleagues didn't seem to find this difficult to handle 'but we who've been around longer find it harder'.

Many social workers were concerned to improve communication so that the relationship between professional and client could be based on more common ground. Immigrant families were thought to have little knowledge of the role of a social services department, the range of alternatives available, and the limits of help available (for example, in 'curing' mental illness). There was concern that social workers themselves should have knowledge adequate for understanding 'real' problems. Some felt the need for information about relevant cultures and religions and lifestyles, to help judgement of 'normal' or other behaviour, and to ease intervention in situations of family stress.

'Communication' can be seen in this sense as designed to ease performance of the social services task. It can also be seen in a more complex way, involving recognition of difference as something requiring possible rethinking of social services strategies and practice. This is akin to, but not quite the same as, an acceptance of cultural pluralism, a recognition that other ways of defining and handling situations may be fully as valid and held with equal conviction as those held or acted on by staff of social services departments. Some of those interviewed tried to express the progress they felt they had made in this direction, but even when this position is held in theory, it is likely to be difficult to put it into practice. As might be expected, young social workers in particular were said to find the role of women in Asian households hard to accept with equanimity, and empathy with 'Victorian' attitudes of some West Indian parents was found equally difficult. Different views of what is a reasonable method and degree of severity of punishment seemed to present the most difficult problems to social workers grappling with the question of what is 'right', and a few expressed the sense of shock they sometimes felt when they realised how far they had gone along the path of accepting parents' definitions.

The rarity with which social workers seem to recognise *strengths* in ethnic minority cultures and lifestyles has been noted by a number of writers in this field. Certainly lip service is paid to the strength of Asian family support, but many social workers may be hampered by the fact that their most frequent contact is with those in trouble, or at crisis points; they thus have little opportunity to judge the strengths of 'ordinary' lives, and how difficulties are overcome within them. An extreme example of this was an area officer who stated that it was not possible for children to cope with two cultures.

Finally, a somewhat different aspect of the ethnic dimension is recognition of the experience of being black in a white society, the experience of racism, and the associated need for maintaining feelings of ethnic identity, particularly in the case of black children growing up in largely white environments. Concerned white staff, and most of the black staff interviewed, mentioned the difficulty of getting over this aspect to white workers.

How likely are social services departments to be able to take on board any or all of these aspects of an ethnic dimension? Some respondents were hopeful, but some discounted both the ability and the likelihood of departments (as opposed to individuals or groups within them) reorienting in this direction. This was partly because some departments were seen as bureaucratic and unlikely to be able to respond sensitively to differences of any kind, although occasionally this view was tempered by mention of cases where sufficient evidence of specific need had been marshalled to push action, for example, for a hostel for battered Asian women. 'Policy' was seen as largely a matter of responding to needs when they presented themselves as demands, *not* as a matter of planning strategies. As one person remarked, 'If you say 'development' at headquarters, they think you are talking about building.' No one mentioned councillors in this connection at all, or the possibility of political will or the corporate committees, introducing recognition of an ethnic dimension. On the other hand, search for resources had led some of those previously not tapping S.11 to look into its potential, and as a consquence questions about services to those from ethnic minorities had been discussed at senior management levels, sometimes apparently for the first time.

Variation in the degree of recognition of an ethnic dimension to the work of a social services department, and in conceptions of the nature of such a dimension, cut across authorities. Our impression was that specific attention to such a dimension was more widespread in Beeborough than elsewhere. But in all six authorities we found a wide spectrum of views, and considerable concern about lack of relevant information.

Knowledge bases

Relevant information about local ethnic communities might include numbers, and demographic and other characteristics, current use of the department's services by those from ethnic minorities, and attempts to judge unmet need. A systematic review of department policies (such as that recommended in *Multi-Racial Britain: The Social Services Response*, the 1978 report of a working party of the Association of Directors of Social Services and the CRE) would presumably include all these. None of our case study departments had mounted quite this sort of review, although there had been some attempts to survey the field; in two departments this had been in response to requests from the corporate committees. The most wide-ranging review seen was one prepared by a group of interested staff who had met with the aim of discovering 'the particular Social Services needs of the ethnic minority communities and the opportunities for tailoring and developing . . . services to meet those needs; for making minority communities aware of social work and social services'. Their report, issued in 1979, noted that:

> 'The tasks involved turned out to be formidable ones which might have taken years of research to accomplish fully and it was therefore decided to produce a report which would help the Department to become aware in very broad terms of the nature of the minority cultures in . . . and the impact which they make on the Department at present and some possible implications for the Department's work.'

This report was intended to be the first stage in a policy initiative, but there was some disagreement about it at managerial level.

One of the most obvious indications that an ethnic dimension in service provision is recognised is the keeping of records of service use by ethnic origin. In none of the case study departments were such records kept on an overall basis, but a number of partial inquiries were noted. One area officer said he had been independently recording such data for the past five years, but more usually offices in areas of large-scale ethnic settlement had done rough checks at intake on an *ad hoc* or pilot basis, or other services had been monitored as part of headquarters' exercises to see whether S.11 support might be claimed.

None of the fostering or adoption officers interviewed kept records of ethnic origin, but in nearly every case they were able to recall the number of children involved, or were able to pick them out from lists of those awaiting placement. Other specialist staff seemed generally confident that they could estimate service use by those from ethnic minorities, if such information were required.

A report by one assistant director argued:

> 'Since to be a client of this Department implies disadvantage, I consider that there are sound contra-indications to the advisability of ethnic

record keeping for the recipients of the services of the Department. The interpretation of any results is open to too many different and possible damaging interpretations. Without an assessment of need in ethnic minority groups, a low take-up of services could indicate that there was little need, that the community was self-sufficient, that services were not available or not appropriate or that there was discrimination. A high take-up could indicate that the group was particularly unable to cope with its own problems, created a disproportionately high number of problems, was particularly effective in seeking out resources and making demands on them, or that there were adequate services, easily available and that there was no discrimination. The interpretation is clearly so open to being influenced by prejudice that I do not consider it advisable to become involved in such an exercise.'

In general, little enthusiasm was found for continuing record keeping, and some staff clearly felt that it was wrong to keep ethnic records. However, in some cases where short-term monitoring had been tried, previously reluctant staff had seen value in the information obtained; and in almost all the departments there were some people who felt very strongly that systematic record keeping was a necessary basis for any discussion about the meeting of current needs, let alone for revealing gaps in services.

A number of other sources of information about service use and possible service needs were mentioned during the course of the study. In some cases, there had been specific soundings of staff views. In Beeborough, consultation with black staff was seen as of particular use because such staff were thought to have a good understanding of their own ethnic group and also the necessary understanding of the social services role. The specialist social workers for the Asian community, attached to area offices, met regularly with a senior social worker to discuss common issues and provide information and advice to the training section and headquarters; an assistant director frequently attended these meetings. Discussions with staff of West Indian origin had preceded recommendation to the social services committee of the establishment of new posts of specialist social workers for the West Indian community. In Wyeshire, an assistant director had surveyed about 100 staff in area offices and residential services to obtain information about what were seen as the particular needs of children from ethnic minorities, and 'local experiences of cultural tensions within the family and within the community'.

In other cases, individual members of staff had carried out race-related research projects for the Certificate in Social Service or other in-service training courses, or for higher degrees; or specialist staff had obtained information about ethnic origins when surveying a particular service. In Exeshire, the first stage of research into health and social services needs of local elderly Asians had been funded through joint Health Authority and Social Services Department finance and the Urban Programme. An Ayeborough community worker had involved students from a local further education college in a survey of a council estate whose residents were about one-third Asian. In

Beeborough, a specialist social worker for the Asian community had attempted a sample survey of the Asian community in his area. Elsewhere in this authority continuing tapping of the views of those from ethnic minorities about their *own* definition of needs was occurring at a neighbourhood project provided jointly by the education, housing and social services departments.

Implications for practice

In this section we consider some of the implications which recognition of an ethnic dimension in social services provision carries for practice. We look at the accessibility of services to clients from ethnic minorities, at staffing, at relations with CRCs and ethnic voluntary groups, and at the way services have been affected.

Access. In discussions in social services departments we asked whether anything had been done to ease access to and understanding of services by those from ethnic minorities, particularly Asians with little command of English. Location and nature of premises, hours of opening, appointment systems and intake procedures could be off-putting. Certainly, visits to area offices revealed wide variations in visibility (only one was in High Street shop front premises) and in the extent to which reception areas were welcoming: some were bare and forbidding, others were bright and pleasant, with posters and leaflets providing information about a range of department and other statutory services, and about the activities of local voluntary groups. Occasionally, there was a notice in one or more Asian languages. It was very rare to see a black person in a reception capacity, either at headquarters or in area offices.

In most departments no formal arrangements for interpreting seemed to have been made, and there was dependence on social workers or other department staff who could speak the relevant language, or the police interpreting service, or professionals working nearby, for example in a health centre. Sometimes the CRC helped out; children, relatives, and neighbours were often used. In some cases, there was a panel of paid or unpaid people willing to interpret. In Ayeborough, Asians on the social services department's general volunteers' panel were occasionally asked specifically for help with interpreting, and in Seeborough a list had been compiled of languages spoken by staff of all departments.

Considerable difficulties were mentioned in connection with all these methods, with strong feelings expressed that social workers' time should not be 'misused' in this way. It was felt that involving children, other family or neighbours was often inappropriate when the subjects under discussion might be intensely personal and stressful. It was also thought that voluntary interpreters, who were likely to be of a different class from those for whom they were interpreting, might attempt to cover up what they saw as failings, or add their own views. None of this is new, and much of it seems fairly obvious, so the fact that departments have continued with unsatisfactory *ad hoc* arrangements seems surprising. In one authority, there was said to be less of a need for specific

74

arrangements now that the Asian community was more settled, with more English speakers. A number of people pointed to the complex ethnic make-up of their locality, and argued that any more formal system of interpreting would have to include provision for such languages as Polish. An area office which had only just realised that the Asian 'elders who come to the surface' were not carrying out straightforward interpreting had decided that the solution was hereafter to get the CRC to vet those proposed as interpreters.

The only systematic approach found was in Exeshire, where a planned programme of recruitment of interpreters paid by the hour had been implemented, with Urban Programme funding. Those chosen were carefully selected as understanding the department's work, and the appropriate limitations on the role of an interpreter, but they were people who seemed likely to be able to develop a more supportive role in time, and perhaps eventually to train as social workers. Monthly training sessions were held with the group. Relief and appreciation were already obvious in area offices. Here and in a number of other departments some social workers, nursery staff and others were said to have attempted to learn Asian languages; such attempts were frequently and regretfully reported as not having been very successful.

The translation of information into minority languages may be seen as a significant contribution to improving access. In Exeshire, this was being tackled in a number of ways, but in general only fragmentary steps had been taken to translate department information into Asian languages, or to provide such information from other sources, although health authority diet sheets were mentioned occasionally. In Seeborough, there was department-CRC co-operation in production of a booklet outlining the department's services. Some embarrassment about lack of activity on this front was evident, and there were no references to possible illiteracy among those to be reached. A frequent response was that the department relied on the local CRC to do anything which seemed necessary, although it was rarely known whether any material had, in fact, been produced. Those involved in work with under-fives had, in some cases, produced leaflets in a number of Asian languages about child-minding, or about the range of local services for under-fives. In Beeborough, the specialist social workers for the Asian community had produced a resource guide and there were suggestions that the department's pensioners' handbook might be translated.

Staffing. In discussion with one leader of a team for the elderly and han-dicapped, she spoke of how 'fortunate' they were to have in the team an Asian social worker and an Asian occupational therapist, as well as an Asian clerk in the area office; she described their presence as 'tremendously convenient, but quite fortuitous'. Over and over again we were to meet this concept: the 'luck' of having area office staff from ethnic minorities, an Asian psychiatrist at the local mental hospital, a West Indian health visitor, black staff in residential homes for children, an Asian of 'high enough caste to prepare meals' in an old people's home.

During the course of the interviews we spoke to black staff, at levels from family aide to assistant director. Some of those we saw, or whose work was described to us, had been appointed under the Urban Programme or S.11 to work specifically with clients from ethnic minorities. Others had been employed in the ordinary way but with the hope and expectation that they would be able to provide an expertise sorely required — as interpreters or to provide an explanation of particular cultural patterns. Some of those who saw themselves as non-specialist workers had, nevertheless, chosen to work in settings where some of the clients would be from their own ethnic group. Yet others were attempting to pursue their careers with no particular involvement with ethnic matters; this was more feasible in some posts and some areas than others, but in general staff from ethnic minorities (especially trained professionals) were scarce enough on the ground to be in considerable demand for consultation over difficult situations.

While no records were kept, headquarters staff were often able to report, either from memory or a quick look at staff lists, how many of the staff within their area of responsibility were black. Staff in area offices could with even greater ease inform us quickly of the number of social workers and others from ethnic minorities in the office. We found no reluctance to state the ethnic origins of staff or to see these as being of relevance. There was, however, little interest expressed in keeping continuing records of staff origins, and the subject of equal opportunity policies was rarely raised.

Many of those interviewed were eager to see more black staff employed by their department. Nursery nurses, occupational therapists and office staff were among the groups mentioned, but most discussion centred around social workers, particularly *qualified* social workers. This was partly a matter of preference (as the aim of the profession has been to achieve a higher proportion of qualified workers) but also because some departments were currently allowed to recruit only those already qualified. But qualified Asian social workers were seen as rare beings, and qualified West Indians were described by one area officer as 'like gold dust'. The position was particularly difficult when specialist jobs requiring post-qualification experience (for example, in fostering) were at issue.

The desire to recruit black staff was longstanding in some areas. In Beeborough, attempts to ensure that there are black staff in residential homes for children are said to date back to the mid-1960s. In some areas it was a recent interest, derived partly from gradual recognition of need, but also sparked off by the tremendous concern with using all available resources which had driven some managements, albeit reluctantly, to investigate the potential of S.11 funding. Concern to recruit was translated into activity in a number of ways, some very deliberate, some much more a matter of responding to events. Where recruitment for S.11 or Urban Programme-funded posts were involved, advertisements could make plain the ethnic content and qualifications required. In other cases, advertisements might be phrased to indicate that those from ethnic minorities would be particularly welcome applicants, either by stressing knowledge of languages or, as a Wyeshire area officer put it, 'slanting' advertisements to stress the multi-ethnic composition of the area. Or advertisements might be published in a standard form, in the standard journals,

76

but if those from ethnic minorities applied, their applications would be 'jumped on' and followed up with particular interest. In Deeborough, when black girls were on placement in the department's nurseries as part of their qualifying course, their progress was said to be observed with particular attention and if they seemed suitable they were urged to return when they had completed their course. Use of the ethnic press was mentioned primarily in relation to attempted recruitment of foster and adoptive parents.

A number of area officers, in the absence of qualified workers, had made a practice of recruiting unqualified staff (often with experience of voluntary social work) with the intention of subsequently sending them for training. Most seemed to feel this had worked well, although one area officer commented that advertising for unqualified workers brought a flood of applications, mostly unsuitable. Given new restrictions on recruitment, this avenue was no longer available in most departments. Other initiatives had been tried, with varying success. An enthusiastic staff member at a higher education college which acted as the staff college for Wyeshire's training section had set up a course for black volunteers, with the intention of finding them jobs in the department later. In Deeborough, pre-professional training had been instituted in several further education establishments. In Beeborough, the department's training officer was involved in a number of local initiatives to encourage young black people to gain qualifications.

Given the relative scarcity of black staff, there were often daunting expectations that such staff, even when not employed as specialists, would interpret, ease communication with clients, act as consultants to staff at all levels, provide white staff with the experience of getting to know someone from another culture, and act as role models. The S.11 specialist worker for the Asian community in Ayeborough described her work as consisting partly of casework with 18 very complex cases, counselling on short-term cases, and advising social workers in her own and other area offices, taking half her time, and development and education work for the other half of her time. This included forging and maintaining links with Asian religious and voluntary organisations (including encouraging the nearby mosque to appoint a voluntary welfare worker whom the S.11 worker advised and supported), talking to foster parents about care of ethnic minority children, attempting group work with unsupported Asian mothers and with depressed Asian women, and liaising with local general practitioners. Interviews in the department made clear her important role: 'Ask M.' was a recurrent response when questions were raised about what sources of information and advice were used. A less experienced social worker might have coped less well.

Most of the white workers in our study spoke very positively about the roles played by individual black workers, except for a few cases where for example 'patronising', 'upper-class' attitudes had been seen as a deterrent to clients. One West Indian family aide was described with warmth as 'indispensable in making *real* contact' and numerous comments were made, particularly in relation to specialist workers, about how the advent of such workers had helped clarify 'previously unmet needs' and had revealed to white staff that their communication with clients from ethnic minorities had been even less adequate than they had assumed. Sometimes this was reported with considerable chagrin. There was recognition and appreciation of the ability of some (female) Asian social and community workers to judge effective tempo and methods of encouraging Asian women and girls to participate more and act more independently. The advantage to white workers of having those from ethnic minority cultures available for consultation over difficult cases, and gradual accumulation of knowledge of another culture in a way never possible from deliberate training exercises, was particularly appreciated.

Some reservations were expressed about the possibility of the CRC, or groups within the ethnic communities, seeing black social workers as *their* social workers and expecting a degree of identification or advocacy inconsistent with the professional role, or of their blaming individual black social workers when an unpalatable decision, such as taking a child into care, was made. Sometimes these fears were general ones, but on occasion they were based on actual experience within the authority or other authorities where staff had worked. It was obviously a disappointment to some white workers that individual Asian social workers were not able to solve *all* the department's communication problems. Those who were part of a close-knit local community had knowledge and experience particularly useful to other staff, but some Asian clients were said to seem anxious about confidentiality and hence reluctant to deal with such staff. On the other hand, there were some unrealistic expectations that any Asian social worker would be able to communicate effectively with Asian clients of whatever national origin, religion or culture.

Black workers themselves saw some problems in their roles, beyond the common irritant of being used as interpreters. Two Asian social workers described the process of coming to terms with their professional relationship to those from their own ethnic group. Having begun by 'wanting to be just a social worker', they began to feel uncomfortable in this role. They were constantly seeing ways in which their extra knowledge might help both clients and practitioners. Gradually they moved into specialist posts, discovering much greater confidence and satisfaction in their work once they had made this decision. Another Asian social worker was still experiencing conflict about this — seeing the potential of group work with Asian women in a mental hospital, but not liking to be seen to suggest special provision.

A number of Asian social workers expressed the difficulty Asian clients had in dealing with them as professionals, rather than as mother/aunt/older sister figures, but to the extent that the professional role *was* accepted there was likely to be great dependence, and an expectation that clear solutions to problems would be forthcoming. A black child guidance worker said that black parents seemed to feel more confidence in her ability to understand their view of the world, and black children felt easier in describing their experiences of racism at school and elsewhere than they might have with a white worker. On the other hand, parents found it difficult to see why she did not invariably accept and act on their view, but rather tried to get them to understand their

78

children's views; black youngsters sometimes seemed to consider that she had 'sold out' by taking a post in a statutory agency.

Little information was proffered about relations between white clients and black workers, although the assumed prejudice of elderly whites was sometimes noted with concern, and one senior social worker said she had to exercise some care in assigning cases to a Sikh social worker to avoid, for example, youths who were National Front supporters — apparently an increasing problem in some areas.

In all six authorities the potential of S.11 was being explored. In Ayeborough, which had a specialist social worker for the Asian community in post, the joint CRC-department advisory group visited other authorities to find out what use they were making of such funding, and then prepared a report for the senior management group of the department, setting out priorities. This was discussed at a meeting with management, and it seemed likely that one unfilled social worker post would be converted into four S.11 posts — at no extra expense to the department. However, the likely necessity of some additional clerical support was raised by the management side, who also argued that one of the posts must be assigned to maternity cases in the local hospital, where the need was drastic. In Beeborough, where each area office had a specialist social worker for the Asian community appointed under S.11, recruitment of two social workers for the West Indian community had recently been agreed: a substantial number of qualified black social workers applied. Two neighbourhood worker posts were funded under S.11, as well as day nursery posts under the agreed formula, and the conversion of many other posts to such funding had been under discussion with the Home Office for some time.

In Seeborough, a social worker for the West Indian community had been appointed under S.11 in 1974, at the urging of the police. Currently, there are three S.11 social worker posts, but one (intended for work with the West Indian community) has been vacant for two years. The department was said to have been 'trying desperately' to fill the post, but without success. They had therefore, in consultation with regional officers of the Central Council for Education and Training in Social Work (CCETSW) and the local polytechnic, prepared a plan for the appointment of 12 new S.11 workers (three a year for four years). No qualifications would be required (except, probably, secondary education in this country). Those selected would spend six months or a year in the department before embarking on the two-year social work qualification course at the polytechnic; they would then return to the department. The intention had not been so much to recruit people to work specifically with their own ethnic communities, but rather to ensure the presence of black staff in the area offices to advise, etc., but further consideration of their roles was underway.

In Deeborough one S.11 post was located within the CRC, and this was felt by the department to be an unsatisfactory arrangement, as insufficient control could be exercised over work thought to be excessively political. Another S.11 post, attached to an area office, was vacant; reasons given for this varied. Headquarters staff were urgently reviewing use of services such as day nurseries, and the work of community workers, in order to see whether S.11 could be claimed for existing posts, but the ten-year rule was likely to frustrate such moves, at least in some areas of the city. However, it was hoped that such funding might be agreed when the CRC childminding centre, a time-expired Urban Programme project, was transferred to the department.

Investigation of the possibility of converting existing posts to S.11 funding was also taking place in Exeshire, where formula day nursery and six individual posts were currently funded: social work assistants, a childminder adviser, and part-time posts in maternity wards of hospitals. The officer responsible for preparing the case had encouraged some surveys of referrals to area offices and day centre and other service use. Although most of the saving, if application for 12 posts was successful, would accrue to the department generally, he hoped that part of it would be set aside for innovative work with ethnic minorities. In Wyeshire, use of S.11 has only recently been agreed, and it is hoped to have four new field workers.

Relations with CREs and voluntary groups. During the course of the study, we explored relationships with local community relations councils and with organised groups within the ethnic communities. In Chapter IV we discussed local authority-CRC relationships. Those between social services departments and CRCs were fully as varied, and ranged from consultation, cross-referral and joint working between CROs and staff in an area office, to virtual avoidance of contact as likely to be counter-productive. Where contact was minimal, deliberate departmental building of alternative bridges to the ethnic communities was not mentioned.

Relationships with voluntary groups, if they existed at all, seemed largely to be confined to contacts arising from applications for department or Urban Programme funding. We noted no departmental attempts to utilise such contacts to increase the general fund of information or advice, although some of the individuals with responsibilities in this area had found the experience helpful. Contact with local voluntary groups was often thought to be the province of community workers, but again, it was not obvious that the knowledge they gained was fed into the department. The situation was somewhat different in Beeborough, where there were thriving Asian and West Indian groups with views about department activity as well as about the department's responsibilities in relation to their own activities.

The relationship between departments and CRCs, and between departments and ethnic voluntary groups, must be seen within a context of more general department-voluntary sector relationships. The inadequacies in the way departments relate to umbrella groups (such as councils for voluntary service) and to individual voluntary group have often attracted comment. Complaints have been made about lack of consultation, lack of support, too much direction, or excessive reliance on established groups. On the other hand, there are recognised difficulties of timing and of accountability in feeding voluntary sector views into the policy making process. Many authorities encounter difficulties in judging which of a plethora of organisations to consult and to finance, and there are problems in developing and maintaining the most appropriate balance between independence and accountability. It is perhaps not surprising, then, that departments do not, in general, seem to have been actively seeking advice and guidance from the *ethnic* voluntary sector, given the addional unknowns of the situation.

In Ayeborough, there was considerable informal discussion between CROs and some of the staff of an area office, and joint use of the CRC mobile unit; the SCRO and the area officer had had regular meetings for seven years. A CRO had been involved in organising study days on ethnic minorities jointly with the department's training officer. Direct links between the CRC and headquarters staff seemed few; however, regular meetings between senior management and the joint CRC-department advisory group have recently been agreed. Links with ethnic voluntary groups were hardly mentioned, except by the S.11 worker, and the officer responsible for links with the voluntary sector could not recall a single case of an Asian organisation coming to the department for financial assistance. Assistance under the Urban Programme was confined, as far as the ethnic population was specifically concerned, to the CRC mobile unit and a new multicultural centre.

The situation in Beeborough was quite different. Here the CRC had gone through a difficult time, and during interviews in the department no mention was made of contact or consultation, other than through CRC membership of the council's Urban Aid sub-committee. But not only are many of the large and powerful local Asian and West Indian groups known to the department, but also the smaller self-help groups. A number of them, indeed, had been formed with the encouragement of the department's community workers; and the department's Asian meals service had been organised in conjunction with some of the groups.

In 1978, the social services committee approved a policy statement on grant aid to voluntary organisations, which designated community and self-help groups as priorities, particularly organisations working in parts of the authority 'where social needs are high and financial resources low'. About 60 organisation were funded, including a few specifically ethnic groups but including many more which were 'at least as black as white', either in membership or in those served (for example, by an advice centre). Many other ethnic groups had recently applied for funding. The department's voluntary organisations liaison officer was said to be in contact with many groups in addition to those currently funded, providing advice, support and guidance in dealing with other departments of the authority. Her role was a complex one, advising groups on grant applications and then advising on whether such grants should be allocated; sitting on management committees of some of the funded organisations in order to help clarify objectives and ensure smooth running, but also having some responsibilities for monitoring progress. Community workers were able to give her some guidance in understanding the complex world of ethnic groups, but difficulty was experienced in differentiating those which it would be helpful and appropriate for the department to fund, when so many new groups were continually coming to her attention.

Some organisations funded under the Urban Programme are ethnic groups whose projects the social service department supports. In the authority's 1981/82 submission, six of the ten schemes put forward to the DoE were supported by the social services department, and half of these were clearly intended to serve primarily ethnic communities. At the meeting at which the ten schemes were agreed, the openness of the authority in relation to its multi-ethnic population was strikingly demonstrated by the presence of four Rastafarians, presenting their case for a car maintenance workshop; part of their motivation, they said, was 'to show that Rastas are good for something'. The project was listed third in order of priority, and was subsequently approved by the DoE.

Seeborough has two CRCs, one in the north and one in the southern part of the district. As Chapter IV indicated, the links between the authority and the CRC were closer and stronger in the north than in the south. We have already mentioned the discussion on the Urban Programme between the social services department, the CVS and the two SCROs. Recent pressure for improved consultation has come from the CVS, but in terms that closely correspond with the already-expressed views of the northern SCRO. These discussions took place at headquarters level, but there are also close informal links between the northern SCRO and the staff of the northern division of the social services department. The CRC and the divisional office share premises; the SCRO seemed to be very closely informed about the work of the specialist staff of the division, and one of the two black social work assistants was formerly on his staff.

In the southern area the situation was rather different. There had been bitter disputes within the CRC itself over the effectiveness of its role. The SCRO was anxious to relinquish casework responsibilities. Overtures had been made to associate the Asian social worker in this division with the CRC, but his area officer (possibly on instructions from above) had insisted that he keep his distance.

Relationships between the social services department and the CRC in Deeborough were also strained. There was dissension over the appropriate role of the S.11 worker seconded to the CRC by the department, and dissatisfaction with the functioning of the CRC sub-committee on which officers sat. There were some individual contacts between department staff and CRC staff, but those interviewed did not look for advice or assistance to the CRC, which was described as 'a chamber for debate and dissension' and 'lacking credibility among ethnic groups'.

The number of voluntary organisations funded by the department (mainstream, urban aid, inner areas and joint funding) has increased eight-fold in the past four years to 300, and a headquarters officer described his position in dealing with applications as 'like being at the bottom of Niagara'. There was said to have been 'little involvement' by the authority with West Indian or Asian groups until the growth in Urban Programme funding. There was some disagreement among those interviewed as to whether any particular complications arose in funding such groups. One officer denied that there were any differences at all; while someone who had been involved in a cross-department community development working party said that in looking at bids from ethnic groups for inner areas money, they had felt so unable to make judgements that it had been suggested no money be allocated for a year, to give time for gaining knowledge of the groups. The social services community workers had opposed this move, on the grounds that it was unfair not to allocate available money, that however good their intentions a freeze was bound to be misinterpreted, and that perhaps their knowledge of *other* groups was not great. The postponement was defeated.

A representative of the social services department sits on the executive committee of each organisation receiving £1,000 or more a year. With the growth in the number of organisations funded, area officers and senior social workers, as well as headquarters staff, were now involved, and seminars had been held to discuss whether the role of such representatives was to advise, or to monitor. We spoke to a number of those who filled such positions in black organisations, and it was clear that this continuing contact was important for attaining greater understanding themselves, and for communicating to the organisations something of what the department did. One of the area officers involved stressed, too, how much she had learned about the many local Asian self-help groups from the area office's volunteers organiser, who had made a special effort to build relationships with such groups.

In Exeshire, some anxieties were expressed about both CRCs. The future of the one in the south of the county was unclear. However, social services department representatives played an active part in its health and welfare sub-committee and a department officer was a member of a group giving professional support to the CRC's mobile worker. Grant aid to ethnic groups was said to come primarily through traditional urban programme, and inner areas funding. There was said to be 'still little knowledge at city or county officer level of the various ethnic groups', but the fact that bids have to be considered was descibed as 'a breakthrough' in forcing officers to learn more about the different groups. Much of the department's support went to voluntary groups running holiday play schemes. The officer responsible for relations with the voluntary sector stressed that although the department might not on paper (compared with the city) seem to be supporting many ethnic groups, in fact social workers and community workers were continually involved with groups and individuals in the ethnic communities, 'getting one-off projects off the ground'.

There were also two CRCs in Wyeshire. In the case of one, the area officer said there was close contact with the CRO ('we phone each other — he's in this office quite often') and the playgroups adviser spoke warmly of the CRC playgroup liaison officer. There had been a post of this kind since 1970, funded under the Urban Programme and there had apparently been a continuing close working relationship between the department and the CRC in the work with under-fives. Relations were less good with the other CRC, although it was said that relations with previous CROs had been better than with the current postholder, who seemed little interested in social services. The only contact now was in nominations for the CRC's summer play scheme. No information was obtained about relations with the voluntary sector in this authority, but one area officer expressed surprise at the apparent lack of self-help groups, but said he was 'glad, too, as it meant they used integrated facilities, and that must be good'.

Changes in services. We were not able from our study to provide anything like a complete picture of social services response to Asian and West Indian communities in the six authorities. If specialist posts have been established, or interpreting services set up, or Asian meals on wheels provided, then *something* has changed, although further research would be required to judge the appropriateness of the service and its effectiveness in operation. Some of the changes noted as important by those interviewed concerned greater flexibility in practice, or more exhaustive attempts to bring families together, and we cannot judge to what extent these changes have, in fact, taken place. There are fashions in social services delivery, and fashions in ideas about ethnic minorities; some of those with whom we spoke may have been voicing ideals of change rather than something they invariably or even frequently managed to practice. Detailed observation would be required to see what changes have actually occurred.

We were trying to get an idea of what current practice was thought to be, and how this had developed over time. Although many of those interviewed, had been in post only two or three years, some had previously worked in the children's department, or the probation service, or as mental health officers, and had ten years or more of local experience. Such workers were particularly anxious to stress the ways in which questions of practice had to be related to changes in the demographic and other characteristics of local ethnic populations, and employment and housing situations. In a few cases, this was seen as a reason for minimal response, on the grounds (noted earlier) that any apparent special needs were transitional. In other cases, it was seen as a challenge to remain flexible and alert to the implications for social services: the additional difficulties in disentangling 'normal' adolescent revolt from specific cultural conflict as Asian communities became more settled and of finding innovative ways of supporting single young black mothers, recently housed on a council estate in large numbers as a result of housing department high-rise one-bedroom flat allocations.

The overwhelming impression when considering changes in services is one of variation — among headquarters staff, between such staff and practitioners, among practitioners (even within the same area office), for the same practitioner over time. Sometimes what was described as a change to meet the special needs of working with ethnic minorities seemed remarkably like what might be thought of as good social work practice — most notably, exploring every available alternative before taking a child into care. Yet practitioners obviously saw such ways of working as different from ordinary practice, and rarely mentioned the possibility that the 'change' was in fact a closer approximation to the (generally accepted) ideal.

The responses described to us can be categorised in the following eight ways, illustrated by a few examples drawn from the interviews:

Do something negative. The single case given was when a social worker expressed concern at the willingness of the local Asian population to make use of such practical benefits as bus passes, telephones and aids. She said that, as a consequence, her team exercised more rigour than they did for indigenous applicants. This was in contrast to views expressed by those in other area offices, who frequently pointed out that although use of social work services by ethnic groups might be relatively low, use of practical services was more in line with estimated proportions of local population; they welcomed this as an indication that they were able to provide *some* acceptable help, whatever their inability to meet more complex needs.

Do nothing: that is, go on providing the standard service. There are a number of different strands in this:

(a) A local authority department should provide a uniform service, or one responding to *individual* need.

(b) Even though, ideally, a social services department should adapt its services to meet differing needs of differing groups, in practice this is not feasible, given the number of ethnic groups involved, or the number of other 'priority' groups.

(c) Whatever the department might like to do, in the present resource situation only the standard service can be offered.

(d) The standard service has been tried, and has failed, but attempts at adaptation would be too difficult or too time-consuming.

(e) The standard service has been tried, and has failed, but insufficient information and guidance are available to implement possibly more effective measures.

Provide the standard service on a separate basis — For example, mother and toddler groups formed specially for Asians.

Make some specific (but relatively minor) adjustments to the standard service. Among the adjustments mentioned were the provision of vegetarian meals in a variety of adult day settings; providing foster parents and residential care staff with information about hair and skin care; and changing children into play clothes for their day at the nursery, thus meeting the desire of West Indian mothers to take home tidy children. (Such adjustments were by no means universal.)

Make some adjustments to the way in which standard services are administered or delivered. The major adjustments noted related to fostering and taking children into care. Practitioners reported reducing the length and complexity of procedures in attempts (by no means always successful) to recruit black foster parents and working longer and harder to avoid taking children into care, as well as increasing flexibility so that, for example, a child in care might be placed with grandparents.

Provide additions to the standard service, or new services, to meet needs seen as specific to some of those from ethnic minorities. Two departments provide Asian meals on wheels, and this was under consideration in a third. In an Exeshire town an Asian childminder group has been set up, and regular training sessions covering diet, health care and child development are held in the Gujerati language.

Provide additions to the standard service, or new services, aimed at reducing general problems, but with some explict or implicit policy aim of helping those from ethnic minorities, or such an effect in practice. Much childminding development work is of this type. In Beeborough, for example, the flourishing childminders' centre was said to be 'not exclusively West Indian' but involving them very fully. Proposals for a new family centre here made a number of references to the special needs of ethnic minority families. In Exeshire, getting over to Asian parents the idea of the value of play was a main motivation for setting up a toy library and arranging parental involvement in play activities at a nursery open night.

Include an ethnic dimension in considering current and future use of resources. We were not aware of discussions having taken place in any of the six departments about a strategy for social services provision to meet needs of ethnic communities, although individual issues (if only use of S.11) seemed to have been discussed on occasion in all departments at senior management group or committee level. Most instances quoted during the interviews were those where individual members of staff had considered an ethnic aspect of their work in considering priorities, or attempting to plan ahead. A number of headquarters staff insisted that they were too busy managing present services to have time to think about future developments of any kind; sometimes they saw the situation with regard to ethnic minorities as, in any case, too fluid and problematic to make planning possible. This was particularly the case in relation to the elderly. However, in Ayeborough the CRC-department working group has been asked by senior management to explore needs in this area, and in Beeborough a member of the social services department staff has been seconded to the chief executive's department to carry out a review and assessment of all the council's policies towards the elderly, with particular reference to ethnic minorities.

Most of the changes reported to us seemed to have been incremental: gradual responses by individual practitioners or managers to a situation they saw as new and requiring a response somewhat different from that in use. All the authorities exhibited some changes in practice. We cannot judge from our study just how widespread and significant such adaptation has been, although our impression is that it has been most wide-ranging and deliberate in Beeborough. But in all authorities some of those interviewed seemed uninterested in change, while others were trying very hard (often with little interest and support from elsewhere in the department) to meet needs more adequately.

Training and learning

In all six authorities we found some awareness of knowledge gaps and some confusion about appropriate forms of social services work with people from ethnic minorities. We were, therefore, particularly interested to find out what opportunities staff had for increasing their knowledge and their competence, through in-service training arranged by their department's training section or in other ways, and what those interviewed said about the training they had had, or felt they needed.

In-service training for work with ethnic minorities may be diffused or specific: relevant information and relevant issues may be fed into more general study days, courses and workshops, or there may be sessions devoted specifically to the subject. Training may be concerned with presentation of information about diet, language, cultural patterns or it may deal with practice issues. It may be intended to increase sensitivity to the position of those living in a new culture, or to raise awareness of prejudice, including possibly that of the participants. Issues about content of courses overlap with other issues such as who should be trained (or trained first), who should organise training, who should do the teaching, at what stage training should be given and at what sites over what period, and how methods and effects of training can be evaluated.

In our six authorities we found different approaches to in-service training on ethnic issues, from systematic consideration and planning to one-off responses to particular requests. Beebrough has the most developed system. Here, there had, from 1976, been a series of 'study mornings' about working with immigrants, covering such subjects as the cultural and historical background of children from the West Indies and the needs of such children in care, going on to look at similar topics in relation to Asian children 'in order to understand why there weren't more in care' and to prepare staff in case the situation changed. However, training staff were sceptical about how much information was being absorbed in this type of gathering, for 100 or so staff at a time. In so multi-ethnic an area, it was felt important that staff at all levels should be aware of the possible racial, cultural and ethnic aspects of their work, yet if special courses were put on, only those interested would come, and insistence on others coming 'might create antagonisms'. They, therefore, now try to incorporate something on the subject in all courses, although use is also made of more specialised courses arranged by other bodies.

At the other end of the scale is Deeborough, where the first training concerned with ethnic minorities took place in November 1980. This was a one-day seminar (repeated the next month) patterned on previous courses arranged by the authority's central training officer, with talks on the main ethnic groups in Deeborough, naming systems and religious practices, diet, 'family structures and social life'. According to the training officer, response had not been great. This might, he thought, reflect cutbacks affecting the possibility of staff attending training of any kind rather than lack of interest: a residential care senior manager had told him some time previously that his staff could no longer attend courses as, with so many unfilled vacancies, there would be no one to cover for them. There was no deliberate ethnic content to any of the other courses put on by the training section, although where case studies were used, these might concern a client from an ethnic group. The training officer had, however, no impression of unmet demand for such training.

A number of two-day courses on Asian culture had been arranged in

Ayeborough jointly by the training officer, a CRO, and health education and community education staff. The first few had been directed at teachers, social workers, health visitors, and others. The organisers were not convinced of the usefulness of this, and the course held early in 1980 had been aimed at management levels. Those attending included head teachers, senior careers officers, police sergeants, senior environmental health officers, etc. — and one senior social worker and one principal officer from the social services department. The intention had been to help these people advise the staff they supervised, but the level of knowledge was found to be so low that the course had to provide basic information of the same sort provided previously.

As far as other training was concerned, the training officer (who had a longstanding interest in multicultural issues) said she ensured that the department's three-day induction courses stressed the multi-ethnic nature of the area, and if case studies were used in social worker training at least one would relate to an Asian family. Further consideration was being given to the format of the more general course, and also more specific training requested by staff of an assessment centre. Like the Deeborough training officer, however, she had found ethnic issues hardly mentioned in a recent attempt to ascertain training priorities within the department.

In Seeborough, an experimental course arranged in conjunction with staff from a nearby university had proved too stressful for some participants, and this was thought to have discouraged consideration of further training for some time. Within the last year, however, the view had grown that 'we need to do something drastic' about training, and courses had recently been established, in co-operation with an industrial language organisation. The courses were available to interested department and health authority staff; it was hoped that later on all department staff might be reached through induction and refresher courses. The courses run one day a week for six weeks, and aim 'to give people an understanding of the local community', so that the course content differs somewhat if given in the northern part of the district or southern part. Four have been held, each with about 25 participants, who have included hospital social workers, home helps, receptionists, and nurses; 'residential staff are just beginning to come'. Where there seems to be some interest in issues of practice this is to be followed up, and the hospital social workers have met for discussions.

Considerable in-service training of day and residential staff, specifically on the subject of ethnic minorities, has taken place in Exeshire. This was the only one of our authorities with someone at headquarters with responsibility for developing work with ethnic minorities, and the officer has a small training budget. He feels that the department's training should include practice-based and management-based work, and he has drawn up a programme which he hopes will gradually be implemented in co-operation with the training department. This includes seminars for social workers on counselling techniques with different cultures, on-site training in day nurseries, and two or three-day exercises to help middle and upper management to 'further their own knowledge of racial and cultural matters through exploring different approaches to solving problems in the provision of social services'.

In Wyeshire the training officer (who had worked in a multi-ethnic inner city area, and had lived in East Africa) was surprised to find when she took up the post that the prevalent idea in the department was that there was no need for training on ethnic issues. When, however, there was a course on non-accidental injury or on mental illness, 'the social workers were all talking about ethnic minorities', and a particular concern was whether people were being 'treated' for conditions which were really 'normal' in their own societies.

The local higher education college which acts as a staff college for the department now runs a number of courses on ethnic minorities, and the programme for the spring term 1981 shows a three-day 'race awareness training' course and a three-day course on 'working with ethnic minority families'. A social worker interviewed the week after attending this latter course said that by the end of the three days there was an air of despondency — the social workers felt 'Do I know even a smattering about cultural differences? None of us know anything at all. We're asking ourselves whether we have any right to offer facilities that are so alien'. They had, however, felt it was a useful beginning to air some of these problems frankly, and further meetings were planned.

Thus far we have been concerned with formal departmental provision for training about ethnic minorities. As we have seen, this is not very substantial in most of the authorities. In looking at other opportunities available to staff we were concerned with organised training by those outside the department, but also with what those interviewed saw as the ways in which they or their colleagues had learned about ethnic minorities and work with ethnic minority clients.

We were told about study days, seminars, and workshops organised by CRCs and council for voluntary service, and by further education colleges and health authorities, by the London Boroughs Training Committee and regional offices of CCETSW, by the CRE, the National Institute for Social Work, the British Association for Counselling and the National Foster Care Association. These ranged from afternoon 'briefings about the back-home situation' as one area officer put it, to intensive three-day discussions of social work practice, or courses intended to train trainers.

Within the departments there were various arrangements initiated by interested individuals or groups. In Exeshire, a S.11 worker had arranged a study day, and those in other area offices had been invited to attend. In another part of the county a black foster mother had given a talk on fostering black children to a group of other foster parents. In Deeborough, fostering officers had established a course at a local further education college on 'Fostering of Children with Cultural Differences'; the speakers were black members of staff. In one of the area offices we visited in Deeborough someone from the local Asian community had been invited to speak to the staff, and in the other area office a programme of four staff discussions was to include one on ethnic minorities. At a child guidance centre, both of the recent fortnightly lunchtime meetings had concerned ethnic minorities: at one the role of the police in the area had been discussed, and at the other someone from the black community had been on a panel discussing community groups and the social services department. In Wyeshire, a team leader said that she had monthly lunchtime meetings for her team, and one of these had been concerned with Asian courtship and marriage. Some social workers had visited the Brixton Neighbourhood Community Association to see the day centre and other activities for elderly West Indians.

Some of those interviewed stressed the importance of opportunities for continuing informal learning, at the time at which issues arose, and a number of social workers saw the role of seniors as crucial 'for drawing out the ethnic aspects of cases' being discussed with less experienced workers. It was these kinds of opportunities which contributed, too, to white workers' obvious appreciation of access to black colleagues.

During the course of the study we were made aware of both an expressed need for learning on the part of many practitioners, and a frequent dissatisfaction with training available thus far. Obviously, there is no 'right' way to train for work with ethnic minorities, but our research seems to indicate that more systematic consideration needs to be given to the subject than has hitherto been the case in some departments. Such consideration might well have to be at a number of levels, looking both at 'ideal' provision, and at priorities and possibilities when training resources are limited and are likely to remain so. The experience of other authorities could usefully be drawn on if mechanisms were available for this, or if research could draw together information about courses which have been functioning for some time.

Influences on change

In the previous sections we have described the ways in which those in our case study departments have responded to the presence of substantial Asian and West Indian populations. Although we could not, in a study of this kind, look in depth at the influences on these responses, we did stress to those interviewed that we were particularly interested in the question of influences on policy and practice — at a departmental level, and in relation to their own work. *In the event, few could discern any sign of policy discussion or change, and so influences on this were hardly mentioned.* In the case of practice changes, the overwhelming response was that these had not been caused by outside influences, but rather by the interaction of the individual, gradually accumulating knowledge and experience, with the circumstances presented. However, other possible influences were discussed; these can be roughly divided into 'external' influences, influences 'internal' to the local authority, and more personal influences.

Among the possible external influences discussed were the Home Office and the Race Relations Act 1976. Mention was made of the Home Office only in relation to S.11 funding, or when immigration procedures and practices were seen as causing difficulties for clients. In some cases, concern was expressed about the increased uncertainties and stresses for clients (and some staff) resulting from the Nationality Bill. Although a few of the initiatives described in this report were said to have been a response to S.71 of the 1976 Act, our impression was that most managers' and practitioners' responses to the changing situation in their localities had not been influenced specifically by an intention to comply with the legislation. Although a circular about the Act was sent to local authorities jointly by the central departments in June 1977, the Home Office has not followed this up with more specific guidance on S.71.

No one interviewed could recall any direct guidance from the Department of Health and Social Security (DHSS) on matters concerning ethnic minorities, although one senior social worker responsible for fostering, when reminded that the department's 1976 *Guide to Fostering Practice* had included a chapter on 'Caring for children from different cultures', acknowledged a vague recollection. A day nurseries manager referred to the 1978 joint Department of Education and Science (DES)-DHSS circular on *Co-ordination of Services for Children Under 5,* but only to say that the recommendations it contained had already been implemented in her authority by the time the circular was issued. The director of the Social Work Service distributed the Association of Directors of Social Services (ADSS) / CRE *Multi-Racial Britain: The Social Services Response* to social services departments in August 1978, but no additional guidance has been issued by the DHSS.

Despite the fact that some Social Work Service Officers (SWSOs) have among their other specialisms a responsibility for matters concerning ethnic minorities, only one such officer was said to have reported on ethnic aspects of a department's work. In none of the other five authorities could anyone remember ever discussing the subject with a SWSO. In one department, a recent evaluation of child care services had centred on the work of the area office in the locality where the Asian population is concentrated; not a single word in the SWSO's report referred to the office's work with Asian children.

The CRE has only very limited resources to apply to the social services field, and the present social services officer had not been specifically involved in development in our case study departments. The information we obtained about the CRE's role was therefore rather fragmentary. Outside London, only one of those interviewed mentioned any direct contact with the Commission or its regional offices; he had applied unsuccessfully for a travel grant to the West Indies.

A number of those interviewed had attended Community Relations Commission or CRE conferences. Two social workers from Exeshire, for example, had attended all three annual workshops on 'The Elders in Ethnic Minorities', jointly organised by the CRE and the University of Keele Department of Adult Education. Useful information about S.11 had been gained at a meeting by one community worker. A principal officer had been much struck by the idea that Asians needed help in understanding the concept of play, and had subsequently instituted some innovations intended to meet this need. On the other hand, a fostering officer had been irritated by the assumption of speakers that all those from ethnic minorities were disadvantaged; an area officer from another department expressed a similar feeling.

The CRC booklet on hair and skin care seemed to be widely used, but other CRC booklets, although occasionally mentioned in a general way, or noticed

91

on bookshelves, were not mentioned specifically. The CRE's *Youth in Multi-Racial Society* was the subject of discussion at the Ayeborough joint CRE-department advisory group, but was not otherwise mentioned in the interviews. The 1978 report of the working party of the Association of Directors of Social Services and the CRE, *Multi-Racial Britain: The Social Services Response*, seemed little known. The staff group who prepared the review of their authority's services mentioned earlier in this chapter were said to have been 'well aware of it', but elsewhere only a handful of people recollected it; they were those most concerned with ethnic issues, and had found it too general to be of much use: 'It just confirmed what we were thinking, didn't help us to move on.' Even at headquarters only a few of those interviewed recollected seeing the report, and fewer still remembered it well enough to feel able to comment on it. One senior officer described it as 'superficial', but another felt the problem was the lack of subsequent action by the DHSS. No mention was made of the CRE's only social services investigation, into Barlavington Manor Children's Home.

The relationship between departments and CRCs has been discussed earlier in this chapter. Where relations were good, and relations between CROs and area office staff informal and frequent, growth in understanding and incremental influences on policy were likely, although no specific instances were cited. In some cases, the CRC was seen as highly politicised, an arena for conflict among different ethnic groups, and quite uninterested either in advising the department or making its work better understood among immigrant groups. Here the influence was negative, if anything, and it was worrying to find that for some staff of departments, contacts with ethnic minorities seemed to be confined to clients and to off-putting encounters with the CRC: there seemed little basis here for understanding of 'ordinary' Asian or West Indian life.

At the time the interviews were carried out it was striking how little specific influence local ethnic communities seemed to have had on developments in social services departments, although they may have played a greater role in Beeborough than elsewhere. Their concerns may have been with education policy, or with immigration problems, or with relations with the police, but even the issue of taking into care, raised with some vehemence over past years, seemed to have been a matter of discussion only with individual families, rather than presented as a general issue; the same seemed true of ethnic matching in fostering or adoption. Awareness of rights to services was said to be increasing in some areas, and the way this would be expressed seemed quite unknown; in a few cases, where it had involved wholesale condemnation of the department, indignation resulted. Generally, pressure seemed to have taken the form of requests for Urban Programme or other funding for projects to be run by ethnic groups, rather than pressure for change in social services departments' policies or practices. Wider issues of social services policy were, however, discussed in Seeborough's consultative bodies, which included representatives of ethnic groups and of the social services department.

How much do the policies and practices of one local authority affect those of others, either as warning or as pattern? To what extent do events or innovations elsewhere seem to have influence? Only a few of those interviewed mentioned the riots in Bristol in April 1980, and interviews were completed in the week before the Brixton troubles in April 1981. In Exeshire, awareness that such situations *could* arise locally had been brought about or heightened by difficulties during the summer of 1980. Changes to the previously-agreed Urban Programme submission had resulted. In Ayeborough, constant references were made to a neighbouring authority whose Asian population was facing increasingly grave housing and employment difficulties.

A number of those interested in expanding S.11 use had noted an article about Berkshire's proposals in *Community Care* early in 1981, and were thinking of making contact; the Ayeborough advisory group had contacted and visited a number of other authorities in preparing its case for expanded use of S.11. Interest was expressed by some adoption officers in the Lambeth New Black Families Unit, set up in autumn 1980, and the Brixton Neighbourhood Community Association had, as we have noted, been visited by a number of social workers concerned about provision for the elderly.

Specialist officers were asked about contacts with those in comparable posts in other authorities, and whether influence came from such contacts. Although many such officers belonged to regional groups, or met informally on a regular basis with colleagues from adjoining authorities, the subject of ethnic minorities was said to have arisen only very marginally, and never to have been discussed in any systematic way. One playgroups' adviser, however, had attended a regional meeting for under-fives workers, had been very impressed by a speaker from another county with much experience of work with ethnic minority children, and hoped to invite her to speak locally.

Only five people mentioned the Association for Multi-Racial Social Work (AMRSW); one had been a founder member of the British Association of Social Workers (BASW) Inter-Cultural Interest Group. A few others mentioned having read the first issue of AMRSW's journal, *Multi-Racial Social Work*, which was published in 1980, and BASW's 1977 *Studies in Inter-Cultural Social Work*. Several people had attended courses or conferences arranged by the Trans-Cultural Psychiatry Society, the National Foster Care Association, and the British Association for Counselling. Regional officers of CCETSW were playing a role in consideration of training and use of S.11 in one department. No other professional contacts were mentioned as possible sources of influence, although it seemed likely that the virtual unanimity among fostering and adoption officers about the importance — at least in theory — of ethnic matching must have some basis in the discussion of this issue over the years in the relevant professional journals. Similarly, no mention was made of Brian and Sonia Jackson's findings about unregistered childminding, and their innovative development of training and support for minders, yet it seemed likely that the childminding developments in a number of our authorities had been influenced by this work.

We did not, unfortunately, ask specifically about any role of the police in affecting social services policy or practice. In Seeborough, however, the appointment of a S.11 worker in 1974, primarily to work among West Indian young people, was ascribed to the influence of the police, as was the more recent (but unsuccessful) proposal for a Caribbean club. Further investigation seemed to confirm that the proposals had originated in the police consultative machinery described in Chapter IV.

As for internal influences, we sought to discover what influences were seen to come from councillors, headquarters staff, and other departments within the local authority. Remarkably little mention was made of councillors, except in Beeborough, although in Wyeshire it was at the insistence of a councillor that S.11 use was investigated. Of course, most social services staff would have little contact with elected members, but even those at higher levels in departments, in most cases saw councillors' interest in ethnic aspects of work as being insufficient to influence departmental practice. Changes such as providing Asian meals on wheels or appointing a S.11 worker were seen as administrative rather than committee decisions in at least one authority.

It was rare to be told that ethnic issues as such had been discussed at senior management meetings within the social services department, or in the context of discussion of particular types of services, or services for individual client groups. 'Never mentioned', 'never raised as an issue' were constant (and frequently surprised) responses to questions about this. Given this situation, it seemed that except when there was someone at headquarters either with a known interest in the subject, or with a specific brief to deal with it, change tended to be initiated by individual practitioners and the direction of influence was seen to be from area office to headquarters, rather than the other way round.

In contrast, personal influences were seen as of prime importance in affecting views and influencing change. Being from another culture (not necessarily being black), or marriage to someone from a different cultural background, was seen as of great importance. The experience of having lived and worked in other societies was also mentioned frequently. This was partly a matter of the knowledge acquired (where the West Indies or East Africa were involved, very relevant knowledge); and partly the experience of having been a foreigner seeking acceptance. Such an experience could lead to greater empathy and sensitivity to the feelings of ethnic minority clients, but in a few cases it seemed to have worked in the other direction, providing a basis for argument that assimilation was a more appropriate aim than acceptance of variation. Previous posts in multi-ethnic inner city areas were often mentioned as having helped practitioners to overcome an initial culture shock, and to go on to begin effective learning. Sometimes disappointment was expressed at the lower salience of the ethnic dimension in the current authority, but sometimes the main feeling seemed to be one of relief and relaxation. A principal officer who had moved from an Inner London borough with active West Indian groups, often anti-establishment, but who in his present post 'didn't need to negotiate' with the more religious or culturally-oriented Asian groups, said that after the previous harder and tougher time 'I find this a cushy ride!'

Living in mixed neighbourhoods, or having friends (or the husbands of friends) from ethnic minorities were mentioned as important in aiding understanding and thus influencing practice. Other influences mentioned in a few cases were reading (both fiction and non-fiction), specific questioning of clients to gain more information about their cultures and their ways of thinking, and attendance at conferences and training courses where skilled practitioners currently practising in multi-ethnic areas had provided down-to-earth information.

All these had obviously been part of the developing framework of individuals in thinking about ethnic aspects of their own and the department's work. But there was virtual unanimity about the two most important influences on practice: the experience of working with ethnic minority clients gained gradually on the job, and ideas and understanding derived from colleagues from ethnic minorities. Although those involved saw such influences as having been very personal, they are not, in fact, entirely independent of department policy and practice. The learning acquired through working with ethnic minority clients may be hit-or-miss, with unhappiness or dissatisfaction on the part of both worker and client; it may be helped along by careful supervision and suitable training. Similarly, the presence or absence of colleagues from ethnic communities need not always be a matter of 'luck', as it was so frequently described; it may be, as we have seen, part of a deliberate policy of recruitment, whether to specialist posts or more generally. Influences, then, are *not* necessarily so personal as to be outside the realm of department policy.

Concluding comments

Incremental changes seem largely to have been the way in which our six case study authorities have responded thus far to the presence of Asian and West Indian populations. Some headquarters decisions have had effects (notably the appointment of specialist workers), and some professional influences seem to us to have been at work. But our impression from the study is that most changes have come about because individual managers and practitioners have learned slowly from experience, or have been pushed by events (such as the mushrooming of requests for funding from ethnic groups) to learn quickly.

Does change have to go on in this way, or has there now been sufficient effort of this type for more systematic consideration of issues at a policy level, and more general dissemination of ideas within departments and between departments? The present situation seems wasteful. Knowledge and experience in one department might help those in another (in particular, in relation to training); there is a lack of departmental services which could be supplied nationally or regionally (for example, translation); there is knowledge in one area office that might be helpful to another in the same department (for example, 'contracts seem to work particularly well with Asian clients').

As we have seen, there is no shortage of ideas. It is rather a question of how, within and between local authorities, these can most effectively be considered and communicated. As far as individual authorities are concerned, a number of ways of looking at ethnic issues have developed in the last few years. A lead can come from the council, through the establishment of cross-departmental committees of officers or members (sometimes including also representatives of ethnic communities such as those described in Chapter III. Such corporate committees, as we have seen, may call for reviews of the work of the social services department, and may consider general issues (such as employment policy and record keeping of service use) with decisions which affect social services functioning. There may be a race relations adviser in the chief executive's department, with responsibilities which include reviewing the council's services and suggesting appropriate areas for change or development.

The social services committee or the department's officers may state publicly a commitment to consideration of an ethnic dimension in the department's work. Member or officer working groups may review relevant issues and make recommendations. There may be someone at headquarters with either part or full time responsibility for advising on race relations, or for developing services and training for work with ethnic minorities. Small groups of staff may, as we have noted, examine particular aspects of their department's work; or an interested individual member of staff may be released from regular duties for a period of time in order to survey the field.

Although all these arrangements (and doubtless others) exist in local authorities at present, most of them are relatively new, and little is yet known about how they function, what they achieve, and what kinds of difference they make to departmental policy and practice. Clearly information about this would be of use to other authorities contemplating the introduction of any such arrangements.

None of the four corporate committees whose deliberations we followed seemed to have influenced social services department policy and practice at the time the research was carried out; this may change, however. Other changes are taking place. In the summer of 1981, the race relations adviser post in the Beeborough chief executive's department was advertised, and in another of the case study authorities, the social services department issued a policy statement on 'Ethnic Minorities and Race Relations'. This stated that the department placed 'a high priority on progress towards a racially just and integrated society' and went on to quote S.71 of the Race Relations Act 1976 and then to outline subjects for consideration in various aspects of the department's work.

Such public commitment seems likely to be useful as an indication to ethnic communities of a department's interest, and as an indication to department staff that the subject is seen as of sufficient importance to justify specific, and open, consideration. From the evidence of this study, such consideration might usefully include an attempt to grapple with and clarify some of the issues which appear to be bothering many staff. Among these are the nature of any ethnic dimension to their work, whether 'ordinary social work practice' can or cannot 'encompass all the range of cases', how a community aspect can best be accommodated within social work practice, and some of the difficult questions about appropriate roles of social services departments in providing 'special' services to particular groups.

All of these are complex issues, with no simple 'right' answers. The same is true of many of the other issues which will require consideration: questions of staffing, of training, of consultation, of relationships with other departments and other agencies, of changes in administration and delivery of services. But there is a wealth of experimentation and experience to draw on and build on, if ways can be found of doing this effectively. We return to this point in Chapter IX.

References

Association of Director of Social Services and CRE, *Multi-Racial Britain: The Social Services Response*, (Commission for Racial Equality, London, 1978).

Association for Multi-Racial Social Work, *Multi-Racial Social Work*, No. 1, 1980.

Ballard, R. Ethnic minorities and the social services: what type of seryice? in V. Saifullah Khan (ed.), *Minority Families in Britain*, (Macmillan, London, 1980).

British Association of Social Workers, *Studies in Inter-Cultural Social Work*, (Birmingham, 1977).

Cheetham, J., *Social Work Services for Ethnic Minorities in Britain and the USA*, Unpublished, (available in DHSS Library, 1981).

Community Care, issue of 29 November 1978.

Connelly, N., *Social Services Provision in Multi-Racial Areas*. PSI Research Paper 81/4, (Policy Studies Institute, London, 1981).

Social Work Today, issue of 20 February 1979.

VII Education in Schools

In Chapters III, IV and V of this report we discussed aspects of authorities' corporate practices. Whether the discussion was arranged by authority or thematically, the primary focus of our attention was in each case the authority as an organisation. The case of social services provision in Chapter VI provided a sharp contrast. Here much of the disussion centred on processes peculiar to a practitioner-based service; the individual social worker was often the focus of our attention. The case of education, which we consider in this chapter, lies midway between the two. While responsibility in education is diffuse, there are some issues in respect of which our concern must be with the local education authority (LEA) and others where the proper focus of attention must be the school itself, or even the individual teacher.

Our approach to this study centred initially upon the LEA. However, the operational level is for the most part to be found in schools, the headteachers of which have a large measure of constitutional and customary authority. This is also an area of public policy where Parliament, the central government, national pressure groups, the teaching profession and a host of other bodies have sought to influence both LEAs and schools by issuing advice and guidance. At the same time the almost universalistic nature of primary and secondary education ensures a keen parental interest in provision and practice, an interest which leads to locally-organised pressure and advocacy which in its scale has no parallel in the other aspects of local authority activity which we considered. Any proposals for the development of policies for education in a multi-racial society will have to take account of the existence of a network of (sometimes reciprocal) influence within which educational issues are handled. In its simplest form it might be represented as shown in Figure VII. 1.

We consider some aspects of these and other national-local relationships further in Chapter VIII. The important point to be made at this stage is that education is characterised by an opaqueness of policy determination: it is particularly difficult to define where influence lies in so pluralistic a system.

The complexity of the institutional framework and the opaqueness of the policy processes have important implications for our presentation in this chapter. While the authority as such was the focus of our attention in respect of corporate arrangements and employment policy, such an approach would not take us far in an exploration of education. The substantial autonomy of headteachers and the professional and situational freedom of teachers give rise to variations at the operational level that may exceed such inter-authority variations as we could discern. We thus used an issue-by-issue approach to education, bearing in mind that particular issues have a different salience not only for different authorities but often for different (even neighbouring) schools within the same authority.

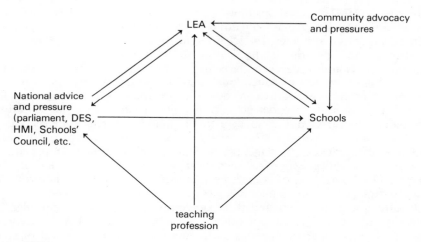

Figure VII.1

As before, our primary concern was not with provision as such (still less with its impact or effectiveness) but with variations in the organisational and appreciative context of provision. With this in mind we visited the six LEAs and discussed a range of issues with senior administrators, advisers and other staff. These topics included the teaching of English as a second language (ESL), the use of funds under S.11 of the Local Government Act 1966, ethnic record keeping, advisory services, teachers' and resource centres, in-service training, the curriculum, cultural diversity and the school-community relationship. We followed up these discussions with visits to a selection of schools and other educational institutions. In four of the authorities, we visited five or six schools by arrangement with the education office. Our request to see a range of schools (rather than the 'show' schools) was, so far as we were able to judge, generally met by those officials who arranged the school visits. In the fifth authority we attended a discussion between three headteachers, the director of education and a group of councillors which covered the same ground, and had access to reports written by other heads. In the last authority we were discouraged from visiting schools as a number of visits had recently been made by other research teams.

99

We are confident that these visits gave us a reasonable impression of the context of educational provision in at least five of the six authorities. Each LEA also provided us with documentation on request. This was sometimes extensive and in three cases included fairly free access to the departmental files. Education issues were discussed on several occasions during meetings of the corporate and consultative bodies in three of the metropolitan authorities and we attended these discussions. We also held discussions with the relevant officials of the DES, with H.M. Inspectorate (HMI) (including, where possible, the HMI with responsibility for our authorities), the CRE, the Centre for Information and Advice on Educational Disadvantage (CED), political parties, professional bodies, the local authority associations and a variety of pressure groups operating in the field of multi-racial education.

While the six authorities were the centrepiece of this study we also asked for information on aspects of educational provision in our wider survey of local authorities in multi-racial areas as described in Chapter II. This information helped to provide the broader context in which to understand the variations among our six LEAs and we made a small number of visits to LEAs outside our main sample. We were aware of the research carried out at Goldsmiths' College for the Schools' Council; Schools' Council Pamphlet 18 provides a picture of the wider scene. Our own work, while confined to relatively few LEAs and schools, has, of course, been concerned less with actual provision than to explore the underlying processes in these six authorities.

In attempting to understand these processes, we have given considerable attention to the degree of operational autonomy which LEAs concede to schools. It was apparent that this autonomy was greater in respect of some issues (the curriculum for example) than others (such as the teaching of English as a second language). In the discussion which follows, the various issues with which we are concerned are grouped into those which are *ipso facto* authority issues in respect of which a LEA-wide policy is normally adopted, those where the LEA will follow a permissive path and provide opportunities and encouragement to the development of practice, and those where an authority will adopt a disinterested stance and leave 'policy making' entirely decentralised to the schools. This tripartite distinction forms the basis of the organisation of this chapter.

This basic distinction must, however, be qualified by differences in the willingness of various LEAs to grant such degrees of autonomy to schools. One authority may well regard as a 'policy' issue a question which elsewhere is handled either permissively or neutrally and may use its power and influence over schools accordingly. Such inter-authority differences, while often slight in their impact, are nonetheless significant. Customary autonomy is a powerful and pervasive force in English education, and many of the issues which arise in the field of multi-racial education do so at the margin where policy and influence are contested between the various parties.

We first consider inter-authority variations in approach to the relationship between the LEA and the school. We then examine in turn, the ways in which the separate local education systems handled issues which may be defined as positive, permissive, and neutral. Finally, we consider what general conclusions may be drawn about policy development in this complex and intractable field.

Policy and influence: the LEA and the school

Education policy-making is distinctive in placing a heavy emphasis on enhancing the capacity of schools to cope with their responsibilities, rather than attempting to secure their compliance with policy. The scope of feasible policy is limited by the autonomy of headteachers and the absence of any effective means by which compliance with policy could be secured. This appears to act as a disincentive to frame any positive policy. Moreover, the general standards of schools and the directions in which their teaching might develop are limited by the capacity of the teaching body to adapt and respond to the needs of a multicultural society. To some extent, the provision of support in the form of advisers, resource centres and training opportunities attempts to address the second of these problems; the first, however, can only be tackled by attempts to deploy an often subtle influence in support of policy.

Influence in this latter respect we found to be generally achieved through the medium of a dialogue with headteachers. This was often conducted by means of close and informal links forged at the assistant education officer (AEO) level. Contacts with heads at this level, by informal visit and telephone call, do provide a useful channel for advice and for exchange of views. Insofar as those contacts may also be important in conveying school needs to the administration, they probably put the more skilful heads in an advantageous position in the competition for resources.

On difficult issues the office might be involved in 'counselling' a head, but where examples were cited this seemed to be little more than the expression, with varying degrees of emphasis, of a viewpoint held by an experienced and sympathetic colleague. Such consultation was evidently the main channel for contact between the education office and *individual* heads in most of the authorities. In Exeshire, the deputy director of education had a special responsibility for multi-racial matters, and a small special fund for disbursement to schools. In Deeborough, the LEA inspectorate appeared to take on the developmental role yet they were probably as concerned to represent the school to the office as to transmit 'policy'.

The periodic, usually termly, meeting of headteachers convened by education directors in each of the authorities provided a forum for pressing a policy view. On at least one occasion in Seeborough a special meeting was called for heads with large numbers of Asian children on their rolls, but this meeting seemed to be intended to facilitate discussion rather than to express a policy on the various questions raised by the director. These questions primarily concerned physical education, but included school meals, absenteeism and religious matters. The director sought discussions to establish 'what is reasonable and how to tackle problems' in order to determine a common approach by schools. Generally, all LEAs used heads' meetings as a forum for discussing issues. Their potential for securing influence over schools on multi-ethnic questions appeared in most LEAs to be limited by the fact that only a minority of schools in each area had a substantial ethnic composition.

The potential of heads' meetings as a channel of influence is in any case limited to those areas where the policy issue is clearly distinct from questions of professional practice. In one authority, the director (a self-described 'constitutionalist') holds meetings for heads once a term but demurred from their use as a forum of policy transmission: 'When you talk about policies this is very dangerous. I'm fully committed to academic freedom. You can express broad strategies but in the end each head has to work out the salvation of his own school.'

In this case (where contacts between the office and the schools appeared firmer and more elaborate than elsewhere) the director confessed 'We had a substantial number of (teachers) who are rigid in their views (on multicultural education). We have to change them to seeing the childrens' needs. There is uneven take-up. With 2,500 plus teachers there are bound to be some who are rigid to the point of ossification.'

In Beeborough, there was a strong emphasis on support services and an initiative to strengthen the inspection of schools had recently been launched, although this made no reference to multicultural education. This proposal to review the performance of schools evidently had had a lengthy gestation period. It was to be a delicate task for 'it involves a group of people evaluating the work of their fellow professionals'. Moreover, 'there is no one "right way" to run a school, no group of people has a monoply of wisdom and good ideas'. Despite these disclaimers, the teaching unions had resisted the proposed review for some years. Because of the teachers' influence within the majority party organisation in Beeborough, it reportedly took the council leader and education chairman 'between two and three years' to get group support for such a new intervention on the part of the office. The rationale for the inspection scheme is one of enhancing standards of performance. Yet the education department and committee probably intend to play a part in defining the criteria against which performance is to be assessed. As these criteria are likely to take account of the multi-racial nature of Beeborough's population, there is an implicit policy initiative here. In a narrow range of circumstances, an inadmissable question of compliance may be redefined as a question of capacity and thus as a legitimate concern of the LEA.

The Beeborough performance review represents a general attempt to reduce the diffuseness of educational policy making. It touches upon the possibility of using school governors to put subtle pressure on a head, sometimes by raising questions which the head would prefer to avoid. Beeborough's director recognised the need to engage governors in the appraisal of schools:

'In most cases governors are not *advised* of the questions that need to be posed to the headteacher and staff. It is the tendency of most governing bodies to repel criticism of their own school. It should be the *responsibility* of the director of education and the education office to *enable* governors to ask the right questions and to insist on the right answers.' (our emphasis)

This degree of explicitness was apparently unique among our case study authorities. This is not however to say that the potential of governors as a lever on a head was not considered elsewhere: in Deeborough, the adoption of a strong policy position by the education committee enabled a senior administrator to claim that

'We are now in a position to say to heads 'this is the policy of the LEA'. I would say this to a head and would expect my colleagues who deal with governing bodies to be softening up the chairman of governors. I would expect governers to ask heads what they are doing'.

Such channels of influence may be potentially to hand. They are, however, unlikely to be recognised as such *except* where there is a distinct policy which is to be transmitted, either obliquely or openly. Most of our LEAs had little that could be described as a broad policy or strategy for education in a multi-racial society. They had, therefore, little occasion to intervene in the schools. Moreover, most senior officials seemed to recognise the practical difficulties of attempting to do so. Sometimes teachers were seen as unwilling to respond, as in Deeborough: 'the majority of teachers would say that (multi-cultural education) is number 99 on the list of priorities'. Sometimes their unions were seen as powerful enough to block the implementation of any policy, as in Beeborough: 'if the teachers in Beeborough don't want it to happen then (the council) couldn't make it happen'.

So far we have been concerned solely with 'policy style' and not with the substance of policy. Clearly there are areas, in particular those concerned with encouraging development in schools, where an authority may have a policy of providing resources but does not deploy influence over and above encouraging their use. Equally, there are areas, in particular those concerning the curriculum, school rules, and relations with the community, where many authorities will have *no* policy but where some education officials will nonetheless attempt to exercise a more or less consistent informal influence. But before proceeding to examine these two areas we must deal with the range of important issues where an LEA will normally adopt an overall policy for *all* its schools: to provide a particular arrangement for English teaching, to keep or not to keep records of the ethnic origins of the children in its charge, to bid for and allocate extra resources for 'immigrant' education, and so on. We turn then, first, to examine these areas of general provision for education in a multi-racial community.

Providing a multi-ethnic service

Teaching English as a second language. The language issue provides a convenient starting point for considering how LEAs respond to the educational needs of ethnic minority children. The DES, in their 1980 memorandum to the House of Commons Home Affairs Sub-Committee on Race Relations and

Immigration describe it as the 'most obvious' of those needs; that LEAs themselves viewed it in precisely this way was evident from our visits. Its preeminence dates from the early 1960s when schools were faced with the practical problems of immigrant children arriving at schools with little or no knowledge of the English language.

The then Ministry of Education issued its first advice on the subject *English for Immigrants* in 1963. In 1966, the Schools Council established a project at Leeds University to develop materials for teachers working with non-English speaking pupils and the production of SCOPE educational materials began. The prevailing opinion of the time saw the needs of immigrant children as being largely a matter of enabling them to overcome the obstacle of language so that they could participate in lessons on the same basis as those born here. Subsequent developments revealed that the issue was more complex than it seemed at first. A second Schools Council project begun in 1967 dealt with the teaching of English to (dialect speaking) West Indian children, thereby establishing the concern with the special linguistic problems posed by West Indian children, an issue which has continued to attract attention (and to pose dilemmas for teachers) to the present time.

The initial policy responses by most LEAs, in making extensive provision for teaching English as a second language (ESL), were based (as was S.11 of the Local Government Act 1966) on the presumption that the language problem would diminish with successive generations. Similarly, the first specialist advisers reflected this supposition in their responsibilities for 'immigrant' education. Further, the progressive limitation of immigration from the New Commonwealth was expected to lead to the phasing out of special provision. This expectation was disappointed, and the DES noted in their 1980 memorandum to the Home Affairs Sub-Committee that: 'the major need was for English language tuition among second and third generation minority group children who, although born in this country, came from homes where English was little used'. The need to continue such special provision is now widely recognised, as is the need to continue such provision through to the second stage of learning in schools.

The persistence of language difficulties has led some LEAs to take a broader view of the educational needs of a multi-cultural society and to accept a degree of pluralism and diversity as an inescapable and, indeed, positive aspect of school life. A view expressed in one LEA is however more typical of the concern expressed to us by educational administrators, that the priority demanded by ESL eclipses such other concerns as, for example, the provision of mother tongue teaching:

'The vast majority of children from minority ethnic groups will have to make their way in their adopted country and it is felt by many teachers that the greatest need is for minority groups children to learn English as a second language in order to take proper advantage of the British educational system. This is a big enough undertaking without introducing complicating factors.'

104

Given such a priority, policy makers have a range of choice as to how they will respond to it. All of our six authorities made such special provision. A typical response of a LEA faced with early waves of non-English speaking children can be seen in Seeborough, where an immigrant centre was initially established to teach children to a standard at which they could be slotted into their neighbourhood school. This particular provision has been virtually phased out since local government reorganisation (although it remains in use for intensive work with some overseas children). For the most part, children are now catered for by arrangements decided upon at a school level, where a separate special English class may be provided, or a normal class placement backed up either by a withdrawal class, or by an in-class language teacher. To these ends, Seeborough employed 53 full time teachers of ESL in 1979.

Deeborough similarly carries out ESL teaching entirely in the schools, having been from an early date opposed to withdrawal to special units or dispersal to 'minority' schools. Here, nearly 100 teachers were employed in 1980 throughout the schools as extra support, in part for 'assistance with language'. Elsewhere, some reliance is placed on special separate institutions. Ayeborough maintain a Schools Language Unit to provide for the needs of first stage learners referred from the schools as in need of specialist teaching. Beyond this, ESL teachers are deployed in the schools and there were claims of considerable problems faced by the Unit, in its dependence on the schools for referrals, its location under the aegis of the local further education college and the absence of a central resources fund. The college lecturer in charge of the Unit has argued for greater centralisation of ESL teaching in Ayeborough.

Beeborough's system is not dissimilar but is more complicated, reflecting more clearly than elsewhere a series of sequential responses made to a developing situation which had long overtaken the basic premise of an early and once-for-all solution of ESL needs. New arrivals are assessed as to their need for special teaching and are allocated to the LEA's language centre as necessary. Of ethnic minority children born in Britain, those at infant level are taught in schools by ESL teachers, those at junior level go to the centre, and those at secondary level are assessed and referred there as necessary. Any language problems of West Indian children are not seen as the responsibility of the ESL teachers. The centre has an establishment of 72 teachers, some of whom are deployed in the schools. In Beeborough, as in Ayeborough, the dependence of the language centre on the schools for referrals was evident, and there may well be considerable further revision of the arrangements there.

Wyeshire we found to have the more complicated and varied provision to be expected of a partly urbanised county. ESL teaching is provided in schools at the infant level. In the northern part of the county, children attend a purpose-built centre which in the view of the education department 'has shown the benefits of intensive help as regards quicker integration at a single centre where teachers with specialist expertise may concentrate their efforts'. In the south of the county, there are seven junior school language units for initial ESL teaching after which children are placed in their neighbourhood school or withdrawn to special classes, as necessary. A parallel system operates for the upper schools. The chief education officer is aiming for the eventual 'harmonisation' of provision in the county.

The work of the primary centre and the secondary reception centre in Exeshire provide something of a contrast. First, the fall off in the number of arrivals has entailed a decline in their basic ESL function and at one point the LEA apparently considered closing the primary centre. Second, both centres are actively involved in producing resource materials for ESL use in schools, that from the secondary centre also being geared to a wider curriculum development role. The secondary centre otherwise provides both assessment and crash course teaching for a duration determined by the needs of the individual child.

It was apparent to us from our visits to LEAs that the considerable diversity in the form of provision both within and between authorities testified to piece-meal, adaptive responses to changing needs over a period of years. All of the authorities recognised and provided for ESL teaching as a priority. That different patterns should have evolved was not surprising. What perhaps was more so, given the considerable experience of ESL that now exists, was the dissatisfaction voiced in most of the authorities at the way ESL provision actually worked. As we have indicated, there were differences of view, particularly on the school versus unit option of providing ESL teaching, but it seemed that development over the past few years had led to a situation where few practitioners felt entirely happy with existing arrangements.

Clearly different patterns of dispersal through the schools dictated different responses, and the 'rippling out' of ethnic minority families to the less urbanised areas (specifically mentioned in Exeshire, Wyeshire and Seeborough) could create new needs in schools that formerly had no on-site ESL teaching. In Seeborough's case, with no specialist unit, those needs would have to be met in school. How far this could be done would depend in part on the availability of extra resources, an issue of particular difficulty for schools with small numbers of minority children with language difficulties. In the absence of a special unit, or where, as in Exeshire, the language unit is primarily concerned with meeting special needs, the question of *resources* for schools becomes paramount.

Resources for schools: the use of S.11. While governments have relied mainly upon the general expenditure programmes of local authorities to meet the needs of the ethnic minority population, extra funding has been provided under S.11 of the Local Government Act 1966. Some extra educational resources are also provided through the Urban Programme but these (even when provided on school premises) tend to be concerned with youth or nursery facilities and are not a significant source of funding for schools.

The rationale of S.11 funding is that the extra staff costs incurred should be attributable to the special needs generated by the pressure of New Commonwealth populations. As the 1980 DES memorandum noted, relevant expenditure was mostly on providing specialist teachers of English or of remedial skills for primary and secondary school children. However, while most authorities fund their ESL provision under S.11, this is usually only part of their S.11 claim. In Beeborough, for example, there are 72 teaching posts allocated to the language centre (including those deployed in schools) but the salaries of 191 teachers are included in the S.11 claim. This extra funding is used, in Beeborough as elsewhere, to provide *general* support and reinforcement to schools.

This characteristic use of S.11 draws attention to the ways in which the entitlements of particular schools and of the LEA as a whole are assessed, and to the manner in which the additional resources are allocated. We are unable to say much about this without the further research which it evidently merits. However, three issues may be touched upon here. First, how closely does the deployment of S.11 teachers match the pattern of ethnic minority concentration? Second, how is the allocation to schools of S.11 teachers actually effected? Third, how do LEAs assess their own overall needs and entitlements?

The first question has often drawn comment as to the disparities in the per capita funding under S.11 that evidently exist between authorities. It is, after all, no more than an opportunity for LEAs to seek extra funding. Moreover, it is one that incurs considerable costs to the authority itself, over and above the 25 per cent contribution which it has to make, for there are also debt costs incurred in any retrospectively-paid grant. It is evident that authorities vary not only in their notional entitlement but also in their willingness to accept these costs. Ayeborough, for example, claimed a little more than a quarter of a million pounds in 1978/79; Seeborough and Deeborough more than twice this sum; Beeborough six times this sum. While their eligible populations vary widely so, too, does their eagerness to seek funding and to meet the local proportion of the additional costs. Ayeborough has in the past shied away from percentage grants, reportedly on the grounds that unacceptable future commitments would be unavoidable should the grant system ever be changed. It was acknowledged in Ayeborough that 'we've got a lot more immigrants in the schools that we could be claiming for'.

A more interesting aspect of this question concerned the deployment of resources within the LEAs. Other than the specialist ESL teachers the 'extra' support sometimes seemed to be invisible, at least at the school level. The head-teachers in Beeborough denied having any S.11 teachers other than those used for ESL (who were not in any case counted as 'their' staff). Yet the heads frequently referred to the generous staffing ratio operated by the authority. Significantly, one head revealed that he had an extra teacher allocated for disruptive pupils, but since he had none he used this teacher for such duties as he thought fit. Similarly, in Exeshire one head remarked that his staff numbered 2½ teachers more than the normal allowance for his school and claimed that it was for him to decide how best to deploy this extra help which was recognisably attributable to S.11 provision. In several of the authorities heads were either unable to tell whether or not they had S.11 teachers on their staff, or were unable to identify them.

As to the second issue, of the process by which teachers are actually allocated to schools, we were able to learn little in the time available. While there are specific rules governing the eligibility of authorities for S.11 support, LEAs generally apportion extra staff to schools on the basis of the subjective judgements of administrators as to the needs of the school. The DES does not require LEAs to identify particular teachers as S.11-funded, and the scheme retains thereby a high degree of flexibility. For this reason, there is only an approximate correspondence between the number of minority children in particular schools and the margin by which any one school might exceed the staffing norm.

Seeborough is a special case. Each head knew *precisely* how many West Indian or Asian children he or she had in school, for a regular return of these figures was still made to the office on a special form. In this authority a detailed claim is submitted to the Home Office, naming those individual staff who could be identified as 'immigrant' teachers. This, however, is a 'notional' list and 'is not revealed to heads . . . the only contact with heads is the form'. The officer concerned recalled that in relation to any particular school 'We say "there is undoubtedly a problem — so we'll give you an extra teacher over your establishment". Provided we're claiming the salary of *a* teacher at that school we're fulfilling the spirit (of the Act).' Given, however, the moderate size of Seeborough's claim — which perhaps can be accounted for in terms of the LEA's narrow interpretation of eligibility — there are relatively few extra teachers to be distributed. Some heads seemed to be dissatisfied with the mismatch between notional entitlement and the actual disbursement of additional support.

Finally, how do LEAs assess their entitlement and thus determine the size of the 'pool' from which extra help can be allocated to schools? Here, it seemed that the most variable factors were the view which the LEA traditionally took of S.11 eligibility, its willingness to make extra commitments and, latterly, the strength of the pressures from the treasurer's department to enter an additional claim in order to reduce current expenditure. In the case of the authorities with the lower levels of S.11 funding, precise criteria seemed to be unclear, each year's submission being based largely on that of the previous year. With, in some cases, a rapidly growing minority school population, such an authority could possibly be underclaiming and all four of the metropolitan authorities mentioned recent pressures to increase the claim.

In the three authorities where we were able to explore this sensitive issue we found an acknowledgement that the rules could not be strictly observed. As one official asked, 'What do we do about those from Pakistan or the second or third generation? Ought we to distinguish them by colour or by other criteria?' In another authority there was a strict attempt to base the claim on assessment of the numbers of 'those teachers who would not otherwise be employed'. One officer, who spoke of the 'ordeal' of district audit and of conversation about S.11 procedure with neighbouring colleagues in which 'we terrify each other' was convinced that 'if I tried to alter the system I'd be reducing it and in trouble with the political masters because this is just taken in by finance as a resource in (budgetary) projections'.

The common themes that emerged from our visits were clear enough. First, the view of S.11 as something of a lottery for schools. Second, the frequent complaint of a lack of guidance from the Home Office as to correct procedure.

Third (and keenly felt in relation to the Home Office stance) the power of the district auditor in vetting the claim. Fourth, the variations among district auditors in their interpretation of the scope and purpose of S.11, variations which inevitably have powerful impacts on the LEAs themselves. Fifth, the relative secrecy (probably necessary, given the foregoing) of S.11 bid preparation. Sixth, the absence of any monitoring (with the apparent exception of Wyeshire) of what was seen as simple staff supplementation to schools. Seventh (and this probably is attributable to the absence of local 'policies' for S.11 or more generally for meeting the educational needs of ethnic minority children), the lack of clarity among key officials as to what S.11 is *for*.

This last theme of widespread confusion can be usefully illustrated by example. In the authority with the most precise statistical base for a S.11 claim, the very quality of the data worked against the provision of a multi-racial service. Here the officer with responsibility for assembling the claim revealed that having received the returns from schools 'As a general rule I ignore the West Indian column . . . there isn't a basic language difference (and) this is the principal area of concern — the basic need is language.' This quotation may represent a simple misapprehension of S.11 as aimed at the linguistic needs rather than at the broader cultural aspects of multi-racial education. But it also touches upon a deeper seated disagreement as to the purpose of S.11. While to some black groups and community activists, S.11 is intended to meet the needs of the minority communities, to most education administrators its purpose is to provide additional resources to areas experiencing particular stress as a consequence of the presence of New Commonwealth populations.

Ethnic records in schools. One important aspect of S.11 funding — the problem of assessing entitlement — leads naturally to the wider issue of the information available to LEAs. Whenever S.11 was discussed, the topic of ethnic record keeping was mentioned to us at an early stage. Records were usually seen as a means of acquiring more resources. However, as we shall see, they may also be seen as a means of monitoring performance. Recording the ethnic origin of children began with the now defunct DES annual return, and with the passage of time that has elapsed since then practice has become highly variable. This is, nevertheless, an area where a LEA can choose if it so wishes to adopt a position in favour of record keeping which must necessarily hold for all the schools for which it is responsible. More than any other area, however, this is one in which actual practice will be largely governed by the willingness of the policy makers to be explicit about the ethnic dimension in policy and provision. It is the reluctance of many of the participants in the educational system to accept that degree of explicitness that militates against the adoption of ethnic record keeping for schools.

Three of the authorities had no such policy. In Beeborough, we were told that opposition from the teaching union rendered record keeping entirely beyond consideration. In Exeshire, we were told that some heads have records but that other heads would 'find it difficult' and although the office had reconsidered asking for aggregate figures broken down by ethnic group this had been rejected because of the difficulties of classification. There was, however, also evidence of acute political sensitivity in Exeshire, where it was felt that 'the maintenance of such records could be positively dangerous if the information fell into the wrong hands.' While records had been kept for a while after the discontinuance of the DES form, pressure from rightwing groups for access to the figures had led to a decision to cease record keeping altogether.

In Ayeborough, the director of education has argued forcibly against ethnic record keeping. However, during an EMSG meeting a group of heads displayed a considerable knowledge of the ethnic composition of their schools (but were adamant that such information, which is not made available to the office, should not be used to monitor the performance of children). Thus, while it had apparently been agreed at some past date that it was 'discriminatory even to count Asian children', the education officers admitted that 'if you want a figure you'd just ring the heads'. This inexplicitness appeared to generate a certain unease and confusion, not least as to what constituted an acceptable index of ethnic origin. One head spoke for several colleagues in claiming that 'when they come into school I enter on the record cards where they came from'; another conceding that he 'manoeuvred' into asking parents 'where they came from'; another education department officer suggested that 'the school last attended' could be used to give 'an unofficial record', presumably for new migrants.

The alarm expressed by Ayeborough heads at the proposal to monitor performance (a proposal which has been strongly supported by the head of the language unit), points up the different expectations which those concerned may have of record keeping. Where records were advocated without success the protagonists usually stressed the advantages that would accrue to the LEA in negotiating extra resources from central government. This argument is reflected also in the practice of those heads who do keep 'informal' records which they admit to using in bargaining for extra allocations for their schools.

Part of the case for record keeping is that it would permit the monitoring of performance or achievement to determine whether or not the LEA was properly discharging its responsibilities to children of ethnic minority origin. This more radical use of records as a monitoring instrument has been briefly considered in Ayeborough but attracted no support within the EMSG there. The education chairman was emphatic that such records as exist in schools are 'non-statistical individual profiles'. A lengthy discussion of the possibilities of correlating spelling ages and maths scores came to the relieved conclusion that as 'you couldn't roll them into one to get a composite measure' it was 'too difficult then to contemplate'.

The situations in Deeborough and Wyeshire present a sharp contrast. In Deeborough the chief education officer proposed in 1978 that 'an ideal policy would include the systematic monitoring of the effectivenss of the educational system in providing for pupils from ethnic minorities, to detect underperformance and to seek to rectify it promptly'. This topic was included in the consultations initiated in 1980 whereby both schools and community organisations were invited to comment on the following question: 'There are now systematic tests of pupils' attainment in Deeborough schools. Should these be used to assess the effectiveness of the system in providing for pupils of ethnic

110

minorities as separate groups?' This view was described in the subsequent report as 'overwhelmingly' supported by the community respondents while 'teachers were more divided in their views with a majority of 3 to 2 against the proposal; opposition was on both philosphical and pragmatic grounds'. The education committee accepted the proposal and the officials began devising a scheme.

Wyeshire's experience illustrates both the administrative and the monitoring aspects of record keeping. In 1977, the chief education officer reported on the problems of under achievement among black school children, arguing that 'in order that rational planning can be carried out it is necessary for there to be more objective information about the numbers of immigrants in our schools. It is anticipated that when such information is available it will be necessary to make further provision for them'. The collection of information was approved 'so as to form a statistical basis on which future arrangements may be planned for the assistance of children whose mother tongue is not English'. In 1979, the CEO reported again on the need for extra provision on the basis that 'information collected earlier this year indicated that the number of ethnic minority children requiring special educational help (has) continued to grow.' From this report arose the extra provision described below of two peripatetic teachers as a support team for the largely white schools, and an Urban Programme-funded language and resources centre in the southern part of the county.

Wyeshire's statistical returns may enable the multi-racial advisory service to extend recent developments in the direction of effective monitoring. The survey of schools was repeated in 1981. The questionnaire not only asked for staffing details (including the ethnic origin of teachers and non-teaching staff) but also provided for the recording of numbers of ethnic minority pupils entering for and gaining GCE and CSE qualifications. The senior adviser has expressed the view that it may be necessary in future to collect statistics on the subjects taken, as he suspected a 'hidden' form of under attainment by Asian pupils opting for relatively 'soft' GCE subjects.

Wyeshire obviously does not provide the last word in the use of ethnic records in education policy making, and it seems likely that the use of the annual return may be yet further extended as an aid to problem identification and policy making. Moreover, only aggregate data are asked for, there being no central register of individual pupils and the clerical and administrative costs of running Wyeshire's scheme are probably small. It is also worth noticing that the scheme was implemented following consultation with the teaching profession.

Perhaps the most stiking conclusion to be drawn from the practices of our case study LEAs is the close association of their position on record keeping with their view on under achievement. In Deeborough, the schools largely denied that minority pupils and West Indians in particular under-attain. However, West Indian organisations and education department officials evidently believe this to be the case. Indeed, some of those most active in Deeborough education saw an acceptance of multiculturalism as a route to increasing minority attainment, citing the Bullock report in this regard. Thus, whether contested or not, the suspicion of under-achievement underlay the proposal from the education office that the ethnic origin of children should be recorded by schools.

111

So too in Wyeshire, the starting point of discussion in 1977 was the assertion that 'black youngsters often under-achieve at school and are often ill-prepared for employment even if jobs are available. Young West Indians are twice as likely to be unemployed as other members of the population at large'. Record keeping was seen as a vital preliminary to providing for a more equal education system. In Ayeborough, on the other hand, discussion of under-achievement centred on the experience of a (selected) handful of headmasters, one of whom told the EMSG that 'when a young person presents himself for employment the parents of ethnic minority children have little to worry about (there are) more desirable end products coming from the ethnic minority community than from the indigenous. I would say that a child from the ethnic minority community who has the full treatment does very well indeed'.

A contrary view was taken by the head of the language unit, who complained that the inquiry was 'not looking borough-wide'. She strongly asserted that 'if I had facts and figures to back me up . . there is no doubt that there *is* under-achievement. But I can't prove it. There are arguments on both sides but I *strongly* come down on the need to know. In secondary I see under-achievement — I would like to be able to say that we need to compensate.' Oddly, however, this impressionistic claim was self-defeating, for elected members, in putting on record their opposition to record keeping, conceded that the head of the language unit 'has the information she wants — *emotionally*'. Precise data would be superfluous.

To sum up, opposition to record keeping often appeared to stem from the undiscussability of under-achievement. Such discussion was sometimes avoided by glowing references to the progress of children from minority groups. We also noticed in Ayeborough frequent references to *the* (Asian) ethnic minority and any problems of the smaller West Indian community were not discussed. Indeed, the dominant assumption in Ayeborough is of a relatively affluent, ambitious and undifferentiated minority community; a suggestion that under achieving minority children 'may be withdrawn for private education' went unremarked. Elsewhere, there was either a reluctance to identify under-achievement, or a tendency to shift the blame to social institutions outside the school or, often, an identification of 'under-achievement' as, in reality, a problem of excessive and unrealistic aspirations. It seemed that the questions of achievement and its monitoring in relation to ethnic origin could only be squarely faced in those authorities where the nature of education in a multi-racial society was itself recognised as in urgent need of re-consideration.

Summary. In this section we have dealt with three broad areas of LEA provision where policies have a mandatory or universal significance for schools: ESL teaching, the provision of S.11 funding, and the collection of ethnic records. Our main concern was with ways in which LEAs provide services through schools but the most striking conclusion is one of massive variations in practice among the six authorities in each of these three areas. While the variations in ESL provision seem to reflect the legacy of past experience and arrangements in each distinct locality, variations in the other two areas seem to indicate wide differences in the ways in which LEAs have faced up to the issues posed by the multi-racial nature of much of our urban society. As the Bullock report concluded in 1975, 'too many multi-racial schools ignore the fact that the community they serve has altered radically over the last 10 years or so'. Given the intricate pattern of power and prerogative in the education service, LEAs seem often to have been reluctant to encourage schools to face that fact. Perhaps this reluctance stems from the widespread aversion to open discussion of race and ethnic diversity. Just as we found in the area of employment practices a belief that anything other than a 'colour blind' approach was *ipso facto* 'discriminatory' so, too, was this apparent in education. In many of the authorities and schools, there was a strong commitment to a deliberate inexplicitness in policy discussion. 'Kids is kids and disadvantage is disadvantage' is how one AEO put it.

Moreover, it was also evident that LEAs, besides varying in their views of multicultural education, vary also in the extent to which they are prepared to steer developments in schools even in regard to these 'universal' modes of provision. It seemed that in many cases LEA responsibility was thought to stop at the point where resources were made available to schools and there was no attempt to monitor either their use or their usefulness. At the end of the day, this must be attributed to the lack of policies in whose terms utilisation and results might be judged. Only Wyeshire, of all the LEAs, claimed to monitor the activities of S.11 teachers and even here this was but an additional responsibility of the adviser for multi-racial education. S.11 is, after all, a central government initiative and schools and LEAs are characteristically both grateful for extra support and not overconcerned about its notional purpose. Provision for a multi-racial education service on the part of LEAs has then a strong element of laissez faire where implementation is concerned. If this is so in relation to such apparently positive areas of policy, it is likely also to be true of the more 'permissive' areas of advice and support to schools and it is to those areas that we now turn.

Advice and support

The multicultural adviser. The second main area of LEA provision which we consider concerns the allocation of resources to support the development of a multi-racial education service in schools. There are several areas where an LEA may make facilities available which schools and teachers may make use of or ignore. The LEA can be little more than persuasive in respect of issues which are ultimately in the hands of the classroom teacher: the style and content of teaching itself. LEAs' emphasis on providing advisory services, resource centres or in-service training facilities and their widespread unwillingness to control the curriculum highlight the degree to which adaptation and adjustment in education proceed at the rate which heads and their staff find tolerable. A committed LEA and energetic advisers may seek (possibly with some success) to accelerate that rate. But, as we noted in our visits, they have little power to do so and only limited influence. The appointment of advisers for multicultural education has been widely advocated in recent years. The National Association for Multiracial Education (NAME) and the Labour Party Race Action Group in particular have pressed for a wider adoption of this general advisory role. The Society of LEA Advisers for Multicultural Education has sought to disseminate the advantages of such provision.

Such appointments (under various titles in different authorities) are then often taken as an indication of positive commitment by an authority to the promotion of the multi-racial ideal in education. We considered two questions raised by this assumption: first, what are the various ways in which authorities handle multicultural issues within the administration? Second, does the impact at school level reflect the general mode of operation of a LEA rather than the specific influence of the appointment of a multicultural adviser? This latter question in turn involves looking more widely at the means by which the administration seeks to influence what goes on in the schools short of laying down specific policies and practices to be followed. The use of advisory services is clearly one element to be considered, but so, too, are the use of other support services (such as teachers' centres) and in-service training.

The question of the appointment of a multicultural adviser has been considered in all of the six case study authorities. In the case of Exeshire it arose in connection with a general review of the advisory service in 1978, but was rejected seemingly on the grounds that such a post would risk 'monopolising' concern with multicultural education. Exeshire's deputy director of education has overall responsibility for ethnic minority education and is highly regarded as expert in this field. One official put what was probably a widely-held view: 'Who needs a multicultural adviser when we have (him)? His advice is authoritative'. The deputy director is assisted by the assistant education officer (secondary) who plays a 'trouble-shooting' and counselling role, but day-to-day support for the schools is effectively left to the general team of advisers, together with, in the largest city in the county, the more specific resources of the language centre. The county's other resource and teachers' centres do not have any specific ethnic minority direction.

Beeborough appointed an adviser for multicultural education in November 1980. Previously, two of the 14 advisers were designated for compensatory education, and in practice a large part of their work was concerned with the education of ethnic minority children. Responsibility within the administration for multicultural education seems to rest with the education officer (schools); he, for example, is responsible for the language centre.

Deeborough, which has inspectors rather than advisers, has recently decided to appoint an inspector specifically for multicultural education. Previously the work had formed part of the responsibility of one of the senior inspectors, although one of the curriculum development leaders (described as a 'ginger group' but occupying a similar position to advisory teachers in other authorities) had an exclusive responsibility for multicultural education. Other changes taking place in the support services in Deeborough are discussed below. Within the administration, responsibility for multicultural education

114

rests with the senior assistant education officer (services), an official who is clearly a forceful advocate of multicultural education within the department.

Wyeshire have the most elaborate arrangements in this field of any of the six LEAs. One of the constituent authorities had appointed an adviser for immigrant education in 1967; another, an immigrant liaison officer in 1969. The county currently maintains an advisory and inspection service for schools, headed by a chief inspector. Multicultural education is the responsibility of a general adviser for multi-racial education, who has been in post since 1974. This adviser has responsibility for the two resource centres (in the north and south of the county). He is also able to deploy a support team of two peripatetic teachers of ethnic minority children as a flying squad to offer professional support on application from schools to the adviser. These teachers are generally used to support schools which have a small number of minority children on the roll, reflecting the gradual diffusion of the minority population away from the two main urban centres. The general adviser for multi-racial education works closely to the senior assistant education officer.

Seeborough also has a substantial experience of providing advice and support in this field. The senior adviser for compensatory education (in effect a multi-ethnic adviser) had been appointed organiser for immigrant education in one of the constituent authorities as long ago as 1968. In recent years, two advisory teachers for multicultural education worked directly to him. Paradoxically, however, this senior advisory post was abolished in a staffing review carried out in 1980, the senior adviser taking early retirement and his duties falling to a primary adviser. The reverberations of this controversial change were very much in evidence during our visits and strong views were expressed by officials and headteachers both for and against this apparent demotion of multicultural education.

Finally, Ayeborough apparently considered the question of an adviser in the late 1970s. The then director of education was reportedly hostile to the proposal on the ground that it would highlight ethnic minority children as 'special'. As another official explained: 'The trouble is, an adviser is a very highly-paid person' and 'finance knocks this on the head'. Moreover, the Asian settlement in Ayeborough is heavily concentrated in the middle part of the borough and ten schools have the predominant share of minority children; 'the argument goes that you'd be giving an adviser for ten schools when (in other topics) you've only got one for 75 schools'. However, some headteachers continue to press for such an appointment. Meanwhile, as elsewhere, the adviser for compensatory education includes the multicultural aspects in her own duties.

There is thus a wide variety of formal arrangements, but it is by no means clear that this variety is necessarily reflected in what happens in the schools. The view that advisers are what their name implies and can only operate by persuasion in the schools was put most strongly by the two Beeborough advisers for compensatory education. They suggested that, at least in the multicultural field, much depended on having a receptive staff and headteacher if ideas were to be put over successfully. The other side of this coin is that if a head and his staff are resistant to suggestions on multi-cultural education there is not much that advisers can do about it. Perhaps not surprisingly, the heads of Beeborough schools whom we interviewed had differing views on the value of advisers; one, for example, thought that advisers tended 'to leave you out on a limb' and saw progress on the multicultural front as depending largely on the efforts of teachers themselves, another had always found advisers very helpful.

There is no necessary conflict in these views in terms of the role of advisers. Rather they show that the relationship between advisers and schools, at least in relation to multicultural education, is a very variable one. Much the same impression derived from visits to Deeborough and Exeshire. In Deeborough, because of the hitherto somewhat diffused nature of responsibility within the inspectorate for multicultural education, the curriculum development leader (CDL) is the main point of contact for schools on many multicultural matters. Nevertheless, one head who was enthusiastic in describing how helpful the authority were, did not in general seek the advice of the CDL. The usefulness of the CDL as a provider of information was, however, mentioned by other heads. This aspect of support to the teaching service is likely to become more significant with the considerable expansion of multicultural advice provided by a specialist unit (headed by the former CDL) approved by the LEA during 1980.

In Exeshire, yet another aspect of the advisory relationship was touched upon. The head who was most critical of the authority for failing to have a policy on multi-racial education and who particularly deplored the lack of a multi-cultural adviser drew attention to the efforts made by some individual advisers (he mentioned in particular the religious education adviser) who happened to have an interest in multicultural education. In fact, in so far as Exeshire may be said to have a policy on multicultural education in relation to their advisory services, it is that advisers should *all* take the multicultural element into account in their work; that is, it is very much left to the individual adviser to make his own response.

This view underlies the recent changes in Seeborough and there were some indications that it represented more than a hasty rationalisation of the recent cutbacks in staffing. As in the other authorities, some heads mentioned close and continuous contacts with the former senior adviser, while others could less easily identify a positive benefit. These differences seemed to be precisely paralleled in the evaluations of the support provided by the other subject advisers. While the religious education (RE) adviser in particular has been very active in disseminating advice to schools on a multi-faith basis, one of the heads we visited was clearly perplexed by the problems of a multi-faith school, but had had no contact with the RE adviser. Moreover, the former senior adviser promoted development with the aid of a small but enthusiastic 'community relations panel' of teachers. Since his retirement, however, his successor in this (now very part-time) role has, in the absence of any readily available body of experience and material, taken steps to establish a local branch of NAME. Concern for multi-racial issues in education has then apparently been opened out to a wider body of practitioners. Some of those whom we met believed that the former arrangements had 'closed off' multi-cultural education almost as a private concern of enthusiasts.

Despite this ambiguous experience, the appointment of a multicultural adviser should in theory enable a much more positive and co-ordinated attempt to be made to provide schools with advice and help in this area. Advisers are, after all, the people who make the most direct and regular contact between the central administration of the LEA and the schools. It seems clear from our interviews and other material, that to translate this theory into practice requires a strong commitment by the authority to multi-cultural education and a particular thrust by the advisory services as a whole towards this end. A great deal depends on how much scope the adviser has, and on attitudes within the administration; we noted in some authorities a frequent involvement by senior administrators in 'advising' headteachers. Such headquarters support may or may not reinforce that provided by a multi-cultural adviser. In particular, the second point draws attention to the relation-ship between the adviser or advisers responsible for ethnic minority education and the remainder of the advisory service. We noticed, for example, that the support of a physical education adviser might in some circumstances strengthen a headteacher's resolve to maintain rather rigid physical education dress rules in cases where a multicultural adviser's counsel might be to do otherwise.

Deeborough again provides a useful illustration of the general point. In the first place, the authority is already seen by some heads as having a commit-ment to multicultural education in spite of the fact that until now there has been nobody in the inspectorate with exclusive responsibility for it. As against this, there is the view of those interviewed in the administration that there is a need to work from within to convince colleagues, and in particular the inspec-torate itself, of the importance of a positive attitude to ethnic minority educa-tion. On the other hand, a senior inspector for secondary education (who was said to be one of those with a personal concern and interest in this area), was at pains to emphasise how limited were his opportunities to influence schools in this direction.

It is, of course, only possible to speculate at this stage what will be the prac-tical consequences of the appointment in both Beeborough and Deeborough of a multicultural adviser/inspector. Much will turn on the status of the post and the calibre of its holder. It is also relevant to recall here the view of the ex-perienced multicultural adviser in another LEA (outside our main sample) that to be successful a multicultural adviser has to be a 'political being' to a much greater extent than other advisers. It may then be concluded that although the appointment of such an adviser can perhaps be regarded as expressing a positive policy intention on the part of an authority, it is, given the nature of the advisory services, little more than an opportunity to schools to make what they will of what is offered.

Resource centres. The support and advice provided by authorities to schools may include the establishment of specific institutional arrangements such as teachers' centres and the provision of in-service training. Advisers often have a large share of responsibility in relation to these. Teachers' centres are widely regarded as a particularly effective way of exchanging ideas and information and disseminating 'good practice'. Their use by teachers (a topic currently the subject of a study by the National Foundation for Educational Research), being voluntary is, of course, variable and necessarily restricted to the more enthusiastic teachers. So, too, is in-service training, the importance of which has been stressed by the Community Relations Commission, the Labour Party Race Action Group, NAME and the National Union of Teachers (NUT).

It should be noted that there are complexities of status within the support services. In Exeshire, there were three reading centres, one of which had on its staff an advisory teacher for immigrant education (although with the closure of the centre as part of current economy measures she has been transferred to the language centre). She was, in effect, the only person within the advisory service with a specific responsibility for multicultural education in primary schools. However, not only was her status as an advisory teacher lower than that of an adviser, but in accordance with Exeshire's general view, her role was restricted to ESL.

Similarly, the curriculum development leaders in Deeborough are formally no more than advisory teachers responsible to the inspectorate. However, Deeborough is the one authority of the six which has attempted a 'package' of measures for multicultural education. Not only have advisory teachers been brought in as part of the preparations for this (for example, to help in the consultations preceding the preparation of proposals) but they will be prominently involved in some of the new measures, notably the establishment of an *ethnic studies unit*.

This new unit will be responsible to the senior assistant education officer (services). The unit's tasks will include the curriculum development work previously being carried out and also in-service training work and the provision of teaching materials. Clearly, the greater resources being devoted to this work and its changed status within the authority will have to be judged, in part, against its relationships with the inspectorate and with other elements of Deeborough's support services.

Apart from the language centres already referred to, five of the six authorities have established teachers' centres and/or other kinds of resource centre. The extent to which these are specifically geared to multi-cultural education naturally varies. In both Beeborough and Deeborough they were cited by heads visited as places with a good deal of information and materials on multicultural education, and the Deeborough centre in particular seems, on the evidence of the interviews, to be a useful source of ideas in this field for teachers. In Exeshire the reading centre which has been closed down was, in effect, a teachers' centre for primary schools and was mentioned, among other things, for its usefulness in the provision of in-service courses, while this would also appear to be a major function of the Seeborough teachers' centre. Teachers' centres, although established with the financial support of LEAs, are also to some extent a joint venture with teachers' representatives, and the nature of particular centres no doubt reflects this as well as the personality of the teacher in charge. The various kinds of resource centres which have been set up are a more direct LEA responsibility. These too, however, are often far from being exclusively concerned with multicultural education.

Wyeshire has made the most explicit resource provision within our sample. The purpose-built resources unit in the north of the county, opened in 1977, has an ESL role which figures prominently within the wider remit on multicultural education. The head of the centre has been active in promoting multicultural education nationally. The more recent (and at present, smaller) centre in the south of the county is explicitly for multi-racial education and is intended, over and above building a resource bank, to give 'assistance in connection with in-service training, education procedures and support to teachers — and, in this latter context, to provide a focal point for multi-racial education in the south of the County'.

The other authorities have to date made less specific provision. Deeborough has its Language Literacy and Numeracy Support Service, part of which is clearly directed at ethnic minority pupils since nine teachers working for it are S.11 appointments. As its name implies, it in part fulfils the function of developing materials in support of language teaching which elsewhere (for example, Exeshire) is being attempted by the language centre, but its role is wider than this. Exeshire has (or had) various kinds of resource centre, but none of these had any very direct relevance to multi-cultural education. Beeborough has no specific resource centres beyond the language and teachers' centres. It should also be added that neither in Deeborough nor Exeshire did these additional resource centres appear as significant sources of ideas for heads and other teachers.

In-service training. In-service training is not, of course, exclusively an LEA responsibility. The greater proportion of such training is provided by DES short courses, organised on a regional basis by HMI. To the extent that it was seen as an important source of ideas by heads (or even by education administrators) it was not always clear how far they were distinguishing the contribution made by authorities from that provided by DES and HMI. One head in Exeshire who did clearly make the distinction saw the authority provision as being inadequate largely because, in the absence of any LEA policy, what was done depended mainly on the interests and efforts of individuals (the RE adviser was again cited). However, in Exeshire, but more especially in Wyeshire and Deeborough, in-service training by the LEA was seen by a number of heads as an important means for the provision of information and advice. The impact of LEA in-service training depends not only on how much provision it makes and on its quality but on the response made by teachers to the opportunities offered to them.

Deeborough makes a considerable effort to mount courses, although one official there felt that these courses overemphasised 'content'; the heart of the matter as he saw it was to shift teacher attitudes and to develop their abilities in a multicultural context. At least one head was sceptical how far such courses were reaching the people who could most benefit from them; since they were held after school hours only the committed and the enthusiastic tended to go. This was a point often made elsewhere. Beeborough's advisers for compensatory education are well aware of this problem and make deliberate efforts to get people on to quite lengthy courses (one day a week for two terms) who will act as 'catalysts' in spreading ideas from the course to other teachers in the school. This approach seemed to be vindicated by one head who said that all his staff had gained information either from going on a course or by having it passed on to them by those who had. It was not possible for us to attempt to evaluate these claims and counter-claims.

These general observations about the impact of provision seem to apply to each of the authorities where we have specific information and indeed to permeate the entire issue of advice and support. We have already cited the variable response to the activities of the former senior adviser in Seeborough. The response to training provision there reinforces this general point. Some officials (and the warden of the teachers' centre) pointed to an impressive list of in-service training courses mounted with the support of the adviser and the 'community relations panel' of teachers. The list however turned out to repay a closer scrutiny, for while some evoked an enthusiastic response, lack of response to others was such that they were in fact cancelled. The differences between the courses in each category was revealing.

A one-day course on 'the needs of Chinese children' was established in two successive years and cancelled each time (attracting on one occasion one applicant, and on the other occasion apparently none). A six-day course, 'teaching children of minority ethnic groups', was cancelled because there were only 12 applicants. A five-session course on 'the Asian child in the early years of school' attracted six applicants and was cancelled. So, too, were 'some aspects of Asian life', and 'working with minority groups' (for which there were no takers). 'The needs of minority group school leavers' attracted just one teacher while six were too few to justify 'the West Indian pupil in the secondary school'. The in-service training files in Seeborough also illuminate which courses were popular. Religious education predominates among the well-subscribed courses. 'Attitudes to death: beliefs and practices', 'an approach to religious education and worship in primary schools', an RE book and audio-visual aids exhibition and a 'one world' course all did well. A visit to a Hindu temple and a Jewish synagogue enticed the impressive number of 42 local teachers. Outside this area of obvious keen interest in multi-faith issues the only other apparently successful multi-ethnic course since 1977 was (possibly significantly?) 'sub-cultures and disruptive pupils in secondary schools'. Comparable information from the other LEAs is not at present available to us (although it is claimed that Beeborough's ethnic minority courses are over subscribed).

The differential response to Seeborough's courses and the small numbers involved indicate the reliance of advisory and support services on teaching staff actually according some priority to multi-ethnic education. 'Preaching to the converted' is a common dismissal of the services which we have considered

120

here. Such differences as were indicated among the authorities appeared, so far as we could tell, to be more than differences of degree in the forcefulness of the preaching and the warmth of its reception. Advice and support evidently depend for their ultimate effectiveness on the acceptance by teachers of the realities of a multi-racial society, an acceptance which is today still highly uneven.

There would appear to be two alternative strategies for those engaged in the provision of support. The first is a 'political' mode, one which attempts to reach as wide an audience as possible. The other is a mode in which considerable support is offered to those who seek it, aiding and comforting the enthusiasts while proselytising among those who have yet to recognise the changing nature of education in a multi-racial society. The implications of such approaches spill over unavoidably into the area of concern where authorities commonly take a neutral stance and often profess 'to have no policy'. This is commonly so with regard to school-community relations and we turn now to discuss that issue.

The school and the community

Two sections of this chapter have dealt respectively with aspects of provision which only the LEA can determine, and with the provision of facilities for advice and support whose take-up rests ultimately with the schools and their teaching staff. In this section we examine a number of questions where traditionally LEAs have been reluctant to intervene and instead have left the determination of practice to the schools themselves. There are of course, variations between authorities, for some LEAs may see a need for action on a question which elsewhere is regarded as a 'non-policy' matter. Nevertheless, there is a range of questions which LEAs are generally content to leave to schools, and where attempts to intervene are likely to conflict with the desires of headteachers to maintain their own prerogatives.

This is not, however, to say that schools are entirely insulated from external influences in respect of such questions as the curriculum, school dress, or religious observances. These are areas where there may be considerable pressure to bring about change, whether it be from DES, the Inspectorate, the teaching profession, the Schools Council, parents' associations or community leaders. Such pressures could possibly eclipse any influence which the LEA may try to exert, either through its advisory services, through governors, or through the 'counselling' of senior administrators. Such pressures (and particularly those of local origin) may themselves be deprecated or resented by those heads and teachers who jealously guard their administrative and professional prerogatives. That pressures for change exist ultimately derives from the location of schools within a multi-cultural community, a situation which some heads will prefer to deal with by denying it explicit recognition. The issues which we discuss here are those which arise from changes in ethnic composition of the cities, changes which call into question the appropriateness of what schools provide for their pupils. Two broad issues may be singled out for special attention here: the curriculum, and questions of cultural diversity.

121

Curriculum issues. Earlier in this chapter we dealt with the teaching of English as a second language and it will be recalled that the initial assumption underlying the development of this provision was that needs were basically temporary in nature and would be solved by the increasing fluency in English of ethnic minority children. The 1970s saw much discussion of the adequacy of this assumption and in particular of whether it was realistic or desirable to base educational policy on so simple a concept of assimiliation. The fact that there were in the schools some — and in some areas large numbers of — children not simply of a different linguistic background but with distinctive cultural traditions which did not necessarily disappear even with passing generations came to be seen as raising important issues for schools. Moreover, since the late 1970s, the concept of cultural pluralism has accumulated more support, and assimilationist policies have been viewed as a threat to a desirable diversity of cultures. Thus, more recently, it has been argued that schools should go some way to reinforce some of the very characteristics that in the past they had sought to change.

Nor were these the only aspects of change in educational philosophy. Proposals for a multicultural curriculum have been developed partly as a means of incorporating the backgrounds of children from ethnic minorities, partly in order to eradicate ethnocentric biases that might contribute to under-achievement, and partly in order to provide an education to fit all children, black and white, for life in a multi-racial society. Not all of these questions could be resolved by changes in the curriculum in its narrower sense and there was doubt as to whether the training of teachers was adequate for this new situation which was developing. There was also concern with more specific issues such as the extent to which text books used in schools embodied racist perspectives or the extent to which more teachers should be recruited from ethnic minority communities. The over-riding question was, however, whether issues like these were simply to be regarded as matters of practice to be solved by the professionalism of teachers confronted in their classrooms with children from ethnic minorities or whether some action should be taken to encourage teachers to revise their basic assumptions about education in a multi-racial society.

It would perhaps be optimistic to imagine that these recent and profound developments in the philosophy of education would in themselves and by themselves be immediately reflected in schools. Rather, the evidence tends to suggest that the teaching profession itself is adapting to change less readily than the situation might be felt to demand. As one head commented apropos his local multicultural adviser, 'We didn't always see eye to eye. He wanted to see differences where I want to see similarities'.

The take-up by teachers of curriculum developments is somewhat less than those contributing to the debate on the curriculum would wish. Collectively and individually, teachers play a crucial and inescapable part in determining the rate at which innovations are adopted. As one deputy director of education put it 'the people who will solve the problems are the people in the classroom'. This is a sobering truth. The conservatism of teachers was cited as an obstacle in several authorities. One head considered his biggest problem to be the prejudices of his own staff and his greatest dilemma how to react to racism in the staffroom. One senior official commented that 'some of our teachers are racist but no one will ever admit it'. It is against such a background of control of the curriculum by often conservative practitioners that both the setbacks and the achievements in the multicultural curriculum must be viewed.

The most visible changes in the curriculum which we encountered concerned the religious practices of schools. Religious education occupies a rather special position both because of the provisions of the 1944 Education Act which requires an 'act of worship' (not necessarily a Christian one) and because many of the parents of children now in the schools hold to religious faiths which even thirty years ago were hardly within the consciousness of teachers in English schools. Authorities have generally reacted on a purely *ad hoc* basis through the advisory services and in-service training. The question of assembly in particular has been very largely left to heads to decide with the result that even within the limited numbers of schools visited a remarkable variety of approaches was indicated from more or less traditional Christian assemblies with the occasional reference to Hindu, Sikh or Muslim festivals to what seemed to be a more or less universalistic approach concerned with moral themes.

One Seeborough primary school head emphasised that she centred her assemblies and RE (in a school in which nearly 200 of the 270 children are from various Asian backgrounds) around the theme 'God the Father'. A former member of a working party which produced Seeborough's impressive syllabus and teaching materials, she jokingly claimed to have 'the most non-religious school in Seeborough. Some of her colleagues in largely Muslim schools, however, showed less flexibility and this sometimes brought them into severe conflicts with the local Imam. Another head indicated his uncertainty as to what direction to take in assembly with the remark that 'you're yattering on about Jesus when you notice all the black faces'. In the absence of support, advice and guidance from advisers, heads were evidently tempted to resolve the religious dilemma by ignoring it. As one Ayeborough head put it, '70 per cent of my children are not Christian. But we are State schools in a Christian country and cannot turn our backs on the great events in the Christian year.'

Such a view was perhaps not typical and visits to headteachers' studies in areas of large Muslim populations usually revealed a copy of the Q'ran and a wider selection of discourses on the Islamic faith on the bookshelf or desk. Yet in Seeborough more than anywhere else we found particular heads clearly embattled on the religious question. One incident, where a class teacher reportedly had used a copy of the Q'ran to prop up a slide projector, had assumed major proportions and led to mass withdrawals from assembly. Generally, however, withdrawals seemed almost unheard of in any of the authorities and this testified to the heads' sensitivities on this issue. In several schools we were told that the only withdrawals were of the children of Jehovah's Witness and on the occasions when our visits happened to coincide with assembly this was, indeed, apparently the case.

More broadly on religious education, what is done in the schools seems to illustrate the blend of advice from above and individual initiative characteristic of much of the English educational system. Exeshire and Deeborough alone of the authorities visited have produced or are producing an agreed statement on the approach to RE after discussion with local community and teachers. In Exeshire's case, it seems that this arose out of a combination of local pressures and the fact that the RE adviser was very committed to multicultural education. The new RE adviser in Deeborough is appparently pursuing a similar path of consultation as the first step in an agreed statement. Seeborough's RE adviser has produced a substantial programme of material for teaching what are emphatically described as 'religious and moral' questions. Beeborough and Ayeborough do not have RE advisers. It was noticeable in all of the authorities how keen heads were, especially in primary schools, to emphasise how much they had done to make RE a multi-faith subject. True, in some cases this seemed to amount to nothing more than grafting some discussion of, for example, Hinduism onto a traditional approach but clearly many heads had gone much further in trying to present a balanced and well-informed view of different religions including bringing in outside speakers, visiting mosques and temples and celebrating different festivals. At the secondary level, a broader approach to RE is helped, as one head argued, by the fact that the subject is non-examinable.

One question for our inquiry is the extent to which what is done in the schools is influenced by specific initiatives taken by the LEA. In the case of RE, for the most part it seems to depend on a blend of advice exercised through the activities of advisers, teachers' centres and in-service training combined with the responsiveness to community feeling of individual heads and teachers. This latter quality has apparently been crucial, particularly in 'difficult' areas.

Perhaps something similar can be said about the remainder of the curriculum, but here other elements come into the picture. Not least is the fact that, as one Ayeshire head put it, nobody questioned that it was a 'good thing' to learn about other religions, whereas in other subjects even those committed to multicultural ideals are not always in agreement about what to teach or how to teach it. Certainly the impression gained from interviews was that although many heads in schools with a considerable number of ethnic minority pupils genuinely saw themselves as committed to and moving towards the provision of education in an atmosphere which was unmistakably multicultural, they were on the whole very cautious in their approach to the formal curriculum. This was particularly so in secondary schools where there are conflicting pressures, particularly in the more 'academic' subjects.

The part played by LEAs in this seems for the most part to be a very restricted one. Even the curriculum development leader (CDL) in Deeborough, despite his title, is very much part of the advisory mechanism. Thus, while no other LEA in our sample had so explicit a commitment to encouraging curricular change, the limits were still apparent. The CDL is responsible for visiting schools to advise and assist heads and staff, for arranging in-service training courses and for developing new teaching materials. Resource boxes for teachers and pupils have been compiled.' Moreover, his work is clearly directed towards those who are willing and interested in re-orienting the curriculum. These limits testify to the persistence of the traditional view that curriculum matters (what is taught and how it is taught) are ultimately for the schools to determine. Differences betweeen authorities are largely in the extent to which they offer opportunities, support and information in the cause of what is everywhere seen as a school-based process of change. The CEO of one of the more 'progressive' authorities perhaps spoke for many colleagues elsewhere in resisting any attempt to establish policies for the curriculum: 'I've been reluctant to press for policies of different kinds. There is a danger when you've got a young and enthusiastic council that they'll press for full control of the curriculum', wherein the CEO saw a direct comparison 'with Nazi Germany and the Soviet Union'.

Two other rather different aspects of the curriculum are also important. On mother-tongue teaching, only Deeborough has made a specific commitment by allocating teaching resources for this purpose outside normal school hours. A major development in this provision, which Deeborough believe will make them the leading authority in mother-tongue teaching, is in preparation. Some limited experimental provision has also been attempted in Ayeborough following representations from Indian organisations. One of the other authorities has been involved in the EEC-sponsored pilot project on mother-tongue. This project has been the subject of two substantial evaluative reports. Not only did the project have a series of ambitious objectives (which it apparently failed to realise) but it differs considerably from the generally more piecemeal experience of our other LEAs in being an example of 'top down' programmed innovation.

Beeborough has been holding consultations with schools and the community on the question. While the CEO is openly sceptical, no decision has yet been made, although the freedom to determine the curriculum has enabled at least one secondary school to include Gujerati as an optional subject. We found a good deal of scepticism among both administrators and heads about the value of the mother-tongue teaching, quite apart from the practical difficulties of providing it. There was sometimes a deeper-rooted source of this lack of enthusiasm. One director of education claimed that leading figures in the council 'cannot understand why ESL has to be increased and not reduced' and made the observation that 'in their families their first language could be Polish or Lithuanian' — they are assimilated (and ask) 'if we do it why don't the Indians do it?' In such a political climate, it can hardly be expected that mother-tongue teaching will attract support at the policy level. On the other hand, the autonomy of heads could work the other way, for one head of an infants' school in Exeshire said that she had become convinced by research findings that encouraging the use of the mother-tongue might also benefit the learning of English, and had introduced a limited use of Gujerati on her own initiative.

Most of this discussion, as indeed most of the efforts of LEAs and schools, has been about education in schools where children from the ethnic minority communities form a substantial part of the school population. Broader issues are raised by the question of how education in all schools might be adapted to reflect the multi-ethnic nature of our society. In particular, the question where the curriculum in 'white' schools should be adapted or modified is inevitably a focal point in any discussion of the issues. Neither Beeborough nor Exeshire has made any positive stand on this, and therefore, initiatives are left to the individual schools and the more informal channels of communication. The issue had apparently not arisen in Ayeborough or Seeborough. Generally, our school visits were to schools with substantial minority populations (in some cases, over 90 per cent of the roll). However, we did visit a small number of schools of a largely white character during the course of the study and it was noticeable that heads and administrators were more concerned with the resource problems of teaching the minority in a largely white school than with the question of multicultural education for all their children.

Deeborough specifically drew attention to the question of what needed to be done in schools other than those with substantial numbers of pupils from the ethnic minorities as one of the five issues in multicultural education on which it carried out consultations with the schools and the community. The upshot seems to be at least a tentative move in the direction of some form of pluralistic approach, and a declaration that this is a desirable aim. What will emerge in practice is difficult to predict at this stage, but that progress is likely to be slow is suggested by the comments of the (otherwise enthusiastic) head of a white school on the need for a cautious and opportunist approach.

Coping with cultural diversity. The question of how far schools responded to different cultural practices, particularly those regarding diet and dress, exemplifies the type of issue where LEAs are prepared to concede almost total responsibility to the head teacher. Questions of dress in particular are generally seen as falling within the province of the articles of government which give the headteachers sole charge of the disciplinary aspects of the school. Yet there are other areas where there may be a permissive or even a mandatory policy on the part of the LEA but where the application of that policy is *de facto* a matter for the head's discretion.

The provision of school meals is an issue where a variety of special diets may be needed if certain religious requirements are to be strictly observed. Beeborough, Deeborough and Exeshire are among those who have adopted a more or less explicit policy to provide a vegetarian alternative to the meat dish of the day which, in the schools visited, might take the form of fish or more often an egg or cheese dish. The rather more rigorous approach proposed in a recent DES course — specifying a number of forms of alternative provision and telling the children the contents of, for example, sausages — seemed somewhat in advance of the practices of the LEAs we visited.

There were some indications of a residual resistance to catering for the dietary requirements of a multi-faith school. One head, who had been slow to adapt his own provision, claimed that a colleague in a neighbouring school had refused to adopt the LEA's optional menu, asking 'Why should I make them more different than they are already?' He claimed that other heads would also refuse the option 'on principle' — they 'wouldn't put any stumbling blocks in (the way) of full assimilation'.

One frequent source of complaint among headteachers and administrators was that the Muslim community was difficult to deal with, because of the absence of an authenticated and institutionalised priesthood. Administrators, in particular, often referred to the competition for influence of rival Muslim leaders and school-community conflicts were readily interpreted in these simple strategic terms. It was perhaps only in such circumstances of fluidity in the religious life of the Muslim community, that the senior administrators of a LEA could feel free to dispute with community leaders the precise requirements of their own faith. On several occasions heads and administrators told us, somewhat triumphantly, that the Q'ran nowhere specified a particular practice in relation to female dress. Moreover, such interpretations had evidently been presented to Muslim leaders as a definitive judgement and their own interpretations disputed.

There were some indications that local education officers and teachers may view the Muslim community through the prism of their own very different experience, seeking a familiar priesthood and a tradition of agreed textual interpretation that was not there to be found. It was interesting to find that the then senior adviser in Seeborough had drafted an internal report which recognised the disparities between textual authority on the one hand and custom, usage and interpretation on the other. There were a few signs that this contribution had been accepted by his colleagues.

Given the ethnic composition of the northern parts of Seeborough, 'the local Imam' loomed large in the consciousness of headteachers there. Two of them described the ways in which, as new heads, they had gradually established good relations with local religious leaders. One recalled how the Imam had monitored her activities for several weeks before introducing himself and expressing his acceptance of her. Both schools were evidently very open to the community and to parents. In the second, (which had an almost entirely Muslim catchment area) the head was evidently proud of her standing in the community. A walk with her among the neighbouring streets in the vicinity of the Mosque seemed to confirm her claim of a respectful familiarity. In some other Seeborough schools, the heads — from the evidence of the records as well as visits and discussions in the office — seemed in contrast to be extremely protective of their schools, actively discouraged the unscheduled visits of parents and were evidently outraged that other locally prominent Muslims should express concern at their school practices.

Clearly, the autonomy of heads can work in either direction. In most of the authorities heads often seemed to use their autonomy to adapt their practices in whatever ways seemed prudent and reasonable. In Exeshire, the AEO commented that most of the heads take a pride in the fact that relationships are good. The heads of the schools which we visited there either admitted to a relaxed attitude on contentious issues or claimed a mutual understanding with parents. As the same AEO put it 'our heads have got used to coping and trimming'. Autonomy in Exeshire enables the heads to accomodate the school to the community and they are encouraged to do so. In Seeborough, by way of contrast, the variations in school practice which are inescapable in a decentralised system were seen as accentuating these difficulties. 'X is more flexible, but this exposes Y' was the rueful comment of one administrator on the problems of headmaster Y. This was evidently so; representations from community leaders often pointed to the disparities between schools.

Recent events in Seeborough have, however, brought the conflicts directly to headquarters. After a series of skirmishes with parents, the LEA have recently been faced with a far wider dispute over Muslim parents' objections to their daughters swimming in anything but the most rigorous conditions of propriety. In this respect (unlike the issues of school dress), they have found an issue which is a matter of LEA policy, for swimming lessons are mandatory in Seeborough schools. The office are unlikely to feel able to advise heads to ignore policy; whatever the views of officials on the issue, to do so would be to violate the heads' reasonable expectations of support from the office.

While Seeborough has a central place in this discussion of cultural issues in school and community it should not be inferred that the authority's officers or its teaching staff are more intractable than elsewhere. Clearly, one variable factor is the nature of the local communities: in this case an indigenous community with a reported preference for 'assimilation' which is reflected among the senior LEA staff (many of whom were local to the area) and an 'immigrant' community of markedly traditional faith and culture. In these circumstances, the LEA's interest in harmonious relations is actually frustrated by the system of 'tremendous autonomy' (in one head's view) which, while it facilitates experiment and adaptation, cannot temper conservatism. These possibilities of cultural conflict are common to LEAs in multi-racial areas but only in Seeborough did we find them so highly charged, as may be seen from a brief review of the dress issue in the other authorities.

In Deeborough we were told that the anxieties of some Asian parents as to dress and religious observances had been expressed on a number of occasions, yet no problems of conflict over dress norms were reported by heads there. In Beeborough, the CEO seemed inclined to support whatever rules on uniform a headteacher might make. A dispute had arisen in the past and representations had been made by Muslim elders in favour of the girls of their community being allowed to wear the shalwar at school. The CEO had disputed the requirements of the text and the problem faded away when the girls in question were withdrawn to continue their education in Pakistan.

Incidents in other authorities were similarly rare. At one school in Ayeborough, Muslim parents had contested the school uniform rule; representations were made by the Pakistan Association and a compromise reached whereby girls were allowed to wear the shalwar *to* school but were required to change on arrival. A similar resolution appeared to have occurred in one Exeshire school but the county had also experienced conflict over a requirement that boys should wear ties, which one Imam interpreted as a Christian symbol. Once again the office were drawn in as mediators. Here the issue was resolved when the family at the centre of the dispute left the area. More generally, in Exeshire the office seemed keen to head off conflicts by early intervention. It was accepted that 'schools have individually made their own decisions' but 'if the school and community do fall out we've got a problem — we'd want to avoid that'. Thus, the advisers might be actively used in situations where a dispute threatened to arise, to offer advice on the experience of some other school in the country which had overcome the problem by a change of practice.

The contrasts with Seeborough are marked. Here the Muslim communities in different parts of the borough have repeatedly raised issues concerning dress for school attendance and for physical education. Heads and advisers have taken a strict view in some cases and there has been one major incident involving mass suspensions and the eventual prosecution of one parent by the LEA. This last rather harrowing incident has clearly left its scars, not least on the relationship between the headteacher of the school concerned and the office. Yet the general position of the LEA is still to apply or to re-affirm the rules when they are disputed and generally to support the stand taken by any head who is not prepared to make concessions. The director of education insisted apropos of a dispute over dress for physical education that:

'It is necessary for the proper functioning of the school that some standards of dress are set. The authority would only intervene if unreasonable demands as to uniform were being made by the school. In the case of physical education the authority would expect the school to insist on an appropriate form of dress that was both hygenic and safe in the interests of the pupils.'

It is, of course, precisely what is 'reasonable' which is in dispute in such cases.

The question of school autonomy then, is less straightforward than at first seems. There was a great deal of evidence that the circumstances of even neighbouring schools could vary greatly and in so sensitive an area it is inevitable that school practice will have to be made to fit the precise situation faced by heads. But an LEA is in a strategic position to mediate in any conflicts that arise. CEOs and their chairmen may choose to back the judgement of a head in the interests of the school (as in Beeborough), to defuse the situation in the interests of good relations (as in Exeshire) or to give rather distant support to a head and hope that the situation improves, possibly with retirement (as in Seeborough). What it cannot do is attempt to dictate to a headteacher, or hope to do more than shift his or her attitudes in a more acceptable direction over time.

One significant way of bringing the school into closer touch with the community is by increasing parental involvement. Once again, the extent to which particular schools and heads have made serious and conscious efforts to involve parents from the ethnic minority communities shows very wide variations. Some heads appear to make no particular effort to make contact with ethnic minorities; others, at least by their own accounts, go to con- siderable lengths to build up liaison with parents. These are clearly individual initiatives depending very much on the personality and attitudes of the head and other teachers, or in one rare case, on the presence on a governing body of representatives of minority groups amounting to half the total.

The discussion in this section has concentrated on ways in which the relations between the school and the community which it serves have been left to the good intentions of heads and their staff. The tradition of headteachers' autonomy leaves LEAs with little room for manoeuvre in this field although, as we have seen, the ways in which informal influence is exercised are highly variable. In the long run, the LEA may put its faith in training or an increased advisory and support staff. There are, however, three other areas where an LEA may make a contribution to school community relations without trespassing upon the prized prerogatives of headmasters: the appointment of teachers from the minority communities; the provision of a special home-school liaison service; and the development of the community school.

On the question of the appointment of teachers from the ethnic minority communities, the comment offered by Beeborough's CEO is fairly typical of what we have heard elsewhere: 'Wherever possible, committee and officers appoint such teachers provided that they have the right qualifications and experience'.

Among the secondary heads whom we met, the prevailing view was that the first essential in appointing teachers was to look for the most able and competent for the particular post. This was sometimes accompanied by remarks that some (usually Asian) teachers inherited by that particular head were good at their subject but could not cope in the classroom, although in cases where young Asian teachers had been recently trained and appointed, heads were noticeably more enthusiastic. We also met ethnic minority teachers who cited their experience of what they felt to be repeated discrimination in employment. One or two heads said that they would favour appointing an ethnic minority candidate if there were two candidates equal in merit, one white and one black. But whatever the views of the heads, it was universally stated that very few teachers from the ethnic minority communities in any case applied for teaching posts.

The appointment of ethnic minority teachers is thus a kind of no man's land. Very few teachers are in fact appointed; in the schools we visited they ranged from nil to about 20 per cent of the total staff. Yet willingness to appoint is always claimed. So in a sense the question is put back a stage to encouraging ethnic minority candidates to apply for and be trained for teaching. Only Deeborough has taken positive steps in this respect in response to the DES initiative to increase access of minorities to training courses. As it is, evidence that LEAs and schools regard the appointment of ethnic minority teachers as an important aim was scanty.

The appointment of special teachers to strengthen the relationships between the home and the school is an innovation which has been more consistently applauded than followed. Beeborough appointed four cultural liaison teachers (CLT) in 1975. They are attached to high schools specifically to deal with educational problems arising from the clash of different cultural and social values in home and school. That this should involve them in working in the schools and making contact with parents seems implicit in the concept of a CLT, but a broader role of contact with the community was set out by the director of education in 1976 and an even broader one taking in curriculum development and in-service training in 1980. It is perhaps not surprising that one head had doubts about the role of the CLT in her school. The one CLT we interviewed claimed that each of the six currently in post had developed his own role according to his degree of interest in either the 'social worker' side of the role or, as in his case, the curriculum development side. Once again, however, the dependence on the head is also apparent for the direction taken by the CLT was seen as determined by the interest of the head and the CLT's relationship to him or her.

This particular Beeborough initiative is thus a somewhat curious and indeterminate measure so far as it relates to strengthening the links between schools and the local community. Several authorities have, however, also made some kind of more institutionalised move towards the local community. In Exeshire and Deeborough, the idea of a community school or of a centre incorporating a school with other facilities of value to the local community has been tried out. In Beeborough, the move does not seem to go very much beyond making school premises available either for the community groups or more specifically for neighbourhood English classes; one head mentioned a youth club run by the school offering among other things mother-tongue teaching after school but it was not clear how much this owed to LEA prompting and how much to the head's individual initiative.

Deeborough has developed the provision of multipurpose centres based on colleges of further education. The one which we visited consists essentially of providing on one site a number of institutions and facilities, including secondary school, youth club, further education college, district library, and luncheon club for the elderly. These are all separately provided but with some sharing of facilities between them (for example between school and youth club). At the same time, although English classes are provided for Asian adults, the establishment of the centre was not specifically an initiative in the multicultural field. It serves a wide area in the northern part of the city, only part of which has a sizeable ethnic minority community. It exists rather to make provision for community needs conceived in fairly conventional terms. Apart from the English language work (and the special preparatory course at the college stimulated by DES) there does not seem to be a great deal which links the centre other than incidentally with the local ethnic minority community; indeed, some of those we interviewed were critical of the establishment of the centre as 'counter productive'.

The factors governing the relations between the school and the multi-ethnic community are then extremely varied. At first glance it would seem that there are significant differences in policy. On closer inspection, however, the common thread is apparent: what actually happens in practice is largely determined by the circumstances and dispositions of those who translate intentions into effect. In this, once again, the *de facto* autonomy of headteachers stands out as the most salient aspect of the landscape of multi-racial education. Equally, however, formal and *de facto* autonomy distract attention from the ways in which the LEA can attempt to influence the school-community relationship through the style and timing of such intervention as it might make. In this, the AEO dropping in for coffee may be a crucial if shadowy figure in the pattern of developments. Here again, however, an important caveat must be entered. Intervention by the office is probably effective in inverse proportion to its frequency. It occurs most readily in times of approaching crisis. It may have a steadying effect but our evidence does not suggest that LEAs are able to steer the schools by these informal means to any significant extent in more normal times. Whatever the schematic representation of Figure VII.1 may suggest, the ultimate power to resist change lies in the headteacher's study and the staffroom.

Concluding comments

This chapter has considered some aspects of education provision in multi-racial areas. Our concern was not to document detailed provision in respect of any particular service but rather to focus upon the very different approaches adopted by LEAs to the questions raised by multi-ethnicity. The discussion focused then upon two questions: the broad pattern of relationships between the administration and the schools in each of the six authorities and their approaches within these relationships to a set of positive, permissive and 'neutral' policy questions.

Even this sketch of the broad contours of educational provision reveals considerable variations in provision and approach. Deeborough and, to a lesser extent, Wyeshire have adopted an explicit and positive stance in relation to direct provision, advice and support, multiculturalism and under-achievement. Beeborough, despite their fairly extensive provision of services to schools, have little in the way of explicit policy. A pamphlet on *Multicultural Education in Beeborough* was published by the LEA jointly with the local NUT branch, but with explicit disclaimers as to any policy status. Beeborough's approach may be summed up as one of attempting to alleviate disadvantage on a broad front by the extensive commitment to education expenditure. Exeshire's approach is somewhat similar, while both Ayeborough and Seeborough have made more modest provision and have avoided any identification of the special needs of minority children.

The bare facts of variation reveal little. Any national initiative to equalise or increase provision would have to address the problem of the multiplicity of influences at work within the complex network of educational policy making. Both LEA policies and school practices are arguably the resultant both of these influences and of the internal dynamics of both schools on the one hand and LEAs on the other. If then, any general attempt to account for variations between schools and across authorities is doomed by 'the real world of too many variables' might this not also militate against the success of any single policy initiative?

Suspecting that this might be the case, we asked senior education administrators and a number of other people just how they would approach the problem of improving multi-ethnic education were they to become Secretary of State for Education. Significantly, no two people gave the same answer. Responses ranged from conferences of politically sympathetic education chairmen to the provision of 100 per cent grants for special provision. Given the very diffuseness and opaqueness of education policy making these divergent responses are perhaps unsurprising. Yet the problem of assessing influence and determining the feasibility of policy initiatives is not confined to education but runs throughout the relationship between central and local government. We now turn therefore to look more closely at national influences upon local policy development as a preliminary to discussing our overall conclusions.

References

Committee of Inquiry into the Education of Children from Ethnic Minority Groups, *West Indian Children in Our Schools*, Interim Report (Rampton Report), Cmnd 8273. (HMSO, London, 1981).

Department of Education and Science. The education of ethnic minorities. Memorandum (June 1980) to House of Commons Home Affairs Sub-Committee on Race Relations and Immigration. Published in House of Commons Home Affairs Committee *Racial Disadvantage*. Fifth Report, Session 1980-81. HC 424. Vol. II, pp. 234-55; and additional memoranda, vol. IV, pp.16-22.

Kirp, D., *Doing Good by Doing Little: Race and Schooling in Britain*. (University of California Press, Berkeley, 1979).

Kogan, M. and Van der Eyken, W., *County Hall: The role of the chief education officer*, (Penguin Books, 1973).

Little, A. and Willey, R., *Multi-Ethnic Education: The way forward*. Schools Council Pamphlet 18, (Schools Council, London, 1981).

Matthews, A., *Advisory Approaches to Multicultural Education,* (Runnymede Trust, London, 1981).

Tomlinson, S., The educational - performance of ethnic minority children, *New Community 8*, 213-34, 1980.

VIII National Influences on Local Policy Development

Chapters III to VII of this report were focused on the experiences of the local authorities where we carried out our fieldwork. The presentation was also shaped to some extent by our necessarily more superficial knowledge of the other seventeen who comprised our pool of relevant authorities. Our concern was with the variation in approach and provision and with the processes by which multi-ethnic issues were advanced or suppressed within these authorities. Wherever there was a significant local influence on these processes we gave it some attention. However, as our general discussion in Chapter IX will indicate, by and large local policies were not notably responsive either to local needs or local advocacy.

This unresponsiveness is hardly surprising, and largely accounts for such influence as has been exercised from the centre to encourage, persuade, or require local authorities to take closer account of the ethnic dimension in their policies and practices. Our concern in this chapter is with that influence and with the promotional activities of nationally organised non-statutory bodies. Our first concern is with the part that central departments have played in this field. Our second concern is to examine the impact of the Race Relations Act 1976 on the local authorities; we also consider the promotional role of the Commission for Racial Equality before examining the activities of a host of other organisations. Finally, we attempt to draw some general conclusions as to national influences on local policy development.

The influence of central departments

As we were commissioned to explore the question of 'policy implementation' in the field of racial disadvantage, we decided at an early stage to familiarise ourselves with the substance of government policy. We therefore arranged a series of meetings with senior officials of the Home Office, the Department of Education and Science, the Department of Health and Social Security, the Department of the Environment and the Commission for Racial Equality. We later extended this aspect of our research to include some meetings with the regional or 'field' arms of the Whitehall departments and the CRE. Finally, we attempted in our work with the local authorities to identify the local impact of central guidance from either Whitehall or the regional level.

In this section we give a brief account of our findings. Our own study was concluded at the same time as the investigation into racial disadvantage carried out by the Sub-Committee on Race Relations and Immigration of the House of Commons Home Affairs Committee. The report and minutes of evidence, published in August 1981, contain a great deal of information on the activities of the central departments in relation to racial disadvantage — information which we would not wish to duplicate here. Our concern was exclusively with central – local relations, and this part of the study was intended to throw more light upon the question of how the central agencies have organised to promote racial equality at the local level, and the means they have chosen to do so.

Home Office. The Home Office is the department with the central responsibility in the field of race relations. At the time of our interviews there were two separate divisions within the Home Office: I.2, which handled relations with the CRE, local community relations councils, and community relations generally; and I.1, which had a more general role in relation to local government through consultations on the inner cities and traditional urban programmes, and in relation to the allocation of S.11 funds. There is also a race relations adviser appointment within the Home Office. During the closing months of our study certain administrative changes were made to create a single division (I division) with responsibilities for race relations. It does not, however, appear that any policy or operational changes have flowed from this reorganisation, although the marked reduction in staff has further reduced the ability of the department to keep abreast of local developments.

Before we turn to the Home Office's dealings with local authorities, something may be said about its role as the focal point at the Whitehall level for discussions of race relations. These discussions mainly occur through inter-departmental consultation on S.11 applications (where DES, DHSS, or DoE might be concerned) and to some extent within the Home Secretary's Advisory Council on Race Relations (which is serviced by an I division principal).

S.11 liaison seems to be largely routinised, reactive, and precedent-bound. The Home Office officials do not see it as their responsibility to encourage innovation nor do they solicit applications for funds from local authorities. Inter-departmental contacts are minimal, *ad hoc* and conducted by telephone or memorandum. Officals have apparently rarely met to discuss inter-departmental issues in race relations, the recent exceptions being the review of S.11 procedure and the Tavistock report on the Civil Service. It has been stressed that the Home Office do not play a co-ordinating role in respect of race relations.

One reason for the limited nature of S.11 consultation appeared to be the largely routine nature of the scheme's administration. There are proportionately few new types of proposal coming forward, and most decisions on applications can be taken on the basis of precedent. A social services S.11 application would, for example, be referred by the Home Office to the DHSS for comment only if it were in some way novel or unusual. There were indications that in the case of some education proposals, HMI would be consulted and might well take a more sympathetic view of local bids than the Home Office. Officials had anticipated playing a greater role in monitoring and co-ordination when the Ethnic Groups Bill was still before Parliament.

As they have no 'field' function and a role in S.11 processing that is largely responsive, Home Office relations with local authorities are inevitably remote. The Home Office said in their evidence to the Race Relations and Immigration Sub-Committee that they kept in touch with local developments through some thirty or so visits made annually at principal level. Some observers misunderstood this to relate to a liaison role with the local authorities. This is incorrect. These visits, in fact, relate to the community relations concerns of the former I.2 division. Certainly, where S.11 is concerned there are no such attempts to acquaint the Home Office with the circumstances of local authorities. Among the local authorities themselves there is relatively little experience of S.11 procedures outside education departments. We found several instance of perplexity on the part of local officials considering a S.11 bid in the social services field. There was widespread misunderstanding of the procedure and, in some cases, unsuccessful (because ill-informed) attempts to contact the appropriate point in the Home Office. The status of the scheme as 'under administrative review' was not widely known in the local authorities. The Home Office feel that it is for authorities to inform themselves as to the availability of S.11 funding.

In the case of education departments, there were several complaints that the Home Office did not understand their own system and were unable to give much guidance on eligibility. There was apparently some slackening of central scrutiny when the Ethnic Groups Bill was still expected to pass into law and a corresponding tightening of control since May 1979. Many of the local policy makers with whom we discussed S.11 deplored the loss of the bill to replace it, while some felt that the very failings of S.11 in effect gave them more scope for independent local action.

The Home Office also play a minor role within the inner cities partnership and (to a lesser extent) programme arrangements. Here the officials have been mainly concerned to ensure that the needs of ethnic minorities are taken into account in the local strategies that are formulated. This concern initially extended beyond commenting on projects to advocating particular sub-committee and working party structures within the partnership machinery, seeking thereby to ensure the consideration of ethnic minority issues. On one (apparently isolated) occasion, Home Office officials evidently pressed their views quite hard, submitting a paper through the partnership machinery; this may possibly account for the authority concerned professing a greater concern for ethnic minorities in the second year. Visits from and pressure by a Home Office official were also recalled in Deeborough as having been influential. There were complaints that the Home Office had withdrawn from this more positive and supportive stance since the change of government in May 1979. Given the precarious support for Deeborough's embryonic strategy for ethnic minorities, the retreat from the former interventionist stance may have been critical. Generally, however, Home Office officials claim to have neither the staff resources nor the local knowledge that would enable them to make a useful contribution to the partnerships.

The Home Office also comment routinely on appropriate projects submitted under the traditional urban programme. Their possible contribution under this scheme is even less than in the case of the partnerships. Officials feel that useful comments cannot be made in the absence of that knowledge of local circumstances to which DoE can lay greater claim. It would seem that current Home Office participation in the traditional and enhanced urban programme is largely a matter of form.

Local authority views of the Home Office were largely shaped by the way in which the department's S.11 responsibilities were exercised, which was nowhere seen as particularly positive. Nowhere did we find policy entrepreneurs in the authorities looking to the Home Office as natural allies in their attempts to secure ethnic issues a place on the local policy agenda. Home Office contacts through the inner cities machinery are predominantly with *London* authorities. While officials freely admitted that the London authorities are far more successful in incorporating the ethnic dimension into policy they did not see a role for themselves in disseminating experience or broadening commitment. Rather, as one official put it, 'you talk to the receptive authorities' and not to those who are reluctant to face the issues. To sum up, Whitehall's 'lead' department is characterised by a reactive posture, a very weak field presence and an avoidance of any promotional or disseminating role. This would seem to reflect the concerns of ministers and the organisation and traditional style of the Home Office itself as a regulatory department.

Department of the Environment. The operations of the DoE present quite a sharp contrast with those of the Home Office. First, the DoE now have overall responsibility for both the traditional urban programme, established under the Local Government Grants (Social Need) Act 1969 and for the enhanced Urban Programme associated with the passage of the Inner Urban Areas Act 1978. This latter responsibility takes headquarters principals and assistant secretaries out 'into the field' fairly regularly. Second, the system of regional offices brings the department into a close and continuous relationship with the local authorities. Third, but not directly considered in our work, the DoE research carried out under their inner cities programme gives the department a considerable involvement in the appraisal of urban deprivation. While none of these concerns is seen as having an explicit racial dimension, the breadth and closeness of the department's involvement appears to give DoE officials a firmer grasp of how local authorities in multi-racial areas are coping with some of the issues which face them.

The Urban Programme responsibilities of the department date from 1977. Both the traditional and the enhanced urban programmes are managed by the Inner Cities Directorate. In September 1979, the government announced that the continuance of the former was under review and a study was carried out between then and March 1980. The government announced in August 1980 that following the publication of a consultative document, it had been decided to continue the traditional urban programme. The review process included a study of nine local authorities and 54 of their urban programme projects.

The rationale of the traditional urban programme is to supplement local authority main programmes by channelling resources on a project basis to areas of special social need. Of the recent projects reviewed by the Inner Cities Directorate's study, 18 per cent were specifically geared to meeting the needs of ethnic minorities. A further 18 per cent could be seen to be directed to populations that included a high proportion of ethnic minorities. Another finding was that voluntary sector projects differed markedly from local authority projects in innovativeness (although the small numbers here should not be over-interpreted), encouragement of community initiative, and assistance to ethnic minorities.

There is close liaison betwee DoE and DHSS, DES and the Home Office on the traditional urban programme. In particular, circulars contain a reference to the opportunities provided by S.11, and DoE officials consult with the Home Office before occasionally suggesting that a local authority might withdraw a particular bid and resubmit it for S.11 funding. The Home Office are also asked to comment on any proposals that have an explicit ethnic minority dimension; it would seem that such projects are also forwarded by the Home Office to the CRE for comment.

Our overall impression of the DoE operation of the traditional urban programme is of an awareness of local authority concerns and procedures, and of a fairly explicit concern with the fortunes of ethnic minorities. The sums to be allocated are seen as very small, but as possibly significant in funding the marginal (and sometimes important) project. Officials showed considerable familiarity with particular authorities. Within the priorities established by ministers and the views expressed by colleagues in other departments, DoE officials inevitably make judgements about local authority programmes and apply their department's priorities in order to achieve a satisfactory 'package'. Thus, within the basic constraint of the local authorities' own priorities, the DoE are able to 'steer' the final overall programme to a modest extent.

This headquarters role contrasts with the case of the inner cities partnership arrangements where 'steer' is provided by the local discussions on priorities. Here, the Home Office have a separate presence and the DoE input reflects the more specifically economic priorities of their own Secretary of State, and the continuing emphasis on urban economic regeneration set out in the 1977 White Paper on inner cities. There are no annual circulars, and programmes are now prepared within the broad ministerial guidelines issued in July 1981. To what extent the inner cities programme (still less the traditional urban programme) is successful in redirecting (or 'bending') local authorities' own main programmes is another question which cannot be pursued here.

Outside the inner city areas (where partnership and programme authorities have their own allocations) authorities are in competition for an annual disbursement currently of £44 million. The recommended procedures are cumbersome and the time allowed for consultations inadequate. In some cases we found authorities responding to the circular without consultation, in other cases consulting fully in self-confessed ignorance of what priorities would be indicated in a yet-to-be-issued circular.

The regional offices of the DoE maintain a close and wide-ranging relationship with local authorities. This is particularly important in relation to the inner cities programmes which (unlike the traditional urban programme) are largely considered at regional level. We had reports of close and involved connections between one regional office and the local authorities but we did not visit that region. We did, however, discuss Deeborough with the appropriate regional office. There were, perhaps, peculiar circumstances in this case which might not obtain elsewhere, but two impressions in particular were worth recording. The first is that the staff with whom we had discussions in that regional office talked readily and in some detail both about spatial patterns of ethnic minority deprivation in the city and about the particular strengths and resources of some of Deeborough's ethnic groups. The second is that the regional officials displayed a considerable familiarity with the names and responsibilities of relatively junior local authority staff who would be concerned with both the economic and the social aspects of the ethnic minority population in Deeborough. The regional office claim to be no more than a 'post-box' for Whitehall understates the significance of their presence in the field.

The occasional intervention by the Home Office does not have the on-going quality of the DoE's relationship with local authorities. There are, however, no 'ethnic miniority desks' at the DoE's regional offices, although we were told of one instance where a regional office had pushed for inclusion of 'ethnic' projects in the inner cities' programme. Moreover, the regional director obviously has to work to the immediate concerns of ministers. Nevertheless, we were led to conclude that the web of relationships between Marsham Street, the regional office and the authorities is such that racial disadvantage could if DoE ministers so chose, be steered into a far more prominent place in the policy agendas of the local authorities. So far as we are able to judge, this is a medium of influence of considerable potential importance. The proposal, mooted in some quarters, to return Urban Programme responsibilities to the Home Office at some future date would seem then to be particularly ill-advised.

Department of Education and Science.   The DES has long been involved in developing responses to meet the needs of the ethnic minority communities. However, their basic approach may be summed up as seeing the needs of ethnic minorities as part of, but not distinct from, the wider problem of educational disadvantage, a perspective which, as Chapter VII indicated, is shared by many LEAs. The DES response to such issues as arise is equally conventional: a reliance on HMI to disseminate good practice by visits and courses and general unwillingness to prescribe any particular stance to LEAs.

The early 1970s saw the publication of two limited surveys, *Potential and Progress in a Second Culture* and *The Continuing Needs of Immigrants*. The ᵩuse of Commons Select Committee on Race Relations and Immigration, in ir 1973 report, *Education*, further heightened attention with criticism of the department's 'haphazard' approach to race relations and with expression of 'surprise' that no specific attention was being given to the issue. In response to the report, the Educational Disadvantage Unit (EDU) was established in 1974 within the Schools Branch. The EDU is intended to serve as a focal point for consideration of all matters, at all stages of education, connected with educational disadvantage and the education of immigrants, and to influence the allocation of resources in their interest. The Unit also actively promotes research. One of its roles is to press the issue of disadvantage within the DES, and advocacy on the part of the Unit presumably played a part in the setting up in 1979 of the Committee of Inquiry into the Education of Children from Ethnic Minority Groups, which is serviced by EDU officials.

The DES have taken a number of steps to raise issues of disadvantage with LEAs. In November 1973 (while the EDU was still under discussion), a circular letter was sent to all LEAs calling attention to the high proportion of West Indian children classified as educationally subnormal, and suggesting some specific steps that might be taken. In January 1976 the DES, through the EDU, held a follow-up meeting with chief education officers. The EDU staff also have a programme of visits to LEAs to discuss their strategies for dealing with disadvantage. Both conferences and seminars have been arranged in the past to cover particular issues. The DES officials operate on the basis of a fine distinction between 'policy' (their own concern) and 'practice' (that of HMI) and have apparently advocated broad strategies in their meetings with LEAs. No mention was made of direct contact among our case study authorities, although some initiatives (for example, improving minority access to training) clearly originated with the central department.

The EDU probably has a discernible impact in some more specific areas such as the inner cities partnerships. The EDU liaises directly with some partnership authorities and claims to be able to suggest projects for inclusion in their programmes. EDU also comments on other Urban Programme projects submitted to DoE where they have an educational content. The comparison which we have already drawn between the discretion available to civil servants in relation to the Urban Programme and S.11 funding equally holds for the DES: while EDU may attempt to influence the general pattern of the former, its role in relation to S.11 is again purely reactive. Despite its 'policy' focus, EDU is not concerned to promote the use of S.11 or to suggest possible usage to LEAs. EDU also has an active and important role in the promotion of research.

The territory on the other side of the 'policy/practice' distinction is occupied by HMI. EDU officials emphasise their unusually close links with HMI, on whom they largely depend both for the flow of information in the field, and for the professional judgement which they, as administrators, lack. The multi-ethnic interest is, notionally at least, strongly represented within HMI. There is a 'multi-racial committee' of the Inspectorate, all of whose members include multi-ethnic issues among their divisional responsibilities. The committee also represents a mix of educational phases and subjects. The committee's chairman has the national responsibility within the Inspectorate for these questions, and this apparently active committee feeds reports and papers sideways to DES administrators, and practical ideas downwards through the normal processes of HMI dissemination.

HMI are clearly more 'promotional' than the DES being rather more inclined, for example, to suggest S.11 opportunities to LEAs. They have also been concerned to disseminate experience of innovative LEAs in the field of multi-racial education to others and in some (largely fortuitous) circumstances, apparently attempt to contribute to local Urban Programme discussions. It is, however, difficult to come to a view about how far HMI influence local policy development. On the one hand, the DES readily point to the activities of HMI when describing and justifying their own role in relation to promoting multi-ethnic issues. Moreover, many commentators see HMI as a powerful instrument of policy dissemination; for example, it has been suggested to us that the HMI could form the centre piece of any strategy for multi-ethnic education. On the other hand, HMI themselves largely disclaim any pretension to play such a role. Our interviews with members of the Inspectorate indicate that they see their primary responsibility as feeding information upwards from the LEAs to the 'the office' as a contribution to national policy making. Their influence on those in local authorities they see as exercised, on the one hand, through their participation in conferences and courses, and on the other, through reports on individual schools or subject areas, and discussion of these with LEAs.

We sought in our visits to the LEAs to glean some impression of how far HMI appear to influence local policy developments. Our conclusions lend some support to the Inspectorate's own view of the balance between their two roles, and none whatsoever to the picture of HMI vigorously transmitting national policy concerns to the local authorities. In those authorities most active in the field of multi-ethnic education (Deeborough and Wyeshire within our sample), the two inspectors who are active nationally in this field were spoken of with great respect. However, these evaluations seem to arise in part from common membership of a broader-based network of enthusiastic officials, and in part from the LEAs' status as innovators. Wyeshire, in particular, saw innovative experience as flowing *from* them *to* HMI.

So far as the main operational body of HMI are concerned we found no education officer willing to concede that they had *any* influence on local policies. We pressed this issue repeatedly in interviews, sometimes almost to the point of perplexing our respondents. Their judgements of HMI tended to be general and neutral (even in a case where the HMI concerned thought himself to have a 'positive' influence on the LEA in question). In one or two cases, we encountered an even more dismissive view of HMI, and sometimes personal incompatibilities were cited as reasons for a distant relationship between the LEA and HMI. Elsewhere, while education officers could be provoked to reflect on their relationships, they were often at a loss to say *why* they would not turn to HMI for advice.

If HMI have such a minor role in this respect despite the presence of a multi-ethnic specialist in each division, the relations between DES and the LEAs appear rather different than the DES sometimes claim. It may, of course, be the case that HMI exercise their influence at the school level, but in those schools we visited we found no evidence of this being a substantial factor, although we found appreciation of the training courses for teachers arranged by HMI, and of their occasional role in drawing attention to the experience of schools elsewhere.

The reasons for this low visibility are undoubtedly threefold. First, as we noted earlier, HMI see their primary role as advising headquarters of local circumstances rather than as transmitters of central policy; the work programme of the multi-ethnic committee exemplifies this role. Second, the Inspectorate are 'too thin on the ground' (in the words of one AEO) to have a broad impact even if they chose to play that role. Third, as our few interviews with HMI suggested, even the multi-ethnic 'specialists' have other and more pressing responsibilities. Our visits to the LEAs themselves indicated serious lacunae of advice and guidance in the multi-ethnic education field. LEA officials were overwhelmingly more likely to identify other LEAs as sources of ideas, usually either the leaders in the field (ILEA apparently playing a role outside London) or the past colleagues of the education officer concerned. Local authorities have their own informal 'reference groups' and, for all their possible deficiencies as conveyers of good practice, it is to these that they turn for advice rather than to HMI.

The importance of lateral rather than vertical networks of dissemination leads to the question of the Centre for Information and Advice on Educational Disadvantage (CED). Like the EDU itself, the CED's work was not confined in its brief existence (1975-80) to racial disadvantage. Grant-aided by DES, it had its own governing body drawn from the teacher's associations as well as from the DES and the LEAs. It was intended as a centre of advice and information on practice, particularly in relation to teaching methods and the curriculum, drawing together the results of research, disseminating advice and encouraging new developments in schools and colleges. Part of its work was concerned with the identification of good practice, sometimes in such fields as the language needs of Afro-Caribbean children or provision for under-fives. In relation to the dissemination role, CED maintained contacts with particular schools and LEAs, held conferences, and published both a regular journal *Disadvantage in Education* (one issue of which was devoted to racial disadvantage) and a 'current awareness service' under the title *Multi-Ethnic Education*. CED also attempted to work through the teachers' associations.

Possibly CED had too little time to establish itself as an important influence on local policy development. None of the LEAs visited in our study made positive references to the Centre. One AEO indicated that its demise was viewed with mild regret by his chief, and this was probably the strongest expression of opinion in either direction which we were able to elicit. Our own direct contact with CED suggested certain internal problems that could hardly have helped its effectiveness. It also seemed that the Centre had set out to operate much in the manner of the Inspectorate but, having failed to gain anything like the deep respect accorded to HMI, had lost confidence and direction. For these reasons, it was unsurprising that CED did not figure as an influence within our sample of LEAs.

We have discussed in Chapter VII LEA views and use of record keeping by ethnic origins. The DES began in 1966 to collect national statistics on the numbers of 'immigrant' children in schools. After widespread criticism of the definition used, of the absence of any comparison with attainment, or any direct relationship to resource allocation, the collection of statistics was abandoned in 1973. The issue has been considered recently by the Committee of Inquiry into the Education of Children from Ethnic Minority Groups and their 1981 interim report, *West Indian Children in Our Schools* (the Rampton Report), argued that 'ethnically based statistics' could 'be of value at all levels and to all parties within education'; they recommended that from 1 September, 1982 relevant information should be recorded, and collected and published by the DES.

Department of Health and Social Security. The DHSS policy divisions on the social services side of the department's work are organised, in general, by client groups such as the elderly, or children. Matters concerning ethnic minorities are the responsibility of the Local Authority Social Services (LASS) division, which deals with other general issues such as organisation of social services departments, manpower and planning, and the voluntary sector. The field advisory service, the Social Work Service (SWS), has a headquarters staff and a regional organisation.

Multi-Racial Britain: the Social Services Response, the report of the working party of social services directors and the CRE, contained a foreword by the then minister, David Ennals. The booklet was distributed to social services departments by the director of the Social Work Service, who referred in his letter of August 1978 to discussions to be held with the local authority associations about the report, with a view to issuing guidance later in the year on some of the issues raised. However, on further consideration, it was decided not to issue such guidance.

There were indications that the department's views would in any case have been very tentative, for a number of reasons. First was their uncertainty about many aspects of work with ethnic minorities, and consequent difficulties in knowing what to advise. There was also some anxiety that discussion of some of the difficult areas of practice might encourage stereotyping and thus be counter-productive. DHSS officials also felt that some recommendations of the ADSS/CRE working party might be difficult to implement uniformly in all relevant social services departments because, for example, of their widely differing practices on such matters as basic record keeping. They were also conscious of the experience of the Chronically Sick and Disabled Persons Act 1970, which had urged large-scale and fairly specific activity on social services departments without giving them any additional resources. In general, given the reduction in the amount of guidance from DHSS and other departments to local authorities since 1979, the DHSS felt that it would not be feasible to provide further general guidance over and above that contained in the ADSS/CRE report.

Some use had, however, been made of the DHSS local authority planning exchanges. These were fairly general; the guidelines issued in March 1978 said:

'The special needs for social care and support in communities with significant ethnic minority populations may require redeployment and special training of staff and may lead to higher unit costs for residential and day care, especially for children. Late entry into ante-natal care represents a special problem.'

Given the views of the new government about the appropriate relationship between central departments and local authorities, development of more detailed discussion or advice was not pursued. The most recent White Paper to come from the department is *Growing Older* issued in March 1981; references to ethnic minorities in this are quite general — but most issues in the White Paper are handled in a general way.

As the urban programmes have moved towards greater emphasis on economic regeneration, the DHSS has pressed for the continued inclusion of social projects. The department is asked by the DoE to comment on social services projects proposed by local authorities for funding under the traditional urban programme. In the case of partnership authorities, the department has some voice in the formulation of programmes, and for both partnership and programme authorities the department has the opportunity of commenting to DoE regional offices on individual projects and the balance of programmes as a whole. The department has supported a considerable number of health and social services projects for inclusion in particular programmes, and many of these projects are situated in locations with significant ethnic minority populations and are aimed at helping with problems arising from deprivation and social isolation. Some work has been done by the department, in association with the Central Council for Education and Training in Social Work (CCETSW), the CRE, and the DES, to encourage those from ethnic minorities to apply for social work training, and to increase teaching about ethnic minorities in all social work courses. The DHSS has also worked with the DES in encouraging the establishment of pre-professional foundation courses. A number of research studies have been commissioned, including Juliet Cheetham's *Social Work Services for Ethnic Minorities in Britain and the USA*.

In the Social Work Service, an officer has a co-ordinating role at headquarters in relation to ethnic minorities; as on the policy side of the department, this is one of the many responsibilities for the individual concerned. The current holder of the post has initiated a study of ethnic minority perceptions of social services, and social services department perception of clients; this is being carried out in one local authority, jointly with a regional Social Work Service Officer (SWSO).

Each SWSO in a region has responsibility for a number of authorities, and for particular specialisms. In each region where there is a substantial ethnic population, one officer's specialisms include ethnic minority matters. In view of the general uncertainties mentioned already and the demands on the regional staff they have not generally acted in a development capacity. On a few occasions, the officers involved have met as a group at headquarters but there has been no recent meeting of this kind.

Similarly, we found contacts between social services departments and regional SWSOs specialising in ethnic minority matters to be almost nonexistent, and the same could be said of discussion of ethnic minority issues between departments and their nonspecialist SWSO. On those occasions when we posed the question we found that senior social services department staff were unaware of the presence within their region of a SWSO with a specialisation in ethnic minority issues. On a few occasions we provided the name and telephone number of the relevant SWSO. Generally, however, there was little sense at the local level that the SWSO could be a useful source of advice and on one occasion our offer to provide details was firmly rejected.

The Race Relations Act 1976 and the Commission for Racial Equality

There are a number of sections in the 1976 Race Relations Act which bear upon the responsibilities of local authorities. In Chapter V, we dealt with the employment provisions of the Act, and we set down our impression that they were neither widely understood nor influential. In this section, we look more closely at S.71 of the Act and at the activities of the Commission for Racial Equality in interpreting that section and urging authorities to adopt appropriate policies.

One important feature of S.71 was that it had no place in the original drafts of the bill. A clause was moved by a Labour backbench member during the committee stage and there was further discussion with the local authority associations (who opposed its inclusion) before the government, who had been unwilling to place a general duty on local authorities, finally introduced a slightly different version. In the form in which it passed into law, S.71 reads:

'Without prejudice to their obligation to comply with any other provision of this Act, it shall be the duty of every local authority to make appropriate arrangements with a view to securing that their various functions are carried out with due regard to the need —

(a)   to eliminate unlawful racial discrimination

(b)   to promote equality of opportunity, and good relations, between persons of different racial groups.'

One of the then government's original objections to S.71 was its merely declaratory form which, in the absence of special sanctions or extra resources, might prove counter-productive. The Act came into force in June 1977 and a joint departmental circular drew S.71 to the attention of local authorities. The joint circular provided no guidance on the interpretation of S.71, and generally confirmed the government's apparent satisfaction with the progress made by local government. The circular recognised that:

'This general duty, which is additional to other specified duties imposed by the Act, represents a new feature in the field of legislation on

145

discrimination. Its effect will clearly differ from area to area and as between different local authority functions. However, local authorities will need to examine their relevant policies and practices to ensure that they meet the requirements of this section'.

We found that authorities interpreted both S.71 and this rather enigmatic guidance in widely varying ways. In Ayeborough, for example, the chief executive took the opportunity to launch a brief review of council policies, using an officer on temporary attachment to his department for this purpose. His report, which argued that a number of policy areas deserved further consideration, was used by the chief executive to establish the strategy group of senior members to review all aspects of the council services. S.71 was repeatedly cited by the chief executive in meetings of the group; but it was clear to his members and his chief officer colleagues that his was a personal and disputable interpretation of the injunction to examine policies.

In Beeborough, as we saw, the employment provisions of the Act produced a very early response by chief officers who also considered the implications of S.71. Not until after the 1978 elections, when the Race Relations Working Party was established, was the review carried forward and directors asked to provide statements of their departments' responses to S.71. In the case of education, for example, this took the form of a lengthy review by the director of education of all the activities of the department that bore upon the needs of ethnic minorities.

In other cases, the response to S.71 lay dormant until called forth by external events. In Deeborough, designation as a partnership authority and a subsequent visit by the CRE evoked numerous references to S.71 in the various documents that were prepared both for briefing and for discussion.

In Seeborough, where policies in relation to ethnic minorities were at least notionally under continuous review, there were apparently no proposals for specific action under S.71. Thus, where there was neither strong political nor administrative advocacy of a policy review in accordance with S.71, nor a specific external stimulus, the general duty conferred by the section went largely unnoticed. Taken by itself, the joint circular failed to provide even the mildest injunction to policy review.

The very nature of our study, with its dependence on access to relatively 'positive' authorities, does not enable us to judge how generally this was so. That we had a number of replies from authorities affirming that no action had been taken under the Act suggests that a negative interpretation might be shared by a number of the less enthusiastic authorities; certainly it was common to two of the authorities which we visited. In one case, the Act and the circular prompted a detailed appraisal of the authority's duties. We discuss it in some detail here as an indication of how an entirely negative construction could be put upon S.71.

The crux of the interpretation adopted in this particular authority was a close comparison of the wording of S.71 with Section 43(1) which established the CRE. The two duties imposed on local authorities, to eliminate discrimination and to promote equality of opportunity, are also imposed in almost identical terms upon the CRE itself. However, S.71 contains a qualification. Instead of simply bestowing such a duty directly upon the local authorities, they are instead merely enjoined 'to make appropriate arrangements' to ensure that their functions are carried out 'with due regard to need'. A report to this authority's working party on the Race Relations Act argued that this difference between the duties placed on the two bodies was significant. Not only were the qualifying phrases added to S.71 but no legal definition of them was appended. Thus, 'it is clear that this Section does not impose a duty on a local authority to eliminate unlawful racial discrimination, and that that duty is imposed on the Commission under Section 43'.

Such an interpretation has of course yet to be tested by the courts and we know of no suggestions that a writ of mandamus could be or has been sought against any authority under S.71. The working party in this particular authority looked closely at the similar injunction under Section 29(1) of the Town and Country Planning Act that an authority shall, in certain defined circumstances, 'have regard to the provisions of the Development plan'. In the case of Enfield London Borough Council v. Secretary of State for the Environment the court decided that an authority was thereby required to do no more than consider the Development Plan among other relevant factors. On this precedent, the working party was advised that the requirements of S.71 would be satisfied providing an authority 'considered' these aspects of race relations in its decision-making.

This interpretation (which has been neither tested nor challenged) became the basis for formal policy in this authority. When one of the senior departmental officers attempted to use the joint circular to open the questions of special provision and record keeping he was told 'there is no practical advice whatever on Section 71', that advice to keep records was not given in the circular, that 'guidance is required' in relation both to this, to Section 38, and to the assessment of special needs before action could be considered. Moreover, 'having ascertained what these special needs are, it will cost money to set up services to meet them. There is nothing in the circular to indicate where such money is to come from.' This is possibly an extreme case of a negative interpretation of the Act and the circular providing a basis for resistance to policy change. How typical it is we cannot tell. It is however worth recording that a neighbouring authority (which had co-operated in the provision of legal advice in 1977) continued to share this interpretation of S.71 in 1981.

There is then a vast gap between some authorities' strict interpretation of the Act and the policies advocated by the CRE and its predecessors. The Community Relations Commission was the first body to provide an interpretation of the 1976 Act in the form of a guidance note for local authorities. One of our six authorities responded to the note by accusing the CRC of making 'quite specific assertions about the Act's requirements without indicating the legal authority for those assertions, some of which could impose considerable burdens on local authorities'. The lack of a more specific basis in statute and in national policy has apparently hampered the CRC and the CRE in turn.

The CRE has attempted to fill the gaps between law and practice in a number of ways. The Commission, like its predecessor, has sustained a fairly full publications programme. It has arranged visits to some of the larger authorities with substantial minority populations. It has pursued a programme of more limited meetings and seminars at which officers from several local authorities are brought together. And it has attempted to work jointly with some of the professional associations to elaborate more specific policies. Wherever possible, we attempted in our work with the local authorities to assess the significance of these activities.

Several of the Commission's publications have been in the field of employment practice. In some cases, these have been of a highly specific nature while not being aimed exclusively at local authorities. *Why Keep Ethnic Records?*, for example, is a set of questions and answers aimed at clearing away some of the more common misapprehensions concerning record keeping. Where such publications were in circulation within local authorities their reception not surprisingly depended upon the general stance of the authority and its officers.

Our main concern here is with the publications relating to S.71 in general and with particular aspects of local authority services. Some of the pamphlets had been issued some time ago (for example, the CRC's *Guide for Local Councillors*) and in the authorities were occasionally resurrected as briefing papers. As noted earlier, the joint ADSS/CRE publication *Multi-Racial Britain: The Social Services Response* was circulated in 1978 to all social services departments by the director of the Social Work Service. However, in interviews in the local authorities we found few social services staff who remembered the booklet. During a meeting of the North Seeborough JCC the local SCRO produced it to a somewhat surprised group of officials and secured their agreement to talks between the CRC and the social services department, taking the ADSS/CRE report as a starting point. In contrast, *Youth in Multi-Racial Society* attracted considerable attention. In some cases, we saw the brief version of the report circulated quite widely, and it came up for consideration in a number of working parties. In Seeborough, a special team was formed to investigate the implications of the report for Seeborough's services.

There are evidently two views as to whether CRE publications should stress the avenues for development in particular services or should attempt to promote 'corporate' issues. Two recent papers by Commission staff have followed the latter path. A fairly substantial (if insensitively titled) paper on 'The CRE's Expectations of Local Government' was published in abbreviated form in one of the local government journals. A later paper on 'social policies' was aimed more specifically at the London boroughs. We found both of these papers considered within the corporate committees established by the London authorities. Where we sat in on such discussions, the CRE papers were taken as sensible and appropriate reviews of the issues.

The 'expectations' paper, which in particular argues for a corporate approach to multi-racial areas, has also been used in a number of meetings and seminars arranged by the Public and Community Services Section of CRE. As we were not present at these events, we are unable to comment upon them. However, our general impression of local authorities' sensitivities as to the source of 'advice and guidance' suggests that the current CRE practice of reaching local authorities through seminars to which experienced local government officers contribute is a realistic approach.

The Commission also have a programme of visits intended, in the first instance, to cover the 20 or so authorities in whose areas more than 20 per cent of births in 1976 were to mothers from the New Commonwealth or Pakistan. We were unable to witness any of these visits and only one of our six authorities had experienced such a meeting. However, other authorities which we visited or contacted as part of our wider survey had done so, while two of our six had also been approached by the Commission.

What general conclusion can be drawn from the promotional work of the CRE among local authorities? It is fair to say that we found very few positive evaluations of the Commission's work among our six case study authorities, the main exceptions being the provision of detailed advice on the implementation of equal opportunity policies. From the limited evidence of our visits, advice on *service* development was not seen as significant. In those areas where service department managers were likely to be receptive to CRE advice, the salience of the Commission was eclipsed by other professional sources of advice. Advice on corporate arrangements, on the other hand, was not generally duplicated elsewhere. It is, of course, true that we did not investigate policies and practices in relation to housing, an area where the ethnic dimension has been widely debated for some years and where the CRE claims to have had considerable impact. Moreover, the inner London authorities were excluded from our sample and here again the CRE has been particularly active. It is also possible that CRE influence has been indirect, shaping the thinking of policy makers who would not acknowledge the CRE as the source of their proposals. There were certainly indications that this might have been the case in some instances.

We suggest in our final chapter that the CRE, in attempting to shift the ways in which race is viewed within local government, has an almost impossible task. That the Commission is unable effectively to challenge prevailing norms or definitions is in the first place a comment upon the inherent limits of a special purpose body of this sort. Many local officials hardly seemed to recognise the CRE as a statutory body, but saw it more as a pressure group — 'like CPAG' (Child Poverty Action Group), as one chief executive put it. Local government is a legalistic and (for the most part) a rather 'constitutionalist' world. The more unsympathetic officers and many councillors, of all parties, would probably respond more willingly to a ministerial lead than to what is often seen as (faintly improper) 'hectoring' from the CRE.

In a sense, then, we were unable to make an appreciation of the potential role of CRE as in most authorities the Commission's authority was not recognised. This said, it is still possible to make some observations. First, the Commission's advice is seen as very general. While it is often rejected by the unsympathetic authority as unacceptable in principle, some of those who were working towards new initiatives in this field claimed to find their own experience, judgement and contacts a better and more exactly tailored guide than CRE advice. Second, the Commission faces real difficulties in providing continuity of contact or follow-up advice. Visits and meetings seemed in some cases to have created expectations of follow-up that cannot possibly be met with so small a staff. Allied to this problem is the lack of a regional dimension to the main promotional role. The centralisation of promotion possibly leads to an undue preoccupation with London authorities and may tend to isolate staff from provincial developments. The Commission understandably finds it difficult to achieve the detailed grasp of local events that is necessary to effective promotion.

For these reasons, the CRE policy of associating with and working through professional associations, as in the case of the joint CRE-Royal Town Planning Institute working party, as well as with such other national bodies as CCETSW, may well pay dividends. Similarly, the recent overtures to the major political parties may enable CRE to make real progress at the point where the need is greatest: among the often unsympathetic local councillors, who urgently need to be appraised of the issues before their own authorities can be expected to become more receptive to CRE advice.

The influence of non-statutory bodies

One part of our study involved contacting a large number of the apparently relevant non-statutory organisations operating nationally in the three main fields with which we were concerned: local authority employment, social services, and education. Some of these organisations were special-purpose promotional bodies, concerned solely to advocate and influence adaptation to the needs of the minority communities. Some were professional associations who had to varying degrees accepted the responsibility of influencing their membership in this direction. Yet others were bodies on the fringe of government, concerned, like the Schools Council or CCETSW, to enhance the capacity of practitioners to cope with the new demands of a multi-racial society. We found that many of the organisations which we contacted had, in the event, taken few initiatives aimed at influencing local authorities. Of those that had done so, fewer still were cited locally as having been influential and several were apparently unknown.

The CRE's advocacy of corporate arrangements to develop co-ordinated policies across the board was, as might be expected, echoed by few other organisations, for most of the bodies which we contacted were concerned with more specific responsibilities. The National Association of Community Relations Councils (NACRC) has tentatively suggested tht local CRCs might press for a co-ordinated policy on racial disadvantage. The Labour Party advocated a 'running programme' to review local needs in the section of the 1979 campaign handbook that dealt with race and immigration. *Labour and the Black Electorate,* containing proposals by the party's National Executive Committee on local responses to black communities, was sent to all local parties in March 1980. The party's subsequent survey of local parties nevertheless skirted the question of local authority provision for ethnic minorities. The Labour Party Race Action Group (LPRAG) has frequently advocated a broad approach to race questions on the part of local authorities in its periodical newsheet *Labour and Race.* LPRAG has also drawn the attention of Labour groups to, for example, the possibility of obtaining NDHS cross-tabulations of race-related data for the area of their authorities. The Standing Conference of Afro-Caribbean and Asian Councillors has also suggested, in a circular to London boroughs, that they each might establish a special committee to take the lead in developing policy on racial issues.

There were not many visible signs of influence from these bodies at the local level. LPRAG has a very small membership and has only recently begun to receive the publicity necessary to become better known to Labour councillors. Where we were able to note contact, representations from the Group were treated politely if cautiously. In only one authority did a councillor spontaneously mention the Group although there seemed to be a degree of interest among one or two other councillors (particularly those with multi-ethnic wards). The survey and eventual report of the Standing Conference of Afro-Caribbean and Asian Councillors was mentioned in both of our London boroughs; in one it was noted in passing, while in the other it led to an extended but not particularly serious discussion.

On questions of employment policy several of the same bodies have advocated changes in practice aimed at securing equal opportunity. LPRAG, for example, has published a review of record keeping issues. At the same time some more well established bodies have issued statements. The National Association of Local Government Officers (NALGO), the National Union of Public Employees (NUPE) and the National Union of Teachers (NUT) now support the maintenance of ethnic records for employment. Such national commitments are not always mirrored locally. However, the London division of NUPE has produced an 'Equal Opportunities' pack for local negotiators. The Trades Union Congress (TUC) has not only urged unions to discuss the promotion of equal opportunity with employers but has also drawn up an equal opportunities clause which it advises unions to incorporate in their negotiations. The National Executive Committee (NEC) of the Labour Party has called on both central and local government to give a lead on equal opportunities. In Deeborough, as we noted in Chapter V, the TUC model clause (which is less far-reaching than that recommended by the CRE and adopted elsewhere) had been adopted as an affirmation of the council's status as an equal opportunity employer.

The Runnymede Trust is one of the better-known bodies operating in this field. Apart from disseminating information on race relations practice and advocating a more vigorous approach the Trust also established an Industrial Unit in 1979 as a self-financing advisory and consultative service for employers. Particular use has been made of the Unit by local authorities in Greater London and, as we have seen, the Unit carried out a survey of training needs in Beeborough.

The position adopted by the major professional associations is clearly a potential influence of some importance. In the employment field the Society of Chief Personnel Officers in Local Government (SOCPO) has an elaborate organisation. Our impression was that the inter-authority linkages within SOCPO are unusually numerous, and issues are able to travel more readily through the network than is the case in some of the other professions. However, SOCPO has not considered the issue of race in employment at the national level although there has been some discussion in regional groups. The London region has considered a number of papers on the subject, and established a short-lived working group on race relations in 1978. Two relevant papers by chief personnel officers have been published in *SOCPO News*. Our impression was however that this limited initiative had lost momentum. In a sense, as we suggested in Chapter V, SOCPO does have an influence within local government in establishing the particular norms of personnel management in a local authority context. If the society were to consider the issues of equal opportunity at the national level, we have no doubt that the reverberations would be felt locally.

Within the field of social services there have been a few attempts by non-statutory bodies to deal with the questions of policy and practice which arise. The British Association of Social Workers (BASW) published in 1977 *Studies in Inter-Cultural Social Work,* based on proceedings of the association's Inter-Cultural Special Interest Group between 1972 and 1977; a study group on social work with ethnic minorities was established in 1978. The Association for Multi-Racial Social Work, founded in 1978, published *Multi-Racial Social Work* No. 1 in 1980, but financial difficulties have delayed publication of further issues. The British Association for Counselling has established a working group (with interest and financial support from the CRE) on problems of cross-cultural counselling. These initiatives and those of a number of other national organisations, mentioned in Chapter VI, may well show an impact on practice in years to come.

The situation in the education field presents a marked contrast, so far as the activities of non-statutory bodies are concerned. The range of Schools Council activities is indicated by the fact that it distributes 150,000 copies of its newsletters to schools via LEAs. As the Council stated at the end of its first three years, 'nothing the Council does is any use until teachers know about it'. It would probably be difficult to teach in a multi-ethnic school without being at least aware of the materials developed by the Council. In the primary schools in particular, headteachers were quick to mention SCOPE and Concept 7-9 when discussion turned to their practices.

In 1973, the Council launched a three-year research project into need and innovation in multi-racial education. The idea for such an ambitious project came from a number of sources, including the NUT, the Association of Teachers of English to Pupils from Overseas (ATEPO), and the National Foundation for Educational Research. This last body had already been involved in carrying out investigations for the DES into the educational arrangements in schools for immigrant pupils, and it was now commissioned by the Schools Council 'to produce materials in support of the education of all pupils for life in multi-racial Britain'; the project was thus concerned with curriculum development not simply to meet the needs of multi-racial classrooms, but in a much broader sense. The report of the completed project claimed that teacher attitudes were major obstacles to any attempt to introduce positive initiatives in the classroom. This caused considerable dissension, and although a draft of the first chapter was published in *New Society* in 1978, the report itself was not published until 1981, and then in a form disowned by the researchers involved.

Curriculum questions are clearly of major importance in considering racial disadvantage in education, yet the difficulties over publishing this report illustrate the hazards of carrying through initiatives in this field. The NUT was prominent in urging the Schools Council to undertake the project, just as it has been prominent in stating the case for meeting the challenge of a multi-racial society, and resolutions on this theme are regularly carried at the annual conference. Yet it was the NUT in particular, which found the findings unacceptable. Nevertheless, it has continued to press for more work to be done on the curriculum.

The NUT has, as well, issued a series of statements and publications about racial aspects of education, including guidelines for the identification of racist stereotypes and a major report on the use of S.11 in schools. It is probably fair to assume that these and other activities have some impact on teachers' attitudes in the long term. Direct influence on an LEA may be another matter, although in Beeborough the local branch has successfully forestalled any action by the LEA to institute ethnic record keeping, despite the NUT's national policy favouring this.

The recent Schools Council project on *Multi-Ethnic Education,* referred to in Chapter VIII, derived from ideas discussed between NUT and the National Association for Multiracial Education (NAME) in a joint working party of the two organisations which meets regularly to discuss matters of mutual interest. NAME, successor to ATEPO, was founded in 1973 'to play an active role in making the changes required in the education system which will further the development of a just multiracial society'. While the NUT has about 260,000 members, NAME has just over 1,000, of whom over one-third are institutional rather than individual members. NAME individual members are not confined to teachers but include, for example, LEA officials. The organisation is committed to influencing LEA policies as well as school practices. The local influence of such a national body is, however, bound to be limited, and the success of NAME is dependent upon the growth of vigorous local branches. A branch was mentioned in Deeborough as having not been influential and having declined in support; on the other hand, local NAME groups were clearly significant in assisting innovation in Wyeshire and expressed hopes of changing the status quo in Seeborough.

Other organisations have been concerned with specific aspects of the curriculum. The National Association for the Teaching of English, for example, has set up a working party on resources for multicultural education which aims to produce practical material for teachers including a list of literature appropriate to children of particular cultural and ethnic origins. The working party has produced a discussion document (*The Teaching of English in Multi-Cultural Britain*) and the Association devoted one issue of its journal, *English in Education* (Spring 1977), to the same theme.

In the case of many of the other bodies active in this field it was simply not feasible to attempt to assess their influence in this project. The activities of, for example, the Society of Immigrant Teachers or the Caribbean Teachers Association, having been established in part to defend the interests of black

153

teachers, are necessarily limited. In a different way the activities of such bodies as the National Committee on Racism in Children's Books, aimed at influencing teacher attitudes, can only be assessed in the longer term. In two authorities, we encountered discussions of racism in children's books, both of which concerned *Little Black Sambo*; in one case there was considerable disagreement among teachers as to the nature of the book, and in the other some uncertainty on the part of education officials as to how far the use of such books in schools raised policy issues.

There is a sense of unreality to be gained from concentrating on the activities of national bodies. In many cases, they seem to look inward, to the Whitehall (and Westminster) village around which they are encamped. Behind them lie the great diversity of local-level practices in those peripheral local authorities to whom mention of some specialist group, or of the policy position adopted by some better known body, will evoke little interest. The first striking impression of the non-statutory bodies is then that few of them have attempted to influence local authorities toward more appropriate policies for ethnic minorities. The second is that fewer still have succeeded.

Concluding comments

In this chapter we set out to assess the various national influences on policy developments among the local authorities as they appeared to us during the early months of 1980. We began work with an open mind as to how important the central-local dimension of influence might be in this field. However, we had expected perhaps more interest and involvement by the central departments in the development of policies than in fact seems to have been the case, and we were somewhat surprised to find effective responsibility being exercised at such relatively low levels in the administrative hierarchy of some departments. The claim by one civil servant that issues of race in public policy were 'on the back burner' may serve as a motif for our entire study, for this was often as true locally as centrally. If it was fair comment it was also apt metaphor. It is often on the back burner that neglected responsibilities turn suddenly into problems.

An important finding of our study was the depth of misunderstanding of the Race Relations Act and the very wide latitude effectively given in its interpretation. The consequences of an absence of guidance acceptable as authoritative to local authorities were apparent in many areas and it seemed that the CRE was hampered in its promotional work by these lacunae.

Perhaps the absence of influence on the part of non-statutory bodies was less surprising. Yet there were two distinguishable elements here. First, the acknowledged difficulty of central influence upon the periphery. Second, the extent to which the majority of the organisations which we contacted 'kept their heads down' on issues of race and so are not mentioned here. Interest in the political parties was at best residual. Several of the professional associations steered clear of the difficult issues or saw them as having no relevance. The local authority associations generally avoided trespassing into such difficult territory. Each of these factors could, however, assume a different importance over time. Each reflects the much broader tendency to avoid being explicit about race, a tendency which is likely to come under increasing pressure to change. Just what might be susceptible to change at the local authority level, and by what means, is the subject of our final chapter.

References

House of Commons Home Affairs Committee *Racial Disadvantage,* Fifth Report, Session 1980-81. HC 424 (4 vols.), (HMSO, London, 1981).

Edwards, J. and Batley, R., *Politics of Positive Discrimination,* (Tavistock, London, 1978).

Griffith, J.A.G., *Central Departments and Local Authorities,* (George Allen & Unwin, London, 1966).

Home Office, Department of the Environment, Department of Education and Science, Department of Health and Social Security, Welsh Office, *Race Relations Act 1976,* Joint Circular, 10 June 1977.

Jones, G.W. (ed.) *New Approaches to the Study of Central-Local Government Relationships,* (Gower Press, Farnborough, 1980).

Kogan, M., *Educational Policy-Making,* (George Allen & Unwin, London, 1975).

McKay, D. and Cox, H., Confusion and reality in public policy: the case of the British Urban Programme, *Political Studies 26,* 1978, 491-506.

IX Discussion and Conclusions

In the opening chapter of this report we suggested that while local authorities cannot solve all the problems of racial discrimination and disadvantage, their activities as service providers and employers can have important effects on the wellbeing of ethnic minorities. The need for central government to take some urgent initiative in urban policy in the aftermath of the disturbances in Brixton, Toxteth and elsewhere is widely recognised. Encouraging the development of local policies and practices more appropriate to a multi-racial society, taken together with other initiatives with which we cannot deal here, is one of the more important options open to national policy-makers.

In the following section we summarise the three broad conclusions indicated by our fieldwork. First, the striking variations between and within local authorities in their approach to the issues raised by the presence of substantial minority communities. Second, the limits on responsiveness which impede any closer relationship between 'needs' or demands on the one hand and provision on the other. Third, the peculiar characteristic of local policy change as largely internally driven with elected members or appointed officers providing the pressure for innovation and development.

We also consider just what is implied in attempting to encourage such local policy developments. The discussion in this section of the chapter is unavoidably complex; many of the implementation failures of national policies may be attributed to an over-simple view of the nature of local policy-making. Only when the complexity and variability of local situations is properly grasped can sensitive and feasible initiatives be designed for maximum effectiveness. With this injunction in mind we turn in our final section to consider what we have learned about the nature and limits of the various national agencies operating in this field. We end this report by sketching out conclusions as to how a broad strategy for local policy development in the field of race relations could be carried into effect by central government.

Local authorities and race relations

In this section we explore three general themes which emerged from our study of how far and in what ways local authorities responded to the presence in their localities of substantial numbers of people from ethnic minority groups. These three issues are variations in approach, the limits of responsiveness, and the internal sources of development and change.

Variations in approach. Differences among local authorities in their approaches to common problems is the most familiar characteristic of any system of decentralised government. Probably more intellectual effort has been devoted to explaining this than any other single aspect of the English local government system. It was no surprise to find a wide range of variation in local authorities' approaches to the ethnic dimension in policy and practice, not only among the six authorities which we chose for close study, but also (although here we naturally had less detail) among the remaining 17 which completed our pool of 'relevant' authorities as defined in Chapter II.

Nevertheless, the extent of diversity was particularly striking, and the more so when three factors are taken into account. First, our pool of authorities included only those metropolitan authorities with a New Commonwealth-born population in excess of 14,000, and those shire counties with districts containing such a population of at least 5,000, as enumerated in the 1971 census. More recent figures indicate that a decade of demographic change has doubled those minima in some cases; all, therefore, have substantial ethnic minority populations. Second, we excluded from the pool the inner London boroughs, who by common consent include several which are regarded as the front-runners in this field. Third, our detailed knowledge is confined to those authorities who were willing to afford the fairly unrestricted access which we required.

When these three factors are taken into account, our six authorities represented a relatively narrow range of circumstance. The variations in their formal provision are then even more striking. Consider for example in the field of education, the differences between Wyeshire and Deeborough on the one hand, and Ayeborough on the other. Compare the approach to employment issues adopted in Seeborough with the recent developments in Beeborough. The examples could be multiplied and broad inter-service profiles could be constructed to reveal the variations in 'performance' between the six authorities. That, however, is not our intention. Such an aggregation of measures would obscure the variations *between* departments in each authority. Seeborough, for example, has elaborate consultative machinery to be set against their unresponsive employment practices. Similarly, Deeborough's rather traditional practices in social services may be thought to be offset by their determined approach in the field of multi-racial education.

The most important reason for eschewing such facile comparisons is, however, that the debate on local government and race relations has been unduly preoccupied with these visible, tangible and essentially formal aspects of variation: *variations in 'policy'*. We have been equally concerned with two other important if less visible aspects of variation, those which occur at the level of *practice* and those which are evident at the level of *dispositions*. Each merits some separate discussion.

The authorities in our study displayed variations in their day-to-day operational practices over and above the more obvious variations in their formal policies. Sometimes the separate departments of the same authority manifested striking differences of style and approach at the operational level. We also found very different approaches at that level within the same department.

The sources of these variations in practice were two-fold. First, there was the differing scope of policy within the authority itself. In the field of education, Seeborough heads have considerable autonomy, while in Deeborough there are attempts — how successful it is too soon to judge — to steer all schools firmly in the direction of a multicultural approach. Diversity in practice is then sustained by an acceptance, stronger in some authorities than in others, that many aspects of practice are 'off limits' for policy makers. The boundary between policy and practice is an elastic one. However, its precise location is never determined by the *fiat* of policy makers, but has to be negotiated within the context of professional claims to autonomy.

The second source of variation at the level of practice is the familiar problem of 'control loss'. Local authorities, in common with other organisations, face problems in securing the implementation of policy decisions. The greater the distance of practitioners from the policy forum and the greater the number of links in the implementation chain, the more likely are divergences in practice to arise. This is inescapably so even in static services or those which are routinely provided. It is even more so in such areas as are dealt with here, where practice is confronted by social change, on the one hand, and by shifting and developing policy requirements on the other. The changing composition of a school or of a clientele forces practitioners to make whatever accommodations their experience suggests, and in the field of multi-racial practice their experience may prove a poor guide. The varied ability of practitioners to cope with this stress tends to make for variable outcomes. The tendency of new policies in relation to the ethnic dimension is to pull in a different direction, toward consistency in practice. Yet the attempt to secure consistency in practice by stating policy objectives and guidelines is never wholly successful.

Development is, in any case, by no means universally imposed in a 'top-down' fashion. Many important changes are initiated at the level of practice, as responses to the perplexing demands of a changing operational field. Some may be passed up to senior management to be elaborated or ratified at the policy level. In other cases, adaptations in practice may be made, particularly in the more professionalised services, in the face of an apparently unsympathetic policy climate. Practice, with its emphasis upon individual professional judgement is inevitably variable; much of the concern with variations at the operational level is quite properly with enhancing the capacity to cope by training, advice, or support, rather than with securing a closer compliance with policy intentions.

Variations in policy and practice are relatively tangible. Our third level of discussion, of variations in *disposition,* is less so. Dispositions may be best understood as very general and taken-for-granted assumptions about both the facts of a situation and its evaluation. Within a broad corpus of more or less consistent assumptions certain phenomena, relationships, qualities and values are held to be self-evident. Certain other issues, if they present themselves, are held to be undiscussable. We have viewed these dispositions as providing the 'appreciative context' of provision in our six authorities.

Four points may usefully be made here. First, such general dispositions, because taken for granted, are subtle and implicit; they can only be elicited by observation, interpretation and inference. Second, while they operate within the 'deep structures' of belief they nonetheless have a powerful effect in determining the broad parameters of explicit policies. Third, what is self-evident and taken for granted within one authority may differ sharply from what is so regarded in another, leading thereby to marked divergences in formal policy. Finally, the issues of racial discrimination, disadvantage and diversity connect with dispositions which are both powerful and, by social custom, often left unexpressed. For these reasons, the variable dispositions of local authorities have far-reaching effects on the policies which they adopt and on the provision which they are willing to make.

The most important single aspect of dispositions in this field is the varied willingness of local policy-makers to be explicit about issues of race and their implications for public policy. Here lies a crucial threshold which, in some 'colour blind' authorities, may not be crossed without transgressing the norms of discussion. Elected councillors generally establish those norms, for theirs are the broad dispositions that set the implicit limits on discussion. In many cases, particularly where political and organisational life is stable, these dispositions come to be shared by appointed officials down through the management line.

In such a case we may speak of a local authority's 'culture' or 'climate', a stable set of uncontested assumptions which may provide the basis for the progressive development of policies, but which act more often as an invisible but powerful constraint upon development. Thus, while local authorities display marked variations at all three levels, the level of dispositions is peculiarly potent, both in its direct influence on policy and its more indirect influence on practice.

Responding to the multi-racial community. The facts of variation are in themselves neither new nor surprising. Nor are they necessarily to be seen as constituting a case for central intervention. An important rationale for local government is the recognised need to adapt the provision of services to a diversity of local circumstances. Thus, one readily-advanced explanation of policy variations is that local circumstances and local needs are themselves variable. Policies and practices are, on this view, the appropriate responses of local authorities as need-meeting agencies.

It is, of course, true that localities vary in their particular circumstances and ethnic composition is an important dimension of variation in circumstance. We found, however, no very direct apparent relationship between ethnicity in the community and the incorporation of an ethnic dimension in the policy agendas of local authorities. It would be naive to expect such a relationship, although it is worth reiterating that the thirty or so authorities of whose variable responses we have some knowledge are the authorities whose areas contain the largest black settlements in English cities. In crude and static terms there is no evidence of policy and provision as a need-reflective response.

Moreover, a satisfactory account of variation in provision as need-meeting would have to satisfy either one of two further criteria. The first is that the

159

relatively recent and rapid changes in the ethnic composition of many areas should have evoked some response in terms of change in provision. Alternatively, it would have to demonstrate that authorities respond to the formal or informal representation of new issues in the community. Neither of these conditions is generally fulfilled on the evidence of our study (although there are some important exceptions) and each is worth examining further.

As to the first, we invited policy-makers, whenever possible, to discuss the changing situation of their localities insofar as they raised new issues for service provision. Migration is, of course, the most visible and immediate dimension of change. We found, however, a discernible tendency to underestimate the impact of demographic change by regarding the new ethnic mix as creating temporary problems which further assimilation would extinguish. This had been particularly the case in areas which in the past had experienced substantial immigration of other minority groups, in particular, the Irish or the Jews. Thus, councillors and officials in areas which laid claim to substantial histories of ethnic tolerance and assimilation were sometimes reluctant to question whether service provision might be failing to meet the needs of the newcomers.

While adult immigration is the most visible aspect of change in a community, the fertility patterns and family structures of minority groups may amplify the calls upon local authority resources in the medium term. Suprisingly, some policy makers were unable to essay an estimate of the minority population of their localities or even conjecture the impact of births to New Commonwealth mothers on local schools. Some had difficulty in assessing the relative proportions of Asian and West Indian residents. In some cases, 1971 census figures were still used, in conversation at least, as a basis for policy discussion. Many authorities have not availed themselves of the opportunity to obtain NDHS cross-tabulations for their own area. Even when available, such figures were often not fed into the policy agenda. Few of the authorities were concerned actively to monitor local ethnic change and even where the data were available there was little sign of their being taken into account.

Discussions of change in the ethnic composition of localities invoked claims that the minority community either sought to avoid differentiating themselves, or that they were not 'in need', or that their problems were (if not actually, then potentially) 'generic' or 'western' rather than 'special' problems. New situations in society are of course inescapably viewed through the prism of past experience; thus ethnic diversity and disadvantage were sometimes interpreted through experience of earlier migrant groups or of the indigenous working class. We were struck by the persistence of images of continuity, of ethnic diversity as a temporary ripple on the still pool of local life. Doubtless this reflected in some cases an unwillingness on the part of policy-makers to accept any differentiation of policies that would conflict with the universalism on which so many public services are based. How far it reflected, in other cases, an undisclosed racial prejudice we cannot guess. An explanation may also be found in the demography of concentration. The variable salience of ethnicity in local politics may flow less from actual numbers or proportions in the total population of an authority's area than from the spatial distribution of minority settlement. In Ayeborough and Deeborough the concentration of large numbers of minority residents into a few wards has possibly led to their political invisibility.

Such a resistance to recognising change is perhaps more easily maintained by elected members and by senior management than by practitioners. It is at the point of 'service delivery' that ethnic change bears most directly upon public services. In the case of social services this may produce a sense of concern among practitioners that case difficulties, communication problems or a noticeable absence of service uptake among minority groups indicate a serious shortfall in meeting the needs of a substantial minority of the population. Such perplexity could also be found in education, where some head teachers were acutely aware that their school population had changed, but were either doggedly maintaining past practices (sometimes in the face of serious opposition) or were discomfited and unsure of their proper course.

Examples can be multiplied from the evidence of the foregoing chapters. Our general impression was one of change in the community impinging more forcibly upon practitioners than upon policy-makers. In a number of cases the implications of change for practice were resisted or denied. While we sometimes found evidence of a serious and profound rethinking of the lessons of experience, the more common impression was of only marginal adaptations being made. In some cases these adaptations were seen by practitioners as sufficient. In other cases officials at the operational level expressed frustration with the unwillingness of policy-makers to recognise the impact of ethnic change on the relationship between needs and provision and to make those modifications to policy which were deemed necessary to permit the proper development of practice.

The impact of change in a locality is only partly expressed through changing patterns of demand upon service departments. Needs and demands may also be expressed on behalf of minority groups and, in some cases, formally represented to policy-makers. Experience in this respect is highly variable. It is perhaps surprising that the particular needs of minority communities are not represented more forcefully or more comprehensively. Seeborough has the longest history of regularised consultation with minority representatives but the issues raised by them rarely touched upon the main lines of policy. There, and elsewhere, the demands of the minority group in some cases were transmitted on their behalf via some other statutory agency or authoritative channel and were accorded more respect for that reason. Some departments disclaimed any pressure from the community and there was a sense that pressure would have provided a convenient justification to those policy-makers who were contemplating new initiatives. That favoured initiatives remained unlaunched *pending* community pressure was claimed in some authorities, but the hypothetical nature of the issue hardly substantiates the view of local services as demand-responsive.

While some authorities (or rather some 'policy entrepreneurs' within those authorities) looked in vain to minority group representatives for pressure, others were less sanguine of the appropriateness, or indeed the propriety, of such submissions. The local CRC might appear to be a suitable focal point for policy-related discussions but in some areas the CRC was seen as discredited or as unrepresentative. Elected members and their officials do not respond warmly when faced with claims to representativeness from outside bodies. Especially when faced with a multiplicity of competing groups, councillors and officers may prefer to fall back on their own judgements. The general pattern of responsiveness to community representations is difficult to discern.

To sum up, we found little evidence of the changing circumstances of the several localities being monitored by policy-makers. Nor did we find the demands of the growing minority communities being effectively represented to them. Some adaptations to practice were being forced by the necessities of life at the operational level but as Chapters VI and VII showed, practitioners can be remarkably resistant. Even where practitioners were inclined to be flexible, the limits of innovation were often tightly prescribed by the maintenance of existing policies and the resource constraints on the adjustment of provision. Variations in provision cannot then be explained in terms of variations in local circumstances for they barely reflect such circumstances.

There is widespread concern that the policies of local authorites *should* take fuller acount of the needs of the multi-ethnic community. However, much of the public discussion of this issue is prey to two important fallacies: the fallacy of monolithic organisation and the fallacy of direct and uniform response to pressure. Variations in actual provision and in rates of service development actually arise from a complex and dynamic interplay of internal and external factors operating upon the dispositions, policies and practices of authorities and their departments.

How development occurs. Considerable tensions may exist between dispositions, policies and practices in a local authority. The dynamics of development reside in the relationships between these three levels and the openness of each external influence. The actual configuration of influences varies between authorities, between service areas and over time. This point is illuminated by our comparative case studies of development, but a bald representation of cases obscures the broader regularities which this briefer, if necessarily schematic, account seeks to highlight.

Developments in practice, we have argued, are constrained by the formal policies which define the 'action space' of practitioners. Beyond certain limits, change at the operational level of service delivery depends on the adoption of commitments and the allocation of resources at the policy level. In a similar way, the broad dispositions of an authority constrain the 'action space' of those who aspire to change and extend those commitments and resource allocations. A disposition to be explicit about race is a prerequisite of the development of policies relating to discrimination, disadvantage and diversity. These dispositions are crucial. Where the ethnic dimension is disavowed, policy entrepreneurs have either to 'do good by stealth' or to place their faith in the (necessarily limited) development of practice.

It is impossible to say *how far* dispositions constrain policy, or policy practice. Nor is it possible to establish how far actors at each level can effectively extend their own 'action space' by stealth on the one hand or by outright advocacy on the other. In every case, these interactions occur within a particular organisational and interpersonal setting (or *milieu*) unique in time and place, providing both opportunities and constraints for any actor or group of actors wishing to produce change. Certainly, change does not occur as the result of the operation of an 'invisible hand' of organisational dynamics. It arises from the activities of policy entrepreneurs who act (sometimes covertly) as advocates of change and who are the prime movers in development.

Policy entrepreneurs seek to place their own particular concerns upon the agenda of the authority and secure the adoption of their favoured policies. Their ability to do this depends largely on their position and the resources which they can deploy in agenda-setting. At the same time, however, they may be constrained by how far explicit and overt discussion of race is permitted. Even a chief executive cannot effectively extend the policy agenda in this area if elected members and departmental managements maintain a 'colour blind' posture. Some would-be policy entrepreneurs judge (possibly correctly) that in an authority whose dispositions do not recognise ethnicity, any attempt to extend the policy agenda would be counter-productive. They seek instead to *prevent* ethnic issues from reaching the policy agenda, and seek to cope by incremental change at the operational level.

Influences at the level of practice are necessarily subject to different considerations. Often deprived of authoritative discussion in a policy forum, developments in education and social services practice have largely followed from the perplexity, curiosity, commitment and enthusiasm of particular practitioners and field managers and their ability to take their colleagues with them. We noted claims to a 'contagion effect' among social workers and teachers, and selective recruitment in schools serving to develop practice as far as possible within the existing constraints of policy.

If the first elementary error of policy analysis is to see local authorities in monolithic terms, the second is to fail to appreciate that the influences from the world outside the local authority bear upon internal tensions in different ways at different levels. Certain kinds of influence serve to promote the development of practice within the limits imposed by the policy agenda. Other kinds of influence may *change* that agenda. Yet other influences may possibly bear upon the overall dispositions of the authority. 'Influences', then, are as complex and varied as the internal milieu of policy-making itself.

Policy entrepreneurs often co-opt external 'influence' to their own purposes. Community demands, for example, rarely evoke a direct response at the policy level, but they may prove remarkably useful to those policy entrepreneurs who judge it a tactical advantage to appear to be responding to the pressure rather than initiating change. This point applies with equal force to pressure from central government or from such agencies as the CRE. Section 71 of the Race Relations Act provides a good illustration. Its significance is not that it compels compliance, for it carries no sanctions; rather, it invites those who wish to establish a place for ethnicity on the policy agenda to point to and argue from a statutory obligation. In some circumstances, this may tip the balance of the argument, and ensure discussion. The importance of S.71, taken together with the earlier White Paper, is that it establishes an ethnic dimension to policy and practice; it serves as a riposte to the frequently encountered reluctance of local councils to consider that dimension. It has, however, apparently had such an effect *only* where councillors, officers, or particular coalitions of either or of both have sought to turn it to that purpose.

The dynamics of development are complex and interactive. Elected or appointed policy entrepreneurs operate within an organisational milieu peculiar to their own authority. In some cases, they operate within an entirely favourable context. In other cases, the disposition of elected members against ethnicity in policy constrains these activities. In yet others, the resistance of officers may frustrate change. In a few authorities policy entrepreneurs seem hardly to exist; some departments seem to lack prime movers. Regardless of these variations, however, practitioners continue to be confronted by the issues in their day-to-day work, coping in a variety of ways from denial, through perplexity, to the enthusiastic redefinition of their responsibilities.

Summary. Variations in approach are not derived in any direct sense from variations in circumstances. Authorities seemed neither to respond promptly to changing needs nor to review their policies and practices in the light of the relatively rare representations from community groups. The key to development seemed to be the presence or absence of groups of 'policy entrepreneurs' — officers or councillors who were committed to change and who could make skilful use of such pressures from the community or from central agencies as were to hand. Pressure was helpful, but ultimately development could only be pressed as far as the dispositions of the council would permit. In Beeborough, we saw a group of councillors effectively leading their colleagues and turning each successive decision to good advantage. Elsewhere, we saw senior officials attempting with varying success to carry their councillors with them toward more explicitly multi-racial services.

A strategy for local development

While our work in the local authorities was intended to identify the internal and external factors that shaped their responses to the needs of a multi-racial society, the ultimate purpose of the exercise was to draw some conclusions about the most effective means of promoting the development of policy and practice at the local level. If local situations are as complex and as variable as we suggest, then the search for a single means of promoting change is chimerical. The clear implication of our findings is that a sensitive and flexible strategy, operating at several levels and engaging a number of agencies, is required.

The purpose of such a strategy would be to tackle four major problem areas which inhibit the continued progress of local authorities. These four, as they are manifested in the town and county halls, are the gross *confusions* as to the nature of law and policy; the absence of any real *communication* of policy from the centre; the weakness in the *promotional* role of the centre; and the obstacles to the freer *dissemination* of experience.

Before discussing ways in which these problems might be overcome, we consider where the key initiative should come from. Our research led us to conclude that the lead would be most effectively given by a Whitehall department. There are limits on the effectiveness of special-purpose bodies and the reasonable and unreasonable expectations of what the CRE can achieve should be more clearly distinguished. The CRE undoubtedly has an important role to play in promoting development, but we feel that its potential impact will only be realised when a decisive lead is taken at ministerial level.

The fifth report of the House of Commons Home Affairs Committee, published in August 1981, contains many suggestions as to how the question of racial disadvantage can be given a greater priority by the establishment of a Cabinet committee and by more assertive action on the part of the Home Office. We saw little in our study that inclined us to believe that such a shift in the Home Office stance is either feasible or appropriate. As we indicate in the following pages, we believe the designation of the Department of the Environment as the lead department in respect of the strategy elaborated here would produce more definite results at the point that matters most: the delivery of local services to a multi-racial community.

Clarifying law and policy. A striking feature of our visits to authorities was the widespread confusion as to the employment provisions of the Race Relations Act. There was a high awareness of the legal and moral prohibitions on direct discrimination. There was less evidence in interviews, meetings or departmental files that the concept of indirect discrimination was very widely understood, or even known to exist. Positive action was usually confused with positive discrimination, and while this sometimes worked to imply that positive action was itself illegal, in other cases, positive discrimination at the point of recruitment (by, for example, quotas) was openly discussed as if it were a lawful option.

It is noteworthy that the only Home Office guidance as to the law on discrimination is the explanatory booklet *Racial Discrimination: A Guide to the Race Relations Act 1976* issued in 1977. It was made available on request to local authorities and we are told that twenty four of them received copies. The emphasis is on the negative aspects of the legislation, and the booklet is lucid on the prohibitions imposed by the Act. Local authorities have not received any guidance from the Home Office on the *positive* approach to equal opportunity and this may account for the widespread confusion as to what is lawful and what is not. Subsequent CRE publications have been uneven in their impact and are sometimes misinterpreted as 'special pleading' rather than straightforward accounts of the current legal context. The CRE would be better placed to advise on implementing equal opportunity if it were operating in the context of an unambiguous explanation of the law as it is understood by central government. The approval of the draft *Code of Practice* would probably go some way toward doing this, particularly if it were accompanied by attempts on the government's part to explain the complex and ambiguous provisions of the Act to local authorities. The somewhat uneven grasp of the issues among officers suggests that such an explanation should be simple, emphatic and directed (there are precedents) at council leaders.

Local councillors' fears of a political backlash would also be relieved both by a ministerial reiteration of policy to which they could refer and, particularly, by a restatement of the nature and limits of *positive discrimination*. No single term arouses greater anxieties in this field. Any ministerial initiative could then usefully address this point: that while positive discrimination in favour of *areas* has been the accepted basis of policy from the Educational Priority Areas to the inner city partnerships, positive discrimination in favour of *individuals* in respect of their employment is not so, except in certain clearly specified situations. Moreover, while area discrimination to produce a more equal matching of resources to needs is almost universally regarded as acceptable in principle, the unlike treatment of individuals is not. It is not mere semantics to insist that the two meanings should not be conflated, for this single misunderstanding also constitutes a barrier to the type of open policy discussion that is the prerequisite of local policy development.

The widespread misunderstandings of the law on discrimination in employment are not the only barrier to local policy development. Nor are the other barriers likely to be removed by a popular exegesis of the Act itself. Rather, they require a well-publicised reiteration of the policy framework established in the 1975 White Paper. That policy framework contains three broad commitments: to eradicate racial discrimination; to reduce racial disadvantage; and to accept and support cultural diversity. However, of these three, only the anti-discrimination goal is widely recognised among local authorities and that seems but poorly understood. That the law prohibits discrimination is easily grasped. However, some councillors and officials seem to imagine that this prohibition ranges beyond the less equal treatment of individuals on account of their race to encompass the recording, enumeration or even *discussion* of the different circumstances of different ethnic groups. Yet an attempt to tackle racial disadvantage — and indeed the concept itself — requires a recognition of those different circumstances. This in a sense *is* 'discrimination' but only in the semantic sense of differentiation.

The overall need is then for an authoritative clarification of policy in relation to discrimination, disadvantage and diversity. This would amount to little less than an educative programme. Local authorities cannot be asked to play a lead role in promoting racial equality until there is a far better understanding among them of the basic premises of a multi-racial society. Nor can they develop policies to achieve it without grasping the need to be explicit about issues of race. While some have already achieved that explicitness the majority of authorities are unlikely to do so until it has been validated by a statement at the national level. *The first component of our suggested strategy is therefore a ministerial initiative to clarify and re-affirm the basis of law and policy on race relations.*

Communicating priorities. We have indicated in this report that the performance of local authorities in relation to issues of race is highly uneven. Indeed, in two of the six authorities where we carried out our fieldwork commitment to action appeared actually to decline during the duration of our project. However, the disturbances in many cities during the spring and summer of 1981, whether or not they are attributed to the ethnic aspects of deprivation, have done much to create a climate of expectation in the field of urban policy. The initial impetus provided by the 1976 Act seems largely to have run its course. The initiative suggested above could renew the now flagging impetus of local policy. It would, however, be no more than the first stage of an effective strategy and would need to be reinforced by more obviously continuous ministerial interest in the activities of *particular* authorities.

The evidence of our fieldwork and our meetings with Whitehall officials leads us to conclude that the major new initiative which we outline here cannot be communicated by circular. Circulars, being generally sent to all relevant authorities rather than to a select few, make it difficult to go beyond (in the words of one senior civil servant) 'rather vapid generalisations'.

Such a strategy as we envisage would be selective. Its primary focus would naturally be that relatively small group of authorities who contain the largest ethnic minority populations in London, the East and West Midlands, and the North and the North-West. These might be the priority or 'target' authorities. The most effecitve means of communicating a new policy initiative on race to these authorities would be by means of ministerial conferences. As a technique it has good precedents in British public administration. There are numerous examples of regional (or, in London, sectional) conferences to promote policy initiatives in the field of, for example, roads or housing. Such an initiative to change perspectives and priorities requires something akin to a ministerial 'task force', with a small but experienced team of officials seconded part-time from their present posts in Whitehall or town hall. They would operate by means of ministerial talks with local political leaders, followed up by meetings at official level, ideally to ensure some progress on developments before a further ministerial visit.

A suitable precedent is to be found in the London Housing Action Group established by the Conservative Secretary of State for the Environment in 1971, and continued under the subsequent Labour Administrations. The Action Group comprised a small number of local politicians under the chairmanship of successive junior DoE ministers. Ministerial chairmanship was thought vital to establishing the priority to be given to land assembly and housing development in the metropolis. The Group had a back-up staff of offi als who worked with local officers to refine the details of those changes in policy and practice which the Minister's group had been able to secure by persuasion. It was in many ways a successful experiment, dealing as it did with highly sensitive social and political issues.

If this theme is developed, the second stage of a strategy might then be as follows. First, a series of working conferences in the metropolitan areas and the East Midlands (with perhaps four London conferences with groups of boroughs). From these conferences a ministerial action group could be formed from a selection of influential local political leaders perhaps half a dozen of whom could accompany the minister on periodic visits to *each* authority. The visits would aim to agree feasible objectives with individual authorities. The body which would exhort and negotiate would be supported by an advisory team of officials drawn from those local authorites with the most substantial experience of developing policies to meet the needs of ethnic minorities in, for example, employment, housing, education, or social services.

The implication of this proposal is that continuous and iterative contact with local authorities via a field presence is essential. Of the departments concerned, only the DoE have the range of involvement with local authorities and the close liaison at regional office level to fulfil this role. It would, of course, extend beyond their existing engagement in managing the urban programmes but would profit by association with that function. The DoE, with substantial local connections and a more promotional style, could then provide the major back-up to the Action Group at regional office level and so achieve some continuity of monitoring and support. The advisory team, drawn largely from local government, could work through the regional office and this would be an appropriate point at which to draw in the relevant HMIs and SWSOs of the region. Some parallels may be drawn with proposals put forward by the Royal Institute of Public Administration in its March 1981 memorandum to the DHSS on 'Development Agencies for the National Health Service in England'.

For reasons which we outlined in Chapter VIII, the DoE officials have a strong and growing involvement with the local authorities in respect of racial disadvantage. The proposal favoured in some quarters to transfer Urban Programme responsibility from DoE back to the Home Office would obviously impede the development of the close working relationship between central and local government which we are convinced must underpin a strategy for local development. It has been argued that for a number of reasons (including those cited in this report but touching also upon the more regulatory role of the Home Office in police and immigration control), the DoE should itself become the lead department in the field of race relations.

This more far-reaching change would seem to us to be entirely feasible and, if accompanied by a transfer of responsibility for S.11 administration, would have the advantage of creating a single focus of responsibility within Whitehall. The Action Group visits would also enable S.11 to be used as a more powerful promotional tool if its administration were also in the hands of DoE. *The second component of our suggested strategy is the establishment of an Action Group or task force, chaired by a DoE minister, including local political leaders and officials, and supported by the regional offices of DoE.*

Promoting development. The third plank of what we see as a feasible strategy is less dependent upon central intervention. The essence of this part of the strategy would be to encourage changes within the local authorities themselves with the object of achieving self-sustained development. The key to unlocking the capacity for such development is to secure the shift in dispositions that will facilitate the explicit discussion of race-related issues. The initiatives at ministerial level described above would be required to bring about that shift. Thereafter, given appropriate internal structures and some external support, local authorities may be expected to develop their own momentum, sustained in part by more attentive community groups, and monitored by more distant contact.

The phenomenon of self-sustained development is apparent in those authorities that have adopted explicit commitments to the pursuit of equal opportunity and the adjustment of policy and practice. We were struck by the sense of momentum developed in Beeborough, where we were able to observe

168

developments over a period of more than twelve months. It seems that once the issue of race had gained a place on the policy agenda this momentum becomes self-sustaining; representations from community groups increase as the limits of political possibility are extended and the representatives of such groups are brought into a participatory relationship with elected and appointed policy makers.

The three main ingredients of self-sustained development are those covered in Chapters III to V of this report. First, the creation of corporate arrangements such as will ensure a prominent place for racial issues in policy discussion, with defined committee responsibilities, inter-departmental links at officer level and the identification of a 'lead' official (such as a race relations adviser) directly responsible to the chief executive. Second, the involvement of community groups in a genuine consultative process, bringing them into some kind of corporate policy forum but reaching beyond them when necessary with wider consultative exercises. Third, the adoption of positive action toward equality of opportunity which will result in time in the advancement of minority groups to positions of responsibility, thereby sensitising departmental services and creating a more representative and accessible organisation. To these we might add the development of an adequate data base to provide information for policy decision, and the introduction of ethnic record-keeping wherever appropriate.

These are mutually supportive. Within a strong corporate structure the activities of more progressive departments can be used to raise the expectations of the others. Shifts of this kind in corporate, consultative and employment practices are likely to provide a vital internal impetus to service development. Moreover, they are likely to make the local authority seem more responsive and accessible to minority groups and stimulate increased black participation in the process of political competition, leading thereby to increased black representation on local councils. Such an interactive spiral of change is not easy to set in motion, but once established its self-sustaining nature reduces the need for further intervention.

These are the kinds of developments which can underpin progress towards a more equal multi-racial society. They are essentially internal and autonomous, and central government can neither expect nor seek to have more than a catalytic effect in bringing them about. The CRE, on the other hand, while it lacks the necessary authority to challenge the dispositions of local councils (and thus provide the catalyst) has an important part to play here, liaising with corporate leaders, with departmental officers, with CRCs, and with community groups. Central government can promote the policy shifts necessary to get ethnicity onto the agenda of local politics. The CRE can advise, consult and encourage during the subsequent process of implementing change. *The third component of our suggested strategy involves a transfer of the responsibility for securing change from central to local government, by encouraging the adoption of such corporate, consultative and employment practices as will make for self-sustained development.*

Sharing experiences. If the objective of a centrally-adopted strategy is to promote local development then it must be recognised that some provision for the interchange of experience among authorities must be made. We were struck during our fieldwork by the extent to which local authorities felt the need for practical advice as to the practices of others. We were also impressed by the extent to which experience and practice is often disseminated laterally, between departments, rather than from the central agencies. Inter-authority contacts seemed more significant by far than the activities of, for example, the education Inspectorate, the Social Work Service or the Home Office. There were even a few examples of surveys being carried out by authorities seeking to inform themselves as to practice elsewhere.

The only positive contribution which we could make to the authorities which we visited was to offer information on the experience of others. On a few occasions, we also provided the necessary 'brokerage' to enable officers from one authority to meet others with relevant experience. At the conclusion of the study, we were asked by one of the six authorities to organise a series of day workshops to promote the interchange of information. It was apparent that adequate arrangements for the lateral sharing of information and the discussion of activity were almost totally lacking. Authorities can turn to the CRE for such advice, but they are unlikely to do so on matters relating to professional practice. Discussions with local authorities led us to the conclusion that this need could be met by establishing a clearing house or advisory service to promote the dissemination of multi-racial practice and the lessons of experience.

Such an advisory service would be similar in some respects to the scheme recently established by the National Association of Health Authorities. It could be centrally maintained, perhaps by the local authority associations in the manner of the Local Authorities Management Services Advisory Committee. Our impression from the authorities is that, while such a service could usefully issue newsletters or listings of reports and innovations, its most constructive role would be to operate a 'phone-in' brokerage service which would enable enquirers to be put directly in touch with colleagues elsewhere who had significant experience to relate. This role requires close links with local authorities. Whether or not it could include the entire range of local services would need further consideration.

That we ourselves in this project were drawn into a limited 'development' role was significant evidence of the need for some machinery for sharing experience. The very good response to our postal enquiries, the frequent expressions of interest (with a number of telephone calls from officials interested in learning more about progress elsewhere) and the requests to discuss the general issues with councillors and to arrange inter-authority contacts convinced us of the need for such a modest but potentially effective device. It is perhaps for local authorities to provide such an advisory service, but a national strategy could derive considerable benefits from a pump-priming initiative. We recognise that while we have uncovered a need we cannot draw firm conclusions as to exactly how it should be met. The first move should therefore be a feasibility study to establish more clearly than we were able to do in our project the precise form, range and type of the information needs of local authorities. *Without prejudice to the outcome of such a study, our fourth suggestion for a national strategy is the establishment of a national clearing house and advisory service to promote the better interchange of experience among local authorities in multi-racial areas.*

Financing a strategy. The emphasis in the strategy outlined above is on achieving some redirection of attention and, by implication, of existing resources. The financial base of the strategy would, as we see it, be contained within local authority main programmes, and the grants made under S.11 of the Local Government Act 1966 and the Urban Programme. Only when it has been shown that these programmes are capable of benefiting the minority communities can arguments for increasing the sums spent be considered.

In the course of the research, we noted a number of problems in the use of S.11, including confusion about the present status of such funding and about how rigidly the constraints in the legislation and the 1967 circular might be enforced, the absence of any appraisal (particularly in the case of education) of the needs which S.11 appointments were supposed to meet, and the absence of any monitoring and evaluation. The House of Commons Home Affairs Committee, in its August 1981 report on *Racial Disadvantage*, noted that S.11 'is intended to be a promotional grant' (para. 48) but 'Nobody from central government attempts to persuade local authorities to undertake new programmes and to reclaim the money spent . . . The known availability of Section 11 is thus expected to have its own encouraging effect' (para. 50). The suggestions which we have made do not require a new initiative from the Home Office to encourage S.11 use. Rather, one aspect of the DoE-led Action Group visits to local authorities would be the promotion of fuller, and more considered, use of S.11. The visits would provide an opportunity for encouraging local authorities to assess the needs of their ethnic communities and the ways in which S.11 could most effectively be used, relating such use to both mainstream and Urban Programme funding.

It is difficult to envisage any such increased use of S.11 without substantial changes, such as abolition of the ten-year rule. The Home Affairs Committee have made a number of suggestions for amendments to the legislation and for changes in the definitions and arrangements set forth in the Home Office's 1967 and 1970 circulars. Until such changes are made, local authorities are likely to be reluctant to put substantial effort into appraising and monitoring current S.11 use, or to think in a systematic way about increasing its use. Our research in the local authorities indicated that changes in administration or legislation would also need to clarify the issue of whether S.11 is intended to meet the needs of ethnic groups through specific posts, or to supplement existing expenditure in areas where the presence of ethnic minority residents increases the call on resources.

The Urban Programme raises questions of a more straightforward nature. At present, the emphasis of the inner cities programme is heavily upon the economic regeneration of the old urban areas while similarly strong encouragement is given to local authorities to submit industrial or commercial schemes under the traditional urban programme. It is often argued that ethnic minorities will share in the general benefits of more prosperous urban economies, a claim sometimes

171

regarded with scepticism. The strategy which we have suggested would depend in part for its success upon the maintenance or expansion of a 'social' element in the Urban Programme, and an emphasis, within the economic aspects, upon the disadvantaged groups in the labour market. Also important would be a more thoroughgoing requirement that local authorities allow for the expression of ethnic minority views within their own consideration of Urban Programme bids. We saw for ourselves that some authorities do this more effectively than others and the suggested ministerial Action Group would be well placed to press a more active seeking out of ethnic minority opinion.

We cannot see that the call on resources of a ministerial Action Group would be very great, although some allowance would have to be made both for the involvement of local councillors and officers, and the redeployment of a small number of officials from (most probably) the Inner Cities Directorate of the DoE. Our proposed clearing house would be best financed by subscription from the local authorities themselves, although the present climate in relation to public expenditure will hardly encourage them to respond positively to such an initiative, and initial provision would need to be made centrally. We have, in any case, suggested a prior feasibility study, which would enable the costs of such a service to be more accurately estimated.

Conclusion. In this final section we have rehearsed a number of suggestions which emerged from our studies of the policies and practices of local authorities in relation to the multi-racial character of their communities. Throughout the report we have highlighted problems, uncertainties and constraints. We have shown that responding to the requirements of a multi-racial society is no easy matter. In this chapter, we turned to the *opportunities* for policy development, mindful all the while of the limits of feasible action as indicated by our research. The experience of the local authorities with whom we were in contact enabled us to sketch out the framework of a new central government initiative: a strategy to promote the development of policy and practice at the local level.

The strategy assumes that local authorities have a leading role to play in achieving a more equal multi-racial society. With the disturbances in many British cities during 1981, helping them to play that role has become an important option for central government.

Appendix: Section 11 and the Urban Programme

Throughout this report we have referred frequently to local authorities' use of funds available under S.11 and the Urban Programme. In this appendix we outline very briefly the history and the administration of these two funding sources.

Section 11

S.11 of the Local Government Act 1966 empowered the Home Secretary to pay grants in respect of the employment of staff by those local authorities who had to make special provision in the exercise of their functions 'in consequence of the presence within their areas of substantial numbers of immigrants from the Commonwealth whose language or customs differ from those of the community'. Grant, originally set at 50 per cent of approved expenditure, was raised to 75 per cent in 1969. Detailed guidance was contained in Home Office circular 15/1967, which said that for purposes of administering grant, 'Commonwealth immigrant' was 'normally considered' to be someone who had been born in another country of the Commonwealth, and who had been ordinarily resident in the United Kingdom for less than ten years, and the child of such a person. Grants were to be paid for salaries of individuals, but also on a formula basis, for example, for staff in day nurseries. Circular 169/1970 presented revised formulae.

Local authorities eligible to claim were those where the proportion of Commonwealth immigrant pupils in the total school population was two per cent or more; 46 were listed in the first circular, but others were subsequently approved. In 1978/79, 88 local authorities plus the Inner London Education Authority claimed grant, and the total amount of eligible expenditure was about £40 million. About 85 per cent of this was for education, largely for specialist teachers in language and remedial skills for primary and secondary school children. It was never intended that the funds should be restricted to educational use, and there has been increasing interest in recent years for use in other local authority services such as housing, libraries and social services.

In administering the grant, a number of 'serious failings' appeared, which led the Home Office to issue, in November 1978, a consultative document,

Proposals for Replacing Section 11 of the Local Government Act 1966. This described the 'major defects' as:

'it prevents aid being given to a sufficiently wide range of ethnic minorities [there was particular concern over the exclusion of those who came from Pakistan after 1972, and such groups as the Vietnamese]; it excludes the second and subsequent generations from the benefits of the grant; it inhibits a comprehensive and co-ordinated approach to the problems of ethnic minorities in particular areas; and it is restrictive in the purposes for which aid can be given and the form it can take'.

The document therefore proposed that S.11 be repealed and replaced by 'a much wider and more flexible grant-aid power'. Subsequently, the Local Government Grants (Ethnic Groups) Bill was introduced, and although it passed its second reading in March 1979, it was in committee, and hence lost, when Parliament was dissolved in April 1979. A subsequent attempt to introduce the Bill in the Lords failed.

The Home Office wrote to chief executives in June 1980 noting that the government was reviewing the operation of S.11. While that review was underway, authorities must 'continue to follow closely' the guidance in the 1967 and 1970 circulars. Decisions about the continued use of S.11, and the form it should take, had still not been taken by 1981, as the government was waiting to judge the effects of some of the changes in the block grant system.

The House of Commons Home Affairs Sub-Committee on Race Relations and Immigration, in their investigation of racial disadvantage during 1980-81, considered the operation of S.11. Their report, published in August 1981, recommended that S.11 'be retained as the major vehicle of central government financial support for local authority programmes designed to combat racial disadvantage'. They noted that some of their specific recommendations, such as abolition of the ten-year rule, could be carried out by the Home Office without legislation, but they urged new legislation amending the 1966 Act to remove the restriction of S.11 to those from the Commonwealth, and the payment of salaries only.

The Urban Programme

The Local Government Grants (Social Need) Act 1969 provided for grants to be paid to local authorities which incurred expenditure as a result of special social need in an urban area. The Home Office initially was the lead department, but responsibility for administering grants was transferred to the Department of the Environment in 1977.

The first circular issued by the Home Office sought bids from 34 local authorities, selected because they contained areas of high household density or an exceptionally high immigrant population. Expenditure eligible for the 75 per cent grant was limited to nursery provision and children's homes. Subsequent circulars widened the programme to include all local authorities in England and Wales, and a much greater range of projects. Voluntary sector involvement was also increased, although funding was via local authorities rather than direct.

Attention continued to be focused on areas of 'greatest social need', variously defined, within each authority, and circulars have drawn attention to the possible special needs of those from ethnic minorities. Unlike S.11, grant was not restricted to salary costs; on the other hand, a limited total was fixed for distribution in response to submissions under each circular.

The 1977 White Paper, *Policy for the Inner Cities (Cmnd 6845)*, announced a number of major changes in the programme. Funds were to be increased substantially; scope was to be expanded to include industrial, environmental and recreational provision. The traditional urban programme was subsequently the subject of a review by the DoE's Inner Cities Directorate, and their 1980 consultative document described the development of the programme and its current use, including projects intended to benefit ethnic communities, and considered arguments for and against retaining it. The programme was continued.

There are currently four categories of authorities receiving funds under the enhanced Urban Programme: partnerships (6), programme authorities (15), other designated districts (14), and any other authority having special social need in an urban area (about 150). Partnership authorities are invited to draw up comprehensive programmes for the regeneration of their inner areas. The programme is discussed and approved by a partnership committee chaired by a DoE Minister and made up of local authority leaders and representatives of the police, area health authorities and central government. Programme authorities are also invited to draw up and submit programmes, but without the full machinery for partnership meetings. 'Other designated districts' receive Urban Programme funding for industrial and commercial projects, but are also elgible for grant for other sorts of projects under the traditional urban programme ('Trad UP'), as are the many other authorities containing areas of 'special social need'.

Ministerial guidelines for partnership authorities, intended to streamline procedures for approval of programmes and projects within them, were issued in July 1981; stress was laid on economic regeneration, and links with the private sector. The guidelines noted that 'Due priority should also be given to projects designed to benefit disadvantaged minorities such as certain ethnic groups, particularly through the provision of work and training'. Urban Programme allocations (England only) for 1981-82 totalled £211 million, of which the traditional urban programme's share was £44 million.

The POLICY STUDIES INSTITUTE (PSI) is a British independent policy research organisation concerned with issues relevant to economic and social policies and the working of political institutions.

PSI was formed in April 1978 through the merger of Political and Economic Planning (PEP), founded in 1931, and the Centre for Studies in Social Policy (CSSP), founded in 1972. It continues the tradition of both organisations to establish the facts by impartial empirical research and to relate the findings to practical policy making. The scope of the Institute's work has been extended by the recent establishment of a European Centre for Political Studies. PSI's work is financed by grants for specific studies made by trusts, foundations and public bodies, with substantial support from donations by industry and commerce, and by annual subscriptions.

The results of the studies are disseminated widely by means of frequent publications, articles and seminars.

1-2 Castle Lane, London SW1E 6DR
Telephone: 01-828 7055

How to obtain PSI publications

PSI publications may be obtained from booksellers or direct from PSI. Postage and packing will be additional to the cost of the publication if it is sent by post.

A full list of recent publications and subscription details will be sent on request to PSI at 1-2 Castle Lane, London SW1E 6DR.

PSI RECENT PUBLICATIONS

Books

Overseas Doctors in the National Health Service	*David J. Smith*	£12.50
Governments and Trade Unions	*Denis Barnes and Eileen Reid*	£12.50
Rational Techniques in Policy Analysis	*Michael Carley*	£12.50 (Cased) £5.50 (Paper)
Parliaments and Economic Affairs	*David Coombes and S. A. Walkland (eds.)*	£13.00
Women in Top Jobs	*Michael Fogarty, Isobel Allen and Patricia Walters*	£14.00
Fifty Years of Political and Economic Planning		£9.50
Evaluative Research in Social Care	*E. Mathilda Goldberg and Naomi Connelly (eds.)*	£15.00 (Cased) £7.50 (Paper)

Reports

No. 585	**Japanese Industrial Policy**	£3.95
No. 586	**Differentials for Managers and Skilled Manual Workers in the UK**	£3.95
No. 587	**The Social Consequences of Rail Closures**	£4.50
No. 588	**Maternity Rights: The experience of women**	£4.95
No. 589	**Shorter Working Time**	£3.95
No. 590	**Microprocessors in Manufactured Products**	£3.25
No. 591	**The Economics of Historic Country Houses**	£4.95
No. 592	**Retirement Age and Retirement Costs**	£3.95
No. 593	**A Report from Hackney**	£2.50
No. 594	**Unemployment and Racial Minorities**	£5.00
No. 595	**Family Planning, Sterilisation and Abortion Services**	£4.00
No. 596	**Maternity Rights: The experience of employers**	£5.00
No. 597	**Case Studies of Shorter Working Time**	**£4.50**

Discussion Papers

No. 1	**Discussing the Welfare State**	£2.75
No. 2	**Diversity and Decentralisation in the Welfare State**	£2.75
No. 3	**Public Policy and Family Life**	£2.75
No. 4	**A New Look at the Personal Social Services**	£3.75

Studies in European Politics

1.	**The Future of the European Parliament**	£3.95
2.	**Towards Transnational Parties in the European Community**	£1.80
3.	**European Integration, Regional Devolution and National Parliaments**	£2.25
4.	**Eurocommunism and Foreign Policy**	£2.95
5.	**Europe Elects its Parliament**	£3.50